W
J
S**

D.

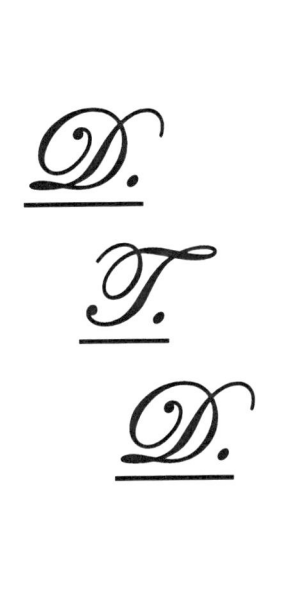

T.

D.

ACCLAIM for "Wisdom To Success"

"What a surprise! Debbi is one versatile, articulate bombshell for bringing creative genius to life. What a privilege and gift to read this book, it was amazing! In fact, I could not stop, and read it completely in two days. The interview format of this book is brilliant! Live, off the cuff, spontaneous, masterful, unrehearsed, compassionate, and inspiring. Debbi's clarity of purpose and huge practical knowledge base really shines through, serving hosts, listeners, questioners, and now, readers. I love the guided meditations in the interviews. Got a nice buzz of deep 'sound of silence' presence-filled stillness from them. I'm surprised and impressed. Readers, remember that there is even more in the author than in the book! I am excited for what Debbi will do next. This is one person on fire. Watch her light up your passion and the night skies of the crazy world we live in. Like her, stand up. Be seen and counted for the unique gift only you can bring to life. That's what I intend to do. This book has just become part of my inspiration for my next, and bigger, mission."

-- **DR. UDO ERASMUS**, *Author: Fats That Heal Fats That Kill; Choosing the Right Fats; Omega 3 Cuisine, Inventor: Methods for Making Oils with Health in Mind, Creator: Udo's Oil 3,6,9 Blend, Next: A Global, Teachable Field of Health Based on Nature and Human Nature*

♦

"This book was a Godshot — one of those instant miracles that changed my life. During a crisis, when I was most resistant to reading anything new, and thought I had read everything, I picked up this book and turned right to a page that snapped me back into divine alignment. Everything I needed to reaffirm my mission in life was right on that page. I couldn't stop reading. I then started it at the beginning and felt the magic in my life come back. Thank you, Debbi, for this thrilling, exciting book — and for continually reminding me that there are no accidents. Miracles are actually natural laws that happen when we let go and tap into our innate power. For me, the miracles and magic happened when I read *Wisdom to Success*."

- **LYDIA CORNELL**, Actress, Celebrity, Author/Founder of Godshots™

♦

"This book will arrest and capture your attention and you won't ever want to be released -- it is spellbinding."

-- **JOHN LEE HOOKER JR.**, *Two time Grammy nominee, Jazz/blues musician*

♦

"Simply the funniest must-read you will ever find! You'll laugh and be deeply inspired all the way to a better you. I loved every page!"

-- **TERESA DE GROSBOIS**, *International speaker, trainer and best-selling author*

♦

"*Wisdom To Success*," by Debbi Dachinger, mixes just the right amounts of Debbi's amazing personal story, with equal amounts of motivation and inspiration, making it easy for anyone to follow their dreams and create a magical and fulfilling life!"

-- **JANET BRAY ATTWOOD** – *NY Times bestselling author: The Passion Test - The Effortless Path to Discovering Your Destiny"*

"*Wisdom To Success*" is amazing and you won't want to put it down. The book is real because Debbi is real and she makes the difficult seem so easy. You will laugh, cry and identify with her style and will be forever changed for reading this book -- a definite must read."

- **DANIEL GUTIERREZ**, *International business consultant, motivational speaker, author, advisor to Obama Administration Department of White House Personnel*

♦

"After reading Debbi Dachinger's book, "*Wisdom To Success*," I must say Deb; you are some kind of wonderful. You walk the talk. You have a way of communicating concepts that is so pragmatic and practical. I feel unbelievably blessed to have you in my life and to have you as an inspiration for me and for all the people we work with. This is a great book - everybody should buy it. I loved it. Thank you for being you, Debbi, and for expressing *you* out into the world."

--**JENNIFER HOUGH**, *President, Speaker, Author at The Wide Awakening: World's authority on awakening, abundance and life flow.*

♦

"As a corporate turnaround man it's wonderful to see that someone has come up with a way to clearly state that dreams are, beyond the shadow of a doubt, the only way to save the world. Thanks, Deb!"

- **PATRICK RETTIG**, *Corporate Turnaround and Restructuring, CEO of The Rettig Corporation*

♦

"A joy to read this book! Engaging and endearing, this book will inspire you to believe that you too can live your dream!"

-- **EVA SELHUB, M.D.**, *Author: The Love Response, and Your Brain on Nature, Instructor in Medicine Harvard Medical School, Associate in Medicine Massachusetts General Hospital, International speaker, Resiliency Coach, Stress Expert*

"Los Angeles can suck the energy right out of people's dreams. Pick up this book and take that energy back. Just as she does on her radio show, Deb exudes a special energy that is contagious. This book helps you achieve your dreams and it also shares real-life stories so you have proof that dreams happen... and now you really have no excuses!"

--**KRISTIN CRUZ**, *L.A. based Morning Radio Host "The Mark & Kristin Show" KOST 103.5 FM*

ACKNOWLEDGEMENTS/THANKS:

- **Philicia Endelman, Photography**
  www.*philiciaendelman*.com

- **Eduardo Roman, Hair**

- **Elizabeth Novak, Book Design & Cover**
  www.*elizabethnovakdesign*.com

- **Nadia Lawrence, Proofreading & Editing**

Other Books by Debbi Dachinger:
"DARE TO DREAM: This Life Counts!"

Bestseller in: Self-Help, Dreams, and Success, Winner of the 2013 Motivational Book / National Independent Excellence Awards, and the NIEA Missy Bystrom Sponsor Book Award. Available at Amazon, Barnes at Noble and all bookstores.

COPYRIGHT© 2013
Debbi Dachinger
10751 Wilshire Boulevard, Suite 1205
Los Angeles, CA 90024

Wisdom

To

Success

❧ FOREWORD ❧

I have had the honor of literally meeting thousands of people over the last thirteen years. Few of them have touched me with their authenticity, caring, humor and brilliance more than Debbi Dachinger. What an honor and a pleasure to be invited to write the forward for this inspirational book.

I am an author, public speaker, life coach, and co-creator of a life-changing body of work called Access Consciousness, and acutely aware of how challenging it can be to be authentic and inspiring.

Debbi shows that our greatest brilliance IS our authenticity—and our willingness to persevere no matter what. She gives clues to what allows a person to be truly successful, and she invites us all to realize, *"Success is achieved through positive thinking and positive doing. It's attraction plus action."*

I met Debbi what seems like many years ago. Within three minutes of meeting her, during our very first pre-interview chat, we were singing a (very bad) rendition of "Jingle Bells" on the phone together. You know...the part about *"Daching-er through the snow..."*

Debbi had invited me, several months before, to be interviewed on her transforming *Dare To Dream* radio show. From simply hearing the title of the show, I was already looking forward to the interview. I thought to myself, *"Whoever is willing to create a show with this name is someone I want to talk to!"* Quite frankly, I had no idea just how wonderful an interviewer—and person—Debbi would be. I had no idea that someone with a syndicated radio show would allow themselves to go to the intense depth and breadth she was willing to go to in that interview (and in many interviews and conversations since).

She invited me to be free to say what I really knew, and to be who I really am, with no holds barred. That's exactly what she invites you to do with this, her latest book. It is filled with the many gifts of wisdom she has accumulated, which will lead you to be inspired to choose success (on your terms) if you're willing to have it.

After interviewing several hundred amazing people in order to pick their brains for the hard-fought awareness that will change her listener's lives, in this book, the tables are quite-literally turned. In this book, it is Debbi's turn to be the interviewee. She shares the wisdom she has learned over many years—not just from having lived through obstacles and overcoming them— but also her journey with phenomenal people whose wisdom has contributed to her own. What follows is a passage of possibilities, and an invitation to become the genius you always knew you were capable of being.

It's that level of authenticity and humor you will find throughout this book, inviting you to be the unfettered expression of yourself in order to empower the life you choose, while allowing her true brilliance and never-say-die "chutzpah" to be revealed. This book format creates a wonderful respite from any possibility of monotony, enlightening and inspiring as you read, with pearls of wisdom too numerous to count.

So many people are looking for the tools for knowing that the dreams they desire are actually achievable. *Dare to Dream: Wisdom to Success* is written by someone smack in the middle of achieving them, for those of us who know they should be possible but sometimes doubt ourselves, experience fear, or who really need someone there to tell us, "*Yes. You. Can!*"

As Debbi says, "*You're sending a light out on the planet. You're changing the vibration of a planet that needs you so much.*" Consider this your pocket-sized book of inspiration from someone who is truly walking her talk.

Dr. Dain Heer, D.C.

Co-Creator, Access Consciousness
International speaker, facilitator
Author of *Being You, Changing The World*

INDEX ✸

Page 17 ~ On Creating a Dream and Achieving a Goal
Page 19 ~ Design Your Life, Interview with Bertrand Dory
Page 57 ~ Programming Goals into the Subconscious
Page 61 ~ On Daring to Dream Bigger, Interview with Kimberly Reid
Page 84 ~ Inspirational Moments
Page 89 ~ Shift Into Wonderful Things, Interview with Psychic Tee
Page 129 ~ The Best People We Know, Interview with Deb Scott
Page 159 ~ Quotable, Beverly Donofrio
Page 161 ~ Children & Their Dreams, Interview with Margaret Ashley
Page 201 ~ If It Scares You, Do It!
Page 207 ~ True Power Comes From Your Heart, Interview with Allana Pratt
Page 228 ~ Quotable, Ayn Rand
Page 229 ~ Awakening to Abundance, Interview with Daniel Gutierrez
Page 263 ~ Wealth Building, Interview with Kris Britton
Page 273 ~ Quotable, Reverend Michael Bernard Beckwith
Page 277 ~ The Art of Joyful Living, Interview with Cindy Briolotta and Linda Cassell
Page 307 ~ Shift, Shine, Grow, Interview with Karen Luniw
Page 332 ~ Quotable, Oprah Winfrey, Harriett Tubman, Erma Bombeck, Anaïs Nin, Lao Tzu
Page 334 ~ Put Aside Distractions, Focus on Your Goal, Interview with Cecelia Li
Page 364 ~ Life Coaching, Interview with Dr. Phil Dembo
Page 379 ~ Figure Out What You Want and Learn How to Ask For It
Page 382 ~ Dream Launch, Interview with Maribel Jimenez
Page 400 ~ New Transformation Strategies, Interview with Debra Poneman
Page 428 ~ Quotable, Debbi Dachinger
Page 430 ~ Instant Transformation, Interview with Farhana Dhalla
Page 457 ~ Practical Techniques Spiritual Approach, Interview with Cindy Briolotta and Linda Cassell
Page 487 ~ Spirit

"When you establish a destination by defining what you want, then take physical action by making choices that move you towards that destination, the possibility for success is limitless and arrival at the destination is inevitable."
— Steve Maraboli

"Someone's sitting in the shade today because someone planted a tree a long time ago."
— Warren Buffett

"By failing to prepare, you are preparing to fail."
— Benjamin Franklin

"A goal without a plan is just a wish."
— Antoine de Saint-Exupéry

Origin of DARE

Middle English DAR (1st & 3d singular present indicative), from Old English DEAR; akin to Old High German giTAR (1st & 3d singular present indicative) dare, Greek THARSOS courage. First Known Use: before 12th century.

Greetings *Dare to Dreamers, Goal Achievers, Those Desiring Different In Their Life, People Here To Contribute, Those Who Sense There Must Be Better, Folks Hungry To Learn, Those Who Yearn for Change, Anyone Seeking A Way Out Of Self Defeating Patterns That Have Held Them Back:*

This book is for you! What a surprise this book is actually since I had another book in mind to write. However I paid someone to transcribe some of the volume of radio shows on which I've been interviewed, and in reading back what she typed (thank you Kat Sparks!), I discovered wisdom offered in a new format, promising the tools to get you to the finish line of your dreams.

*My radio shows are one way I deliver the information on how to achieve goals, also my bestselling book "DARE TO DREAM: This Life Counts!" contains motivating material, my videos on YouTube (**www.YouTube.com/debontheradio**) assist with the message of what's possible, and now I've discovered this new format: radio shows over the years where I've been asked various questions on how to get from where you are to where you desire to be – your dream come true -- as well as how to remove any obstacles from your path. Through each of these venues my one wish is for you to live a joy-filled life.*

The pages to follow are literal transcripts from radio shows I've been featured on as a Goal Achievement expert and guest. I've had the good fortune to experience how eager listeners are to create an inspired life of their own design. I often hear from people who have followed my recommendations and I'm moved by the letters and emails from artists, tractor-trailer drivers, teachers, coaches, entrepreneurs, musicians, healers and people from all around the world who resonate with the idea that we came here to live our dreams out loud! I believe that a life filled with the journey and experience of crafting dreams is a generative, rich life and the one we're called to.

Enjoy these pages and as you go forth to make your dreams your reality know that you are inspiring many. Dreams are free, so free your dreams. What do you dare to dream?

Much love,
Debbi

On Creating a Dream, Achieving a Goal

- *If it doesn't challenge you it doesn't change you.*
- *Know your limits and then defy them.*
- *You are stronger than the burn and the sweat a dream takes.*
- *Say "yes" in your mind.*
- *If it comes up, feel it. Don't force it, feel it.*
- *What you resist - only further exists.*
- *You can do anything. Say "yes" to your dreams. Say "yes" to your life.*
- *Allow and receive everything.*
- *Feel gratitude. Gratitude for everything you have already been and done and for whom you are right now.*
- *Stop trying to figure everything out, just start.*
- *Do whatever it takes.*
- *Stop trying to fix or change who you inherently are. Let your freak flag fly and relish it. It's so much more attractive to be who you are.*

- *No more blending in.*
- *Send thanks and appreciation to everyone who has ever been in your life, every job, every physical experience, every moment of your life's journey thus far.*
- *There is abundance all around you right now. Flow with it.*
- *Your dreams will lead you to the greatness you came here to be for the world.*

<u>SECRET</u>: EVERYTHING YOU NEED IN ORDER TO BECOME WHO YOU TRULY DESIRE TO BE --- IS ALREADY WITHIN YOU.

Debbi Dachinger: Interview - Design Your Dream Life with Bertrand Dory

BERTRAND DORY: Hello Everybody. My name is Bertrand Dory, and I welcome you to Design Your Dream Life. It is always a pleasure and really I'm feeling so humbled by this, to share this next hour with you. I know that maybe you are in this place where life is difficult. Maybe the money is not here. Maybe the relationship is not what you want. Or maybe you have to make a decision. A decision in your life that could change everything but this decision is consuming you and you don't know what to do. Or maybe it's just that life has become boring and you wonder if there is something more. Or maybe you're just in this place where you feel that everything is wrong, and you're angry with everything. I have been here. I have been here and that's why I wanted to bring to you this wonderful lady called Debbi Dachinger. Why? Because Debbi is very successful and she is trying, and she's moving forward, and she's embracing life. And I think this is part of her success. It's a journey of congruence, of persistence, and you all...you heard me many times on this show using these same words. But I do believe that once we embrace this journey and we want to be only the best version of who we are, and we want to shine to the world with our gifts, that life changes. For me that was the case, for Debbi it was the case, and I hope that some of you will be inspired and will take this journey also, and do whatever it takes to make the next steps, take the decision and move forward.

Hi, Debbi. How are you?

DEBBI DACHINGER: Oh, I am so in love with your voice, that's how I am. A sexy man, with...a sexy man's voice with a French accent is, I mean the bomb. That's the best, so thank you. It's going to be a pleasure to converse with you today.

BERTRAND: Thank you very much. It's a pleasure to have you here, and I know that you're doing great things in the world for people and you're helping them to really step forward. So thank you for being here, Debbi.

DEBBI: My pleasure. You bet.

BERTRAND So Debbi, can you tell us a bit more about you and more specifically how you came to become who you are today.

DEBBI: I definitely came out different to start with, and I always had these desires to entertain since I'm a little, little girl, I would sing every opportunity I could, every time there was a play, whether it was in school or, eventually, to summer stock to perform, where my mom sent me. I went to performing arts camps in the summer, and during the school year I was in chorus, I starred in school plays, I was a very good violinist and played in school orchestra and all-county orchestra, I taught myself how to play the guitar; I excelled at most forms of entertainment, some venue of having the spotlight on me, which is what I craved, and the other piece was expressing myself in a way that could move people. As it turns out, entertainment and expression have taken many forms in my life. I could never have guessed I would end up where I am today. And although no one taught me how to achieve dreams, no one taught that I could accomplish goals, I have always had…there is a Yiddish word "chutzpah," which means to have nerve and audacity, in Spanish you might say I had 'cojones,' a way of saying this person the guts or courage. So I have this kind of "*Um!*" energy that says, *I'm going to do it.* I have always possessed tenacity and chutzpah, a crazy belief in myself and my desires.

Part of my journey has also been about having to heal issues inside of me, and rearrange what was going on including negative thoughts. Look, you know, let's face it. Beliefs are thoughts that we think so often they become solid filters through which we perceive and live our lives out of. That's a lot of what I was doing. So I had great natural inner qualities and gifts and talents and then got in my own way. I'd have great times of...where things just came my way and I'd audition for things or I decided on something-- and I really made it happen. But there were other times when I didn't. It was that inconsistency that made me tired. I didn't like it. I felt like there had to be an easier way, because frankly I could just pause at any time in my life and look around on this planet and notice there are amazing people doing amazing things. So how come it didn't stop them? It didn't mean I was wrong, it didn't mean I was bad, it didn't mean that I was untalented or ungifted, or someone else was better or I was worse. It just meant something was going wrong in my space that wasn't working for me.

I didn't realize that I was setting out on a journey, really I didn't. I was just setting out to stop the issues and to increase the pleasure and the joy in my life. What ended up happening is I started achieving things and people started to notice and wonder, "How did you do that? *You just learned how to make jewelry and three months later you have a business and you're selling in five major stores across America."* Or, *"You decided after all this time that you wanted to sing."* I was always a singer but I just decided at a certain juncture in my life it would be kind of interesting to experience singing from a band perspective because I'd always been on stage and in shows. And then I was singing with a big band and with jazz combos. I decided to do a marathon and I ended up successfully completing two. I wanted to travel, I did some of that. I wanted to take workshops that really appealed to me and seemed quite expensive. However, I found a way to make it happen. I was carrying around extra body weight and I wanted to lose weight. I also got to the other side of that, and have been in a normal sized body for a long time now.

And with each succession, it was reflected back from others who saw what was happening. I was just doing my thing. Friends from college said, *"You're the Madonna of careers, Debbi. You recreate yourself all the time."* And each time it had an element of success attached to it. That has been my journey...it's been that "*Um!*" energy that I was telling you about, that willingness to desire something and then go out and get it.

All of that caused me to do whatever it took so that I could learn what I did. And now here I am...I mean who would have thought, I've got a syndicated, award winning radio show. I wrote a best-selling book, I'm a keynote speaker, I'm an oft-interviewed guest on radio and TV shows and my life has changed so significantly and I see how I get to use my gifts of entertainment, my desire to inspire and lead and teach, and that my journey, actually my wound, has become my gift that I can offer to the world. So now I teach how to achieve goals, I know it works, I hear from other people using my goal fulfillment method with great success, and I am known today as a goal achievement expert. It gives me a lot of joy.

BERTRAND: Yeah. I can hear the joy in your voice. What you said here was really profound. Once we get out of our way, miracles are happening. Okay, you use the miracles but this is how my life works so changing but also, you said something else. That now you can use your gift. And isn't this the best present or the best gift you can give to other people?

DEBBI: It is the best present. And many people feel that, they have this defect or something happened or something didn't work out. And they actually desire that thing, but it doesn't seem to happen or something has gotten in the way, and it's amazing to see those people and what they can achieve in spite of that. You know courage isn't to do things without fear. People who are courageous do things in spite of fear. They get it. They see the fear, or the doubt, or whatever it is that's going on in their space. But they don't empower that issue anymore. At some point in their life they just say, *"Bring it. I have let you be the god that leads me and directs me my whole life and when I do you sabotage my dreams and I run away from them. So this time I'm going to behave differently."* And with courage they move forward and take massive action to achieve great things.

Another aspect of what you were saying…I'm not sure that most people realize how big this is, that somewhere in your life, whatever happened to you that you felt was a great deficit, if you have turned it around, that what originally appeared to be a deficit is actually something you can now use to great effect as a gift to the world.

BERTRAND: Oh, yeah. Completely. I was saying my life three years ago was completely different and it was the best that I thought I could have. And then everything crashed and for three years I really had to go over fears, being petrified, being alone and everything. And that was really the biggest lesson of my life. And taking the step forward, that's what I can now bring to people because I understand where they are, I can help them. And I can take the step forward myself. And using the gift of my voice, as you mentioned before, is something that I didn't like before at all. And now it's becoming one of the best assets I have to communicate and share with people.

DEBBI: That's brilliant, exactly.

BERTRAND: It's so true that we have sometimes to go through these depths of pain to be able to find what is really important in our life.

DEBBI: The question is what if that pain was not put there because you're bad or wrong? And what if that pain was not put there because it's meant to dissuade you from moving forward? What if that pain isn't meant to punish you? What if that pain is actually there because your soul said, *"I want, before this person incarnates, I want them to get to a level of understanding about this particular aspect of themselves. And the only way we know if it is, is to have them go through something a little traumatic that may feel painful, but in actuality when they take it on and deal with it and heal it, when they come out the other side they will be a wholly different person."*

Based on the story that you were sharing, Bertrand, about three years ago where you were...or where I was when I was in that place in my life of inconsistency and frustration, the interesting thing is, you just get to a point when you're on your path and finally stop resisting the pain you're carrying and you say, *let me experience this.* You know everything that exists in us, like doubt, like trust issues, like playing small, like fear, lack of clarity, fear of failure. All the things that plague people, they're actually...they've become solid inside of us because we hit up against the same emotional limiting pattern over and over again. And what we do is we run away from it. And we treat it like the big monster in the closet. We never open the closet door to see what is in there and we can't overcome what has been stopping us repeatedly on our life's path to success.

On the other hand, what if the issue was put in our path on purpose by us, by our soul, our highest self, before we came in this life, because in overcoming it we're going to become more and exactly who we're meant to be? Brave people are the ones who say, *I'm not going to fight this anymore because resisting it has only made it more solid, it's never made it go away, it's never made me feel better, it's never given me the reality I prefer. No more struggle. Now I surrender. What if I just stayed still, breathed and felt this issue and pain?* What really successful people do is just stand still. We breathe through it. We get help if we need, and we know we're going to live through whatever this is, we will make it. Fear is not going to kill me. Failure's not going to kill me. Doubt is not going to kill me. If I just stand still for the first time, maybe I can breathe through this and see what riches are on the other side. And that journey is really what it's all about.

BERTRAND: Yes, completely and I must say if I'm really looking back and am bluntly honest, that before I was more or less dead inside. And it's only since I was nudged as you said with the pain, but nudged to become more global and to take the courage to talk about things as important as life but also as vulnerable and authentic about myself that my life really started to take a different meaning and different direction. And without this pain I would never have done this. I know this. Yeah, it is now, looking back, my path and that's what I'm here to do. I had to go through all of this to be able to have learned and to have cleaned whatever I was carrying from my past.

DEBBI: Exactly, and opportunity is the most amazing, miraculous thing that comes our way. Because we can sit back and say, *oh I desire this and I desire that* but then an opportunity comes and we run. What if when opportunity came instead, we said *yes*, knowing that this opportunity can be one of two things? It can be the "it" factor for us, in that moment it's going to be an amazing life changer. An experience that's exactly made for us. Second, an opportunity sometimes shows up appearing a little different. Sometimes we need to say yes to something in order to open another door we cannot yet see, for something entirely different to come to us that is right for us.

I've had a number of those. For example, at one point in my life I wondered what it would be like to be a motivational speaker. I knew I couldn't think my way through to a conclusion to know if I'd love speaking in front of others enough to say, *"okay that's the career for me."* I'd actually have to do it and experience it to know. I had been in Toastmasters several years and had received my Advanced Toastmasters medal so I was confident at speaking and comfortable doing it. I wrote a whole seminar. I found someone to help me and she got me out into Los Angeles and I was speaking at different companies for three months, delivering this workshop. It was fantastic because I was doing it. And I was doing it to see how I liked it. What I started to learn was that I liked it but it also became clear it wasn't the end-all be-all for me. I knew there was much more. And unexpectedly, now--because I stepped into the opportunity and because I said yes to all the opportunities to speak--something entirely different, entirely unexpected, and entirely amazing, *came to me.* This is how life, magic and miracles work. What we know about our energy is that what goes out then resonates back. We are energetic mirrors. And having a positive energy going out, following my path, following my bliss, seeing where it would lead, I received a call out of nowhere from a director who said somebody recommended me for a voiceover cartoon. Patricia Heaton who had been on the TV show "*Raymond,*" had to opt out of the project and could I audition to voice the part? Now I had never done a voiceover in my life. I couldn't even believe someone recommended me. I was thinking *where did that come from*? And it sure sounded like fun! The director sent me the script. Of course I never told him I hadn't done a voice over before. I just flowed with it! I loved the script and a week later I was auditioning. I did a good job. I made him laugh. Apparently none of the other actresses did. And a week after that that audition, I received a call that I was cast in the part. I went to the studio to voice this lead animation character and they discovered that I sing. They asked, *"Now we don't have to hire someone additional to sing. Can we write a song for your character and you'll sing it?"* I said, *yes that would be fabulous.*

Now my heart is soaring, and I'm...I love voiceovers, I love doing voices for cartoons. This is incredible. The greatest experience. So here I am now in another joy. And I decide I love voiceovers. *This* is what I want to do. So I get an agent and I start auditioning left and right. Now I'd book some things here and there but not as much as I want. And about a year down the road I'm going through a huge change crisis in my life, which means a divorce, and all I knew during that time was to *keep on moving forward Debbi, just keep putting one foot in front of the other.* And I happened to see a job notice for a radio show looking for a host. In my mind I thought, *if I do radio, that will get me more exposure and voiceover work.* I'm not sure how linear that thought is, but something inside of me clicked. I got the radio job.

I had a little music show for two months. I didn't love it. I kept thinking *what am I doing here?* Two months later the owners of the station came to me and said *we like what you're doing. We want to give you your own one-hour show; what would you like it to be?* And I just...it poured out of me. Like the path of my life, Dare to Dream. I'm going to inspire people to make their dreams and their goals come true. I will interview really successful individuals on my show who have achieved amazing things in their lives, and seven plus years later; here I am with this award-winning, syndicated show.

I never could have guessed then that this would have been a place that was right for me or where I'm supposed to be. However, it took me saying yes and showing up, and yes and showing up, and yes I'll try that, and yes I've never done a voiceover and yes I've never done motivational speaking and *yes, yes, yes*. They were very positive risks. And was I scared? Of course, you know? With each turn there was a whole other set of values I had to deal with and questions of...*am I capable and can I do this and can I* ...of course, of course. But it didn't stop me. I still showed up and brought everything, my entire arsenal inside and then went for it with a lot of fun and love.

Wisdom To Success | *Debbi Dachinger*

So here I am, and I know where I am right now is not the end...not the last depot in my station. I feel that from here I'm going to continue to grow and that means I need to keep saying yes, and take on new challenges and experiences.

BERTRAND: Yeah. It's completely true. It's very...it's reflecting more or less how my life was and I remember when I started this radio show I was just in tears. So scared of going to do my first show. But you have sometimes to say yes. But sometimes also, some people will never take opportunity because they're petrified by the idea of failure, personal failure or success, or they're just trying everything and nothing seems to come from this. So what will you advise people to do in this case?

DEBBI: Well, I know one thing for sure and that is that we have to take massive action. That's the one thing nobody wants to hear. I'm going to tell you a funny story. I was at a workshop this past week and I was talking to one of the facilitators afterwards and she said, *"It's so great that you came to the workshop, Debbi."* And I said, *"Of course. I said I was going to come and I'm here."* She said, *"Yes, and even though this is a packed workshop and it's very successful, it's interesting to me the amount of people who said I'm going to come and do that workshop, and the day before the workshop is going to start they called and cancelled. And I asked them why and they said well I hoped for the money to pay for the workshop but it never came."* She shared that, and I thought *isn't that fascinating. That's just like life.* So many people wish for things. You know a wish is a longing. A wish isn't real, it isn't a demand. But a goal or a target, well that's different.

Those people who did not attend the workshop, they didn't take the steps to create the dream of attending the workshop. They may have pictured the money, prayed for the money, affirmed the money, visualized--that's great. But those are accessories. The real meat and potatoes? That's taking massive action. You have to do whatever it takes to make something happen. So, in lieu of that, potential issues may get in the way, they may come up…and I get it. I have them, you have them, and we all have them. The most successful people have them. What I know about the obstacles is…the most successful people…they don't let them be deterrents. Some of the most successful people we know, Edison, Donald Trump, rock stars who have hit the bottom and suddenly come back up. There are tons of people we know, we see every day and probably people in your everyday life who have all failed tremendously. But the one thing they did is they get back up. They have resilience. They don't let it define them, they don't let it be their whole life's path, or story. You know, they feel their feelings and then they figure out: what is the lesson. Like what did I bring to the party? Why did that happen? Because once they get the lesson they can go out and do better. Be totally different next time.

So I say that fear, doubt, failure, trust, playing small...here's the truth. They're all energy. They're not real. We make them real. And if you know anything about energy, energy is transmutable. We can transform energy and decide on the energy we're choosing. So if we're choosing the lie of fear or doubt and the things it tells us will happen if we move forward...that means we can make a new, better, different choice. That's really what it's about. For some people when that comes up, get a coach. Get someone to help you through it. For some people, hire a therapist or great energy healer. I'm all about doing it fast, to move through things. Or you can, in your own mind ask, *"what is the opposite of fear?"* And ask, *What would faith do? How would faith move? What would faith look like going towards my dream and my goal?* And choose that instead. Or if it's doubt. What's the opposite of doubt? It's certainty. What would it look like if you were certain that everything you did would work out for you, and you had the stuff it took? And what if you weren't put on this planet to be an unworthy pile of crap? What if you were actually created at this time in this very reality because you were meant to be so big that you shine as bright as that sun? What would that look like and feel like? And just go live in that huge, expanding space because it's energy and it's a choice.

BERTRAND: That's wonderful. Thank you for the wisdom, it's really wonderful. You're saying it's taking massive action but sometimes action is associated with hard work. And from my experience it's not really the work itself that's hard because once you do something you like and you love, it's easy. Even if it's big. But it is really just taking the step and transcending whatever fear we have in our way.

DEBBI: Transcending, indeed. You know there is only the joy of doing what you're doing. And if you focus on that, it's so much easier. Find the joy. Where's the joy in doing what you're doing?

I also think it's fascinating how there's different perspectives on "hard work." Or on what is an opportunity? Bottom line: action creates opportunity. For instance, in certain areas in Africa, some people don't have the means to have an education. These are people who are so hungry for an education they would do anything to get it. And yet, in other more wealthy countries…some of the people do not carry the same value in education, in fact they may take it for granted. It is available so they don't feel the same sense of importance and urgency, that schooling equals opportunity and possibility. It's fascinating, the kind of action somebody will take when they're really desirous of something that's got great meaning to them. I think that's an interesting paradox of life.

So what you're willing to do, I think has to be predicated by a great desire. A great hunger. Something that inspires you that wants to be expressed. And let it start there, let that be your guidance, your GPS, your inner God Protection System that points you in the right direction and points to, *this is what's next*. The truth is we don't have to know all the action steps. We just don't. But we do have to acknowledge what we know…like the next right thing is this, and then you do that. And then the next right thing is this.

Personally, with a big goal, I always write it out. I write out the steps with the caveat that as I go through the steps they may get modified, or things will get added because sometimes you don't know what you don't know. You're on a journey to go somewhere but you've never been on that journey before...it's all brand new. You're learning so much as you go along and you're changing so much.

Listen, we all have one life in this particular body. It's super quick. It really is. Aren't you put here to enjoy it? I don't think we're put here to wake up to a poopy job we don't care about, to be in a loveless marriage, be in relationships with people who are naysayers and dream stealers, to give our souls over to dysfunctional families, or to create unhealthy bodies. Come on, you know? That's all choice. It's really all about choice. And even if you made selections that previously were unkind to you, you can now make new choices that give you the joy of living. Just decide, what is it you desire? What does it look like? What does it feel like? Then choose to do it. Choose to make it happen.

BERTRAND: Yeah, it's completely true and I love what you say here, that we go on a path where we don't know what's going to happen because we don't know what we don't know. And, what I would like to say to the listeners is sometimes when we take these paths and suddenly we meet some amazing people out of the blue, just because we are such…well this happened to me…when I'm really happy and I'm really doing what I love to do when I'm serving and so on, this makes this journey interesting but also easy. But…without being at this level where we are able to cope with meeting this kind of this person, we're able to cope with is opportunity, we will fail so sometimes our journey is a little bit of a learning lesson because we need to grow to certain levels so we are ready to take this opportunity or to meet this person.

DEBBI: Absolutely. I like what you said about it being easy, and that is an important point. There are many things we have to do and take massive action for. Why? Because a dream, a goal, is challenging to us. It's outside of what we currently know. It's outside of our comfort zone. Awesome. That's what a goal is. So yes, you take massive action because you're actually creating a treasure map through the steps you take to get there. There are also very easy dreams and goals that come along that require much less of us. I'll tell you that I do write things down, and I find that the Law of Attraction…sometimes I just vibrate. Am I aware of the vibration? No. It's something, I have…I desire this, and then it just creates.

For instance, I desired to be in a mastermind group. I had heard about them and thought it sounded great; I'd never been in one. Napoleon Hill is the man who recommended Mastermind groups. Hill said that the 'Master Mind' is defined as: *"Coordination of knowledge and effort in a spirit of harmony, between two or more people, for the attainment of a definite purpose."* In his book, *Think and Grow Rich*, Napoleon Hill said: *"No two minds ever come together without, thereby, creating a third, invisible, intangible force which may be likened to a third mind."* So where there are two or more minds gathered creating synergy and nurturing each other toward a goal, it becomes a mastermind…ooh, I was very excited by that idea. I wrote down several things on a list of goals, and one of them was: *"Join a Mastermind Group.'* Literally, two weeks later without my having done a thing, I became a member of an already established Mastermind group. I had had someone on my radio show who introduced me to somebody who was an amazing connection, who then introduced me to somebody else and by that third call I was speaking to the person who said, *"By the way, I run a mastermind group, and I was wondering if you would like to join it?"* I just went *hubbidah, hubbidah, hubbidah.* I didn't have to go out and create it, or find it; I didn't have to

Wisdom To Success | *Debbi Dachinger*

research it. The Mastermind Group came to me, and it is a high level group of people. I'm blessed. I'm so blessed.

And last year, here's an interesting one. At the end of every year I write a list of what I desire to create for the new year. One of the last days of the year, I look over my previous year's goal list and it's amazing for me to see where I'm at, what was created, and then I write a new list for the following year. The list sets up an energy and that energy takes over, some goals start creating by their own volition. Last year, the one thing I wanted more than anything was a feeling of peace. I really wanted peace from my inside out. And here we are, almost at the end of the year. Enough so that I can look back and I'm touched when I say I see that the twist and turns my life has taken thus far, it has created an amazing peace inside of me. All those things that weren't working, have so gracefully been chipped away and all the things that I needed to generate for that space of serenity, calm and knowingness have come in and in that space, peace is there. I am sometimes amazed at how easy it can be. To put it forth with the best of intentions and that it can all work out so gracefully.

BERTRAND: Yes, it does. It does work out this way and yeah. Peace is, especially when we, like you, go through a divorce and the fears and difficulty after this kind of experience, it's difficult to find peace again. But putting this as a goal and something that we want to achieve, when it comes to us because we change our beliefs and we change our thoughts and we are open to receiving peace. That's probably one of the biggest goals. This happiness that we can have in our lives.

DEBBI: There is a special ease in peace, and I know because I've experienced a lot of anxiety. When I was younger I had a tremendous amount of stress and anxiety, which was a result of the environment I grew up in and then took on a life of its own and became self-induced; stress and anxiety is a very difficult place to live and interact from, difficult to create from, so to have this peace now in my life, is meaningful. What's beautiful about it is that if I have peace now, what it means is that I can expand out into it. Everything I choose can become bigger and better. It can have that expansive energy and more. To have that and more, and more and more, is beyond my wildest dreams. It's all energy. So even this peace can continue to expand out and become greater and a new place for me to create my life from.

BERTRAND: Yeah, and that's where it's beautiful because you can then be completely in the now, because once you have peace around you, you're not living in your fears, you aren't living in your past, you aren't living in a potential future that may be better or not. You just know that you're here and that you're surrounded with peace and you know that where you're going is going to bring you more of what you want because it is a normal path we create for ourselves in our life. I think it's really beautiful when we arrive here. But sometimes people are setting goals by fear. And I'm going to give you an example here. Some people are going to say I want to be a millionaire because they don't have the money now. And they will never get there because what is behind this is a fear. So how would you invite people to set up their goals? Yeah. That's the question.

DEBBI: That's a great question. I definitely have a formula, and if you use this formula it works every time. The first thing is what we discussed. You have to have desire… desire it for yourself and the goal causes a feeling inside of excitement. What would that be like? After you have that desire, the next thing is to decide. What do you choose? Do you choose to have those million dollars, or do you choose to just wish you had a million dollars? Totally different energy. If you're going to wish, this is not for you. But if you're going to decide...and by the way, anyone who is listening can fill in any goal or dream they desire here. It doesn't have to be a million dollars. It can be fifty million. [LAUGHTER] It can be anything that you'd really like to experience in your life. The first thing is desire; the second thing is to decide you will step into it.

Quick example: Somebody who wants to quit smoking and they successfully quit for good. Why were they successful? They decided and they were willing to do whatever it took for that to occur for them to never pick up another cigarette again. What about someone who loses weight and successfully maintains the weight loss. What makes them different -- because it is a very small percent? They lose weight and keep it off. They're doing whatever it takes. They did what it took to lose the extra weight, and then understand once they lost it, they didn't go back to eating the old way. They aligned with a weight maintenance tool that worked for their body. In each of these examples they desired it, they decided fully to do it, they took steps to achieve it. If feelings or issues came up, they dealt with it, they kept taking necessary steps and once the dream and desire was achieved they enjoyed their accomplishment. This is what successful people on every level do.

Again, you have desires and you decide. The next thing is to write. Take paper and write on the top of the sheet of paper what your dream is, what is your goal, what is your target. Beneath your dream write what the steps are to get you there. I begin at the very bottom of the sheet and say, this is where I am now. If I want a million dollars, what is the first thing I have to do? I'll tell you the first one I might write down: *Start to understand finances and wealth.* I would do some research to learn more about what solid finances are. How do people make it? What do the successful people do to manifest the money I'm looking for? The next thing I would do is set up a special bank account with a million dollars as a goal. Then the next thing I might do is study a financial subject or take a course in stocks that interests me. Then write another step to take, and another step you'll need to take. Somewhere along the line I may write I acquire a better job that pays me better. The next thing may be I find outside interests that are easy, quick ways like flipping houses or stocks, or hedge funds -- something that will create money quick. You write out all the steps necessary to get you to a million dollars, until the last thing you write may be: a safe bank account with good interest that will make the money accrue even more money. That might be the final item you write and at the very top of the sheet of paper of all these steps is "My Dream."

The next thing is to keep your sheet with you each day. Don't write all that beautiful information and throw it out. Keep it. Because that's your guide, that's your map. You want to read it every day and see what the next step is. *Oh, okay. Today I'm supposed to call banks. Today I'm supposed to look into finances. Today I'm supposed to find out what a hedge fund is, and how I might successfully do that. Today I will look into what classes can help me get the knowledge I need.* If you hear what I'm saying, and I'm hearing me right now and I'm getting excited because I see now this can happen. And every day when I take out my sheet, as I take another step towards this dream, it will happen.

The next thing is to heal and deal. What that means is, the things that we spoke about...the feelings that come up, the limitations, the things that scare us into submission: the doubt, the fear, the failure, the playing small, the lack of trust, the poor time management, thinking we're beholden to others, or what will others think about us. All of that. When it creeps up because

Wisdom To Success | *Debbi Dachinger*

it hasn't been healed yet, it is an opportunity to stand still, to breathe, to feel all that stuff you've been resisting and just allow it to flow through you, know you'll live through it, and if it's too big get help or get a coach, just keep moving forward. Keep taking massive action. The very final step is, when you achieve, celebrate.

BERTRAND: Yes, that's very important. Celebrate and to anchor this into our life and to recognize that we did it and that it's here. What is really interesting with what you said here with your process or method is that you don't really go after the goal but you are learning, you're immersing yourself; you're soaking in this vibration of having it, of getting the knowledge, of being there already. And I think that this gradually, slowly, is planting seeds in our mind and in our soul that is getting more and more possible. From my experience when we do this, then suddenly we find the right people. They're coming to us because we are vibrating this and because we are really soaking ourselves completely with this goal and I believe this is the action that we have to take.

DEBBI: Absolutely correct. And get ready because when you do step into that vibration, when you do start to take action, things and people and circumstances will come to you that you could never have foreseen. Here's a key element. A big portion of this idea, this principle we're talking about right now, is letting go. So right next door to the *House of Taking Massive Action* is their next-door neighbor who is *Letting Go*. Because we do take action and then at some point during the day we can let it all go because there is a universe that cares for us so deeply that has been waiting for us to step up and be who we came here to be. To live our lives with joy …..think about it. The Universe. You want to talk about magic and miracles? The Universe has an endless storage full of it that they're just waiting to dole out. And when we let go we allow the space for that to come into our lives. Because we're vibrating at that level we magnetize wonders to us. And it is some of the coolest phenomena that could possibly appear and you often never foresee coming. So, is it worth the journey? You bet.

BERTRAND: Yeah, it's completely worth the journey and sometimes it is a very, very scary journey. And I'm not going to minimize this, especially when we have to look at what is not healed in our life and what we need to let go. Because it is redefining also who we are and we're becoming, and sometimes it is very safe, or we feel unsafe, or having these things of our past, of our own defenses around us, because this is what we have built to protect ourselves. But in order to arrive to a dream life, in order to arrive to a life where every morning you wake up and suddenly you don't know what's going to happen because you know something good's going to happen, that's just amazing and it's really a worthwhile journey.

DEBBI: I have to say I think as much as those elements of limitations that we put on ourselves feel scary, it is a far, far, greater scare to me to not ever go for what I desire and love. That's scary to me because if you have ever stayed in a relationship way too long and not been happy, you know what that feels like. If you have ever been in an unhealthy body and really desired to be in a body that was fit and healthy and worked for you, you know what that feels like. If you ever dreamed about going on a trip but never gave that to yourself, dreamed with all your talents and gifts to be doing a job where you were really meant to be, but instead your work, your employment had nothing to do with your personality or your magnificence; you know what that feels like. To me, that's real fear. That's soul killing. And instead if we deem our dreams as 'a scary, unsafe journey,' which we make so big and important, when truthfully the fear or lack of safety is not real. This is all an illusion. It's just isn't factual. We just make it so real. But if we just trust, you know. Wow. What we can create.

I don't know of anybody who has been afraid and has died while creating a dream, right? I mean you never hear on the news, "Mr. Jones died because he wanted to go after his dream and he was so frightened he keeled over." [LAUGHTER] You know, you don't. But you do hear stories about how many people die on a Monday because that's the day we 'go back to our jobs, go back to work,' which is often not fulfilling. And you hear stories of those who created amazing things on this planet and when they're interviewed someone will ask, "So Mr. Jones, were you ever afraid?" And Mr. Jones says: "Yes, yes! Sure I experienced fear. But you know I felt I really had to do this, and I figured a way out. And now I am elated."

Here's a little secret. One thing I find that people…something that they gloss over is…research. Research is huge. I research a lot because part of fear is ignorance. I do not mean that as a judgment. We're ignorant when we don't know, when we haven't lived the dream yet, the reality of the dream, we don't know it, we don't know the steps and all the data yet, therefore we're ignorant. And the only way to change that ignorance, to turn it around and shift it, is to learn. Sometimes we need to research so we understand better what it is we desire to move into and how to get the dream into gear. Research the industry you're interested in, research the experience you wish to create, the trips, and the place you dream of going. Once you do the investigative work you'll find that fears start to quell; you start to have a better understanding. Now you're not stepping into the great unknown. Now there's a connection from becoming informed and from that new understanding you have the awareness to take massive action.

BERTRAND: Yes, you're so right. It is ignorance that is scarier because it's the unknown. But it's in the term of knowledge of course, as you mentioned. But also it's a term of becoming the person that we want to become. The person that we are going to become. That can be scary too but it is my belief that we can only become what our soul wants us to become and if we love our self enough to respect what we truly desire, that's where we find real bliss.

DEBBI: Yeah, I feel that we have blueprints to follow. And we also have a lot of gray matter that is desire we create by will—there's a lot of things I can desire and make happen that probably have nothing to do with my soul. I don't know how important it was to my soul that I write a book. I was however, strongly compelled from within to create it. Then there are some things that are so huge in my space that if I don't do them there will be sadness and regret inside of me. That's probably why I push myself in a really positive way. Why I push myself out of my comfort zone is because I can't stand that feeling of not having the experience, of regret. I just can't stand the energy attached to it. I'd rather harness my courage and proceed forward and see what's there, you know? It's not going to hurt me to just see what potentially can happen.

Frankly, we are all potent. That's an interesting aspect. Let's face it, how powerful are we as beings and creators? To pretend that we are otherwise is a great disservice to ourselves. We are so much more powerful and limitless than we allow ourselves to fully know. If we were to step into our complete brilliance and live from there, what could our lives be like? What could we gift to the planet at a time when the planet really needs us to step up as leaders and as chiefs of our lives and also as stewards of the earth and of the universe? You know, what's possible?

BERTRAND: Yeah. How powerful we are, I don't know. I just know it's amazing when you start to embrace this power and I am barely on the start of my own journey so I can only see glimpses of power. But it is amazing to see the impact we have on other people, as we decided to step out and help other people, that we became this person that now, just by being there we are bringing so much to the people. And that I find is the magic of life. To be able to give this gift.

DEBBI: The more I become myself, which means I step out of my own way and let all of me shine through with no judgment and complete allowance, the more capacity I have to love and to show up for others. Also the more capacity I have to set boundaries. To know when it is correct for me to say no because it's not right for me, or just something I don't want to do. And also know when to say yes. I think each of us embracing authentically who we are and sensing there's a reason why I was put together this way: the personality, the gifts, the talents, the quirks, the intelligence, the sensitivity. By the way, those of us who are spiritual seekers are deeply sensitive people. We feel others, we are empaths, and we are intuitive. Because we are so sensitive we need to be especially kind to ourselves. And kind to us means how we talk to and treat ourselves. Kind to ourselves means whom we surround ourselves with - others who honor, support and appreciate us, and kind to ourselves means giving ourselves the things we so deeply desire. Why should we withhold? Why should we put ourselves in a prison of not having? It is our right. It is our right to move forward and give ourselves that which we desire the most.

BERTRAND: That it is. You are right, you are right. Our capacity to love is just enormous when we arrive to this stage because well, I'm not scared anymore of being authentic because I know who I am, and that every part of me is either lovable or either…okay, if it's not, then it's not. I can't do anything about this. And that's really where we have the freedom. The freedom to give the biggest gift of all which is the gift of love and understanding to people.

DEBBI: It simplifies life to embrace yourself and to feel alive when you're just being yourself. I think the coolest people I've ever met are the ones who really are themselves without any agenda or apology; they're the people that I'm often very drawn to. They have a certain charisma in owning all of who they are with no apology. You can notice them when they walk in a room; they're the ones who draw everybody's attention – they certainly draw mine. I think this is the time for us to completely embody ourselves, including our blueprint. Including our who-ness and our is-ness and why we're here. Whatever you're currently doing that is working for you--just keep building and expanding on that and whatever you're doing that you don't prefer, understand that you can choose otherwise. When it's time to make a better choice just do whatever it takes to get through so it doesn't own or control you.

Remember you are the steward of your own life. That's the bottom line. It is your life. It is my life. I can decide-- I can make life as crappy or as phenomenal as I want. I definitely choose phenomenal. I definitely want to fly. I'm a human without wings and yet, in my space I often feel like I fly. That's the greatest feeling for me. And what else is possible? My journey doesn't end here, as long as I'm alive I am growing and growing, and so it can be for everybody. The truth for all of us is: Know you can create your dreams come true.

BERTRAND: Thank you very much. And I think that's the biggest gift that you can do to support people and give them life and give the hope and then nudge them forward through their life so that they can decide then to define their dreams and then take the right actions that will bring them to this dream. So Debbi, if people want to find you it's at http://www.deborahdachinger.com?

DEBBI: Yes, and I have a YouTube channel so anyone who likes inspiration can go to my YouTube channel at: http://www.YouTube.com/debontheradio. I've had businesses write to me that they begin their staff meetings playing these videos. It's thrilling to me that I inspire people at that level. These uplifting videos teach lessons with fun; they're sweet little 5 to 10 minute videos that can really get your day going.

BERTRAND Wonderful, thank you. Any other way we can connect with you?

DEBBI: Sign up free on my web site, get a free audio gift plus the newsletter and that tells about upcoming interviews with a link to everything available from Dare To Dream to make your dreams your reality.

BERTRAND: Wonderful. Thank you very much Debbi. It is really a great pleasure for me to share this hour with you, and thank you for sharing everything that you have learned with our listeners. Appreciate you.

END

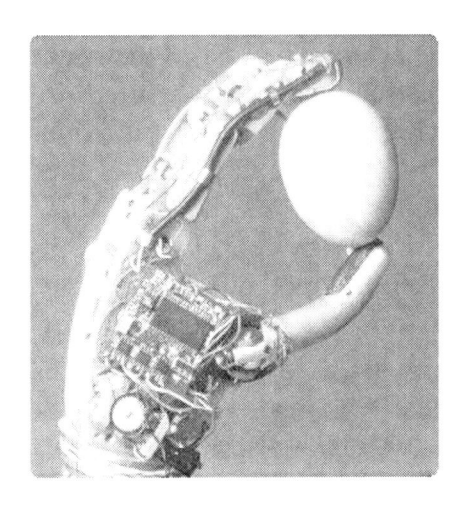

Programming Goals Into The Subconscious

Sharing with you through media - I have to say this really is my happy place. What an amazing job I have, I get to explore consciousness!

My subject today is setting and achieving goals with metaphysical cooperation. Steven Richards said, *"To dream by night is to escape your dream. To dream by day is to make it happen."* Scientists have identified specific parts of each of our brains. It's called the reticular activating system. They call it "RES" for short. And that works with the visual parts of our brain to call our conscious attention to the things that are important to reaching our goals and to also filter out the things that are unimportant.

Once we've decided what our dream is, what our goal is and what we desire to create in our life this RES is activated by programming goals into our subconscious mind. The subconscious mind is the power center and that's the mechanism that explains why goal-setting, why positive choices now are accepted as scientific methods for change. We're discovering that our brain is cybernetic in nature which means that it is literally like a computer. If our subconscious is cybernetic, if it is like a computer, that means it is waiting for a program to be installed because once it's installed it will execute it. Here's the beauty: the subconscious is completely neutral, it's impartial. It's going to carry out any instruction you give it. Then, perhaps, it is clear why people say you create everything. *Everything.*

More good news: you can make a new choice at any time. If things don't work for you, you can make a new decision. There are some things we may re-decide – newly choose – and the shift is easy. Then there are those things that act like a stuck demented pattern and if that experience feels immutable, you just need to go deeper. You need to do the inner work so you have the outer results. You have to look at the beliefs and look at the experiences. You can detect what you resisted that became very solid. It's like a Trojan virus is being executed from your subconscious programming. We need to run a new package to destroy the virus and go to a healthy life operating system.

So we've got a neutral and impartial subconscious waiting for instructions, and now scientists have discovered that we each have a capacity to create an almost infinite number of new neural connections in our brain when we run new thought patterns. Old neural pathways are like grooves in a record, right? So if you're struggling with your issues or negative behaviors, then you've been playing the old records over and over again. And if you were going to carve a new groove into that record it would never play the same way again. The old pattern weakens and the new one takes over. Brand new positive thoughts, feelings; images create new neural patterns.

We can take pressure off ourselves by sometimes accepting that negative thoughts and criticisms may pop up now and then. And if so, you can observe the thoughts. You don't have to make them that important. You can just notice, and then change the polarity of the thought. Change your intention. Change your vibration. You don't need answers, by the way—you don't. You can just change the energy you're experiencing and emitting. It's that simple. Sometimes things happen in your life unexpectedly. You can decide to find comfort even in temporary changes that may feel like an upheaval. You can keep going forward in a positive way and make it work for you. Herman Melville said, *"We cannot live only for ourselves. A thousand fibers connect us with our fellow men; and among those fibers, as sympathetic threads, our actions run as causes, and they come back to us as effects."*

If you want to be successful and you're finding it's not happening, are you taking action? Success is achieved through positive thinking and positive doing. It's attraction plus action. Every person I know who is a super achiever with a myriad of impressive goals --all say *take massive action.* Massive action. There are the two sides to the success equation: attraction plus action. If you want to transform any aspect of your life, choose to change on the inside, and then everything else will follow.

Alan Watts said, *"You're an aperture to which the universe is looking at and exploring itself."* Just know you can be still, you can be here and quietly remember the real presence of and within yourself. You'll know in your soul that while all around you everything changes, within you there is something unchanging. Fearlessness follows this discovery in much the same way as the dark evening shadows leave to reveal the morning light.

Please remember when Plan A doesn't work, the alphabet still has 25 more letters.

On Daring To Dream Bigger

Debbi Dachinger: Interview with Kimberly Reid

KIMBERLY REID: Welcome to the Connect with Kimberly Reid Show. Tools you can use today, where I bring you the best of the best. Thought leaders, speakers, authors and life coaches sharing their genius in business and in life. Are you ready? Because it's your time to shine. Today, joining us is a radio host in L.A., she's had her show for several years and it is a great pleasure to have Debbi Dachinger on the phone with us talking about her latest book, *DARE TO DREAM: This Life Counts*, which you can get on Amazon and all the other bookstores. She is an expert in goal achievement. As I said she is a radio and TV personality, a three-time best-selling author, keynote speaker and coach and helping people attain their goals, and educating people on how to be great in radio. Her work with people in the media, workshops, and through coaching, has been achieved through decades of research, education, and her gifts as a clairsentient and intuitive. I was very surprised to read that actually. It was kind of fun. Debbi's *Dare to Dream Radio Show* is a syndicated, multi-award winning program with four million listeners offering inspiring information and methods on how to achieve goals and dreams. Debbi is a top notch radio personality, an award-winning actress and singer as well as a successful motivational speaker, a professional radio interview coach, and was also a popular jewelry designer. A woman of many talents, please welcome Debbi.

DEBBI DACHINGER: Hi, Kimberly. Great to be on the show with you. Thanks.

KIMBERLY: Thank you. So our topic today is "*Daring to Dream Bigger.*" What can you share about the laws of say, quantum physics, that you feel govern dreams and goal manifestation.

DEBBI: I know of many; I have a funny one right now. It's called the Law Of Being in Many Places At Once, which I'm saying tongue-in-cheek. I'm actually being aired right now in three different venues. That is modern technology! [LAUGHTER] I'm being heard on a Telesummit across the world that's being aired right now, my radio show is also airing, and at the same time here I am being interviewed with you. I love it.

KIMBERLY: Talk about compressing time and space. [LAUGHTER]

DEBBI: Being in multiple places at once is really getting the job done. [LAUGHTER]. So that might go under the law of passive multi-tasking or something. Now to seriously answer your question, there are several laws that govern dream and goal demonstrations. I will share some and if there are any in particular you're interested in, I'm happy to go into more depth. What we live with every day is the law of vibration. We live with the law of attraction, which of course, most people have heard of. We experience the law of cause and effect. There's also the law of resonance, there's the law of growth, the law of abundance—which is kind of yummy. And the law of reciprocity.

KIMBERLY: Huge.

DEBBI: There's actually one that's worth mentioning called the law of reversibility.

KIMBERLY: That's not one I'm familiar with.

DEBBI: Okay. Is that the one you would like me to talk about? You pick it girl.

KIMBERLY: I have great stories about many of the other ones, so tell me about the law of reversibility?

DEBBI: The law of reversibility is like the rubber band effect. This is where a lot of people go wrong with dreams. The reason why they don't come true—is because we have not been taught how. We're full of lots of yummy ideas and desires and then we have no clue how to execute it. We get frustrated, we get overwhelmed and we give up on ourselves. What's cool about the law of reversibility is—the rubber band effect—what it is, is we are here, and our dream and our goal is out there somewhere and we can imagine it, we can taste it, we can dream it, we can idea it. But what gets us from here to the dream manifest is actually doing everything in reverse. It's taking the idea of where we are and moving ourselves in our imagination out to where we want to be, which is living that goal as a reality, then from that space, coming backwards it informs us—in reverse—how I create that. If I was already at the apex of my goal come true, what's the next thing underneath that that would have to happen, for the goal to have been created? And once we write that down, what's the next thing that needs to occur—we write that down. Then the next thing. And these are what we write down that becomes our action steps. We write our dream at the top of our paper and then all the steps are written backwards, until the last step we write, is actually the first step we will take, it is the step closest to where we are right now. That's the law of reversibility and how when we release a rubber band it snaps us to the dream.

KIMBERLY: So like walking backwards in time from where we want to be, and finding out the critical steps along the path.

DEBBI: Precisely. Because these critical steps—"bread crumbs" is a good allusion, is the map to our treasure.

KIMBERLY: Beautiful. There are certain little steps along the way—pit stops and gas stops—[LAUGHTER] we have to go through in order to get to the destination. That's great, awesome.

DEBBI: What I know is, when you make your dream come true it does something. You may think it's just about you, and you're sitting back saying, *"Yay, I created that...yay I'm a best-seller...yay I have this charity organization."* But really the truth is that you're sending a light out on the planet. You're changing the vibration of a planet that needs you so much.

KIMBERLY: I couldn't agree more, Debbi. Could not agree more. So what happens when you use this law of reversibility and you start stepping backwards in time, but the fact is, we don't always know what we don't know? How does that work?

DEBBI: Exactly. We don't know what we don't know and that's part of the journey. So can you let go of control enough to allow that to be? That's the question. Some people feel or believe they have to figure everything out. You don't. You just have to figure out the action steps and have trust. The funny thing about all of this is that it doesn't matter what energy presents itself. Whether it's fear, distrust, whatever issues come up--the truth is it's just energy. We all experience it. The greatest of the greatest transformational people I know go through this as well. They're just upping the ante to pursue bigger and bigger dreams each time. We have to trust that in walking ahead, in spite of issues, it will take care of itself. So, as far as we don't know what we don't know—that is true. We don't. And why a dream is so important—was it presented to us for a reason? We have purpose, we are unique. We have something we're supposed to put out there. So don't be hiding that light under a bushel. [LAUGHTER]

KIMBERLY: Say amen to that sister. [LAUGHTER]

DEBBI: Ha! If you're going to go there, I'm going to preach so that you listen to me. [LAUGHTER] Go after your dream and do your thing. You never know whose life you're going to change. I give you permission and the freedom to fail. I do. Everybody has successes and failure. No one is successful at everything. Everyone is going to fail at some point because that's just how things are. But this is what I know for sure. We learn from the things we do well, and we also learn from the things we have executed poorly. Failure can be a gift along our way. If we don't know something, if we bump up against something, if we mess it up-- what we can do is experience it. Have those feelings then gather yourself with honesty and introspection to inquire within: "Whoa. *What went on there? That was pretty interesting. What did I bring to that party? What created that situation?*" Once we have an idea where we went wrong—and it's not about blame, it's just about ownership.

Once we get that gift of information we can then change and right our path because we've just learned what to do instead. Failure is useful. I'm not saying go out there and make it a wonderful life of failure. Don't hear that. I'm saying that when you're brave and courageous in spite of fear, you're courageous going out there and doing it, what's going to happen is possibly you might fail at something. If you fail allow yourself to be educated. You can recognize instinctively how to do something completely different and better next time. It's an informative experience. So I say, go out there, give yourself permission to fail, don't need to know what you don't know and just do it. Let life happen.

KIMBERLY: So you're saying on this law of reversibility that we come up with these action steps, and have the faith then that what we don't know will come to us in good time and to just keep moving forward. If we happen to make a mistake and get off the path that it's okay, learn from that too and just get back on the path.

DEBBI: I'm saying that. To be clearer, some of what we do is informed by our action steps. Some of what we do is informed because we are pursuing our dream, we're out there and we're starting to see how things work, we start to gain information we didn't have before. So we're continually being educated and through that edification we learn along the way as opposed to having to know it all before we start. Does that make sense?

KIMBERLY: Yes. Absolutely true. Absolutely true. So everything is a learning process if we allow it to be that, and can bring us closer to our dream or our goal.

DEBBI: It is. It is. Now, another law to introduce is the law of growth, it's one that weaves in and out of this. If you've ever been to a beautiful forest or a nature location, you know what it looks like to see a pond that doesn't move, water that's been sitting there for a long time and it's green and you can't see the bottom. It's stagnant, right? That's the pond's energy. It's saying, *"Whoa, I haven't moved in a long time."* [LAUGHTER] We are just like that.

KIMBERLY: Are you saying we get stinky if we stay in one place too long? [LAUGHTER]

DEBBI: We do! [LAUGHTER]. Folks don't care so much to be hanging out with us because we're a little over ripe, let's say.

KIMBERLY: [LAUGHTER]

DEBBI: We have been doing the same thing, over and over again, and we keep talking about those dreams and talking about those goals, and people are starting to look at us like, *"You know, hon, you're not a whole lot of fun to be around. You keep talking about what you want to do, but you never actually do it. Would you just go out there and do it?"* [LAUGHTER] The opposite of stagnant is the river that's flowing, that's running over stones and boulders and you know it is clean and clear, the kind of ionic energy that has, and so it is with us too. When we are moving and flowing and in the moment with what is we are living the law of growth; all I'm saying is keep growing. We were never built to be stagnant beings. We are built to continue to change and make things happen.

KIMBERLY: Interesting. A friend of mine talks about how we're already born great and, it's kind of like two sides of the same coin maybe, in the sense that yes, we're growing. But the other way to look at that is that we're already great and we need to shed some of the things that we've picked up along the way so that we really shine a lot more brightly.

DEBBI: Well, I agree. We are born great. We are born with everything intact. But it's often what's between our ears that stops us. I mean a few dream busters are "out there." Occasionally, yes, we can get past those obstacles. And the majority of what stops us is not "out there," but rather stems from inside us; we stop ourselves from shining our light brightly. For those of us who are fierce about making dreams come true, the idea is *I'm going to do it.* The growth part is an inherent gift in the journey of taking on a dream and a goal. There will be two obvious gifts that result from creating a dream. One is that you are now living the dream as your reality, and the other gift is that there is healing that has taken place. I can tell you that for every single dream I have taken on and created along the way, I've had to look deep inside. If something came up I had to address it. For instance, *"Whoa, okay – Fear. Cool. You've been there all my life – Got it. Really, what is your point here? You aren't stopping me from a dark alley; you're stopping me from a goal, a dream. Let's talk. Let's sit at a round table. Why? Why is it so important to you to hold me back? What is the belief that is compelling you to stop me?"* I would rather have things in place between my ears and in my head so I can propel forward, and replace that fear with the sense of encouragement and nurturing. To nurture a dream into being instead. I've certainly needed to heal at times in my life, and allow those feelings to unearth. To do that I ask the obstacle: *"Where did you come from?"* It doesn't mean I necessarily go back to that exact time, but it means that I bring up whatever 'it' is because it's been controlling my life and now it's really rearing its head. So I pay attention. What I desire to share is, I know the volcano that I am and I'm in a place where I'm dealing head-on with, *"What does it look like to play in the biggest arena in life, the biggest game possible? To be completely visible?"* From there all these amazing opportunities are showing up for me right now. I choose to let myself move into that expansive, infinite arena. Can you feel the ferocity of that? I know what my willingness is, so whatever is between me and *that* dream—living that way—it's going to have to be dealt with because I believe that's what I'm meant to do and frankly, I desire it. I believe that's what we're all meant to do. The question is: what are you willing to do to have it? I'm willing to do the work. That's the law of growth, and the willingness to walk through the emotions and let things positively change — that's what I mean.

KIMBERLY: That's awesome. So Debbi, you talked a little bit about what holds us back and it is the fear, it is the limiting belief, and a lot of people don't realize that those were probably created very young, between zero and seven years old and they don't even necessarily know that those programs are running in their head. I think it was really great that you were asking yourself, having that conversation with yourself instead of being stuck in the mire of whatever the limiting belief was. *"I'm not good enough. How can I possibly do this tremendous big dream goal?"* But to ask yourself questions and to ask really poignant questions about the fear or what's holding you back, and get to the root cause of it, and have that conversation like at a round table. I thought that was a very good visualization on how to actually do that. Are there any other things that hold people back that you know?

DEBBI: Oh my—yes. Indeed. It's interesting how different things run different people and patterns get formed. Doubt, is one thread that hold people back. There are people out there who just doubt it's possible. The dream can sound terrific but they're not sure it could happen and not sure they have what it takes. As in, *I doubt anyone will see me seriously or realize the talent inside of me.* And an interesting one with doubters is some doubt that if their dream comes to be fulfilled—that they can handle it. Next is fear, we went through that a bit—in addition, what holds people back is issues with overwhelm, fear of failing, fear of succeeding, fear of being seen, fear of screwing up, anxiety, stress. What's fascinating is they're manufactured from within. Some people let the idea of others hold them back. It's particularly interesting that people sabotage their dreams by an over-attention (feeling beholden) to "others." There's a sense of, *"Oh my family would not approve of that, I can't do that"* or, there are people who say, *"I need someone to give me the money to do this."* They think the only way to get to their dream is to be rescued; they are convinced that others have the potency and the answers, and they have none. They're looking for a handout out there and it's like wow..... *Tic, tic, tic.* You can hear the clock ticking and the calendar pages ripping off while they're putting their energy into finding someone to save them. [LAUGHTER] Oops! You're going to have to find the potency within yourself. We're more resourceful than that. Then, one that is sort of global, I'm sure most will relate to and that's time management. People have poor time management which overtakes their lives to the point that they say *"Writing down steps? I don't even have the time to sit down and imagine my dream – forget about writing down the steps or even taking the steps."* They believe they have no authority or mastery over their own time. That's an illusion. We decide how to appropriate our time every day and every moment. So with great love I say, *"If you mismanage your time then your life isn't working for you and it's up to you to take a look and restructure that."* [LAUGHTER]

KIMBERLY: [LAUGHTER] No doubt. And is that just an excuse because of some of their underlying fear?

DEBBI: Absolutely, it is. And I know that one. I used to live in that one.

KIMBERLY: [LAUGHTER]

DEBBI: It's also how I kept people away. *"I'm so busy."* There was all that busy stuff going on and it kept everyone out at arm's length. Although being busy felt solid and real, it was one of the obstacles I had to look at quite some time ago. When I did, it was powerful: "Wow. *How's that serving you, Deb? Really? How's that working out for you?"*

KIMBERLY: I really love those questions [LAUGHTER]. *"How is that serving you?"* My clients have heard that one many times. They're probably sick of hearing me say it. So, let's move on to successful people. What are the patterns of successful people? Obviously, you're very successful in what you're doing, and in the many different things you've done in your life and I think one of the things, that we've talked about is being willing to ask yourself the hard questions and go there into that dark space of self-sabotage, or fear, or anxiety, or whatever it is. What are some of the other things that successful people do?

DEBBI: They do the work. To loop off of what you said—they really do, do the work. There is a reason why they are where they are. Because successful people also experience doubt and obstacles and everything else. But they do whatever it takes and go toward their dream anyway. The majority of successful people meditate or they have some form of spiritual practice. They utilize a strong connection with their intuition. They surround themselves with a network of supportive friends. I know stories of transformational people who have really veered off their path and to gain clarity they've vented to their friends. And one of the friends will look at them and say, *"Honey, ha, ha, ha. May I share what I perceive is really going on for you?"* And the friend will just give them insightful wisdom and truth so they can honestly address what's going on— and once they heal and deal, there is a huge shift. A mirror has been held up, and a modification occurs. Successful people are winners because they refocus on the truth and, unlike others who let fear stop them, they allow fear to be transmuted and then with excitement they drive forward.

The successful folks I know write down their gratitude, and they express thanks. And here's one I found interesting the more I worked with well-known leaders: they often have had wounds that have driven them to where they are today. Somewhere early in their lives something happened and the greatest healers I know have turned the biggest wounds into their biggest gifts. That is why I established this Debbi-ism, this quote from me, which is *"Turn your mess into your message."*

KIMBERLY: [LAUGHTER] I'm a testament of that. Definitely a testament.

DEBBI: We're in such good company. So understand that whatever happened to you in the past, the pain of it encouraged you to deal with the issue, and in dealing with the issue and coming through to the other side, you've opened the space for the very opposite experience, the healed version of that issue, to now be lived by you. In only the way you can, and through the wisdom and lessons that you learned—you were brave enough to face that pain head on. You become triumphant in spite of, and because of the wound, which becomes a gift you give to the world. The last bit is that successful people make time for stillness, for reflection.

KIMBERLY: Stillness is absolutely perfect. There just comes a point where I personally had to go, *"Okay, I have options here. I can continue to be the victim, and be caught in that story forevermore. I've seen the effects that that can have, first or second hand based on family members I've seen that have been stuck in that victimized pattern, or I can find a different way."* I'm so glad that I had the awareness to step back and go, *"I definitely want a different way because I see what that life can result in and I really want something different for my life. And I don't know how to get there, but I know that there's got to be a better way. I just know in the very soul of my being that there has to be a different way, than that way, to live."* Because that way to me, wasn't living. So just being able to be willing to step back and gain some awareness and look at life with different eyes than maybe your family did or society is currently or whatever. And ask that question. *"What's true for me? How could things be different?"* And to ask the questions and be willing to ask great questions.

DEBBI: Absolutely indeed. You cry your tears,

you feel your feelings, and you work through it. When you get to the other side you have a new frontier with which to make a new choice. I want to offer something here that may assist people who are spiritual and also doing business however not building the success they would like. Do you mind if I address this in these last few minutes?

KIMBERLY: Yes, please.

DEBBI: I deal with a lot of spiritual people. I love them and I'm one of them. What sometimes stops spiritual people from getting ahead in their business is they don't know how to put out there what it is they do. What happens for spiritual people is, they get lost in the verbiage of giving their businesses names or knowing how to properly write a biography that works out in the world to let us know what they really do. Many spiritual people write information that contains the vibration of what they do however, it makes no sense so they do not generate business based on the title or explanation of their work and abilities; we can't identify who they are or what they do. For instance you may meet a spiritually based person and when asked *"What do you do?"* They'll reply: *"I'm a joyologist,"* if you further inquire *"What does that mean, what service do you provide?"* They'll tell you: *"I make the world a safe place for you to do business."* Huh? What does that mean? Why would I use your services and what niche do you fulfill and how can you help me? Do you see how that does not remotely translate out here? What happens is potential clients cannot comprehend what spiritual people do; their real work is not being verbalized and endorsed in a way that is understood. It is very often clouded in "ethereal" terms which do not register out here and is hampering their success. It's important to turn that around. Work with someone to come up with a business name, your title and your mission in terms that we immediately get what you do and it excites us. What you can do is to be so clear so we can align with your work. The point is: be deeply spiritual and also very successful. The same is true for bios. I see it all the time. Spiritual people are so busy being the beautiful, light beings they are, and often there's no business shrewdness behind them. So I desire to share two pieces of advice I hope will help. The first is that really successful people invest in themselves. So you can be that creature of spirit and also work with a business coach, take classes, invest in the right books—and learn from people who get results and can help you. Whoever it is you choose to align yourself with, go to those individuals and companies—remember the law of growth. Grow, grow, grow. And know that really successful people all get knocked down from time-to-time however they have resilience, they get back up to either change their course or right their course and then they keep on going.

KIMBERLY: Beautiful, Debbi. Thank you so much for sharing with us today. We very much want for you to live your best life in an authentic space, and that is letting your light shine so that others have permission to do that as well. Make it a great day and remember to be more brilliant today than you were yesterday. Thank you so much, Debbi.

DEBBI: Thank you Kim. My pleasure.

KIMBERLY: Take care.

END

Inspirational Moments

It's a good time to set goals and devise a plan. Remember to plan; you need a roadmap, and be prepared for the unintended, the confusing and the closed roads. Amend, adjust, convert, alter, modify, transform and revolt. Be willing to change. Enjoy the journey, and make your life one that causes you to respect yourself.

Whatever feels as though it is in your way of living your dream life, I offer the suggestion that it's actually your spirit calling you to change and grow. I understand that it may seem as if the Universe is out to get you: *"Why me – why is this happening? What is causing this problem?"* I counter and maintain it is the Universe loving you into growth. The challenge and the change upon you is the very growth your soul requires to move you forward in life and on your path.

In The Dream Business This Does Not Cut It…
- This will resolve itself
- My dreams aren't that important
- I'd rather be safe than take a risk
- It's inconvenient
- It's uncomfortable
- It's difficult
- This is a bad time
- It's not worth it
- I'm attached to the way things are
- I am a victim of _____, therefore _____
- I can't help myself
- I am not responsible
- I am so bad at _____
- _____ just happened to me
- I can never seem to _____
- When will you feel sorry for me?
- Why do I have to look at this right now?
- Let me stay in this position of safety
- At least this is familiar
- I'm uncomfortable with challenges
- I can't commit
- I don't know
- I can't figure it out
- I don't have the time
- My mama, my brother, my wife, my dog

- I'm not enough (smart enough, pretty enough, talented enough, rich enough)
- I need guarantees
- It seems like a lot of work
- Life will just work itself out
- I tried
- I quit
- I had a bad childhood
- I don't have what it takes
- Stepping out is unfamiliar and new
- I may be ostracized
- I may be alone or lonely
- What assurance do I have?
- What security do I have?
- Rescue me
- No one believes in me
- At least I know this (crappy life, relationship, body, situation, job)
- I'm scared of what will happen
- What if I make the wrong choice
- I don't trust myself
- It's hard work
- What will people think of me
- Action steps?! You want me to do *what*?!
- I don't want to give this up (even though it's killing me)

I propose that you release resistance. Just release it right now. [Breathe] Using our breath we let go. There may not be many voices in the world that will encourage you to follow your inner superstar and get out there on the cliff edge of your life to look down, look out, and leap. Yet most of us are called to jump into the abyss with a crazy notion that there is someone or something out there that will catch us and catapult us into another stratosphere with a brand new, exciting reality. We feel this longing because we did not come here to do what has been done before. We came here to magnify – arouse, set right, express, generate, and realize the elation of being everything we are meant to be.

In each and every era, unconventional, brave and daring souls have doubted themselves, have been criticized, and have struggled to forge a channel for their genius. Those whose names you have never heard of turned their power over to the world and to the population's world-view at the time. Those whose names have gone down in history and those who have lived the life of conscious evolution instead trusted their creativity, their vision, their truth, their motivated desires, and trusted in dreams that did not even yet exist. They jumped and in their lifetime, they turned the beat around, and the ripples of change and choice were fully lived.

It's going to be alright. It's simpler to surrender to the dreams you have been given and flow with the goals you deeply long for. It was Dawn Clark who said, *"The only truth is love. Anything less than love is just begging to be healed."*

I am here right now with you– we are at the tip of the limb of the tree of your existence, we are at the edge of the cliff of your life and out there is your dream. I am holding your hand and on the count of three we will jump. We will leap together. And we will fly. Eyes opened or closed – your choice – take a deep breath, expect amazing things, feel the dream calling to you, toes on the edge of the cliff – and.... One... Two.... **Three....**

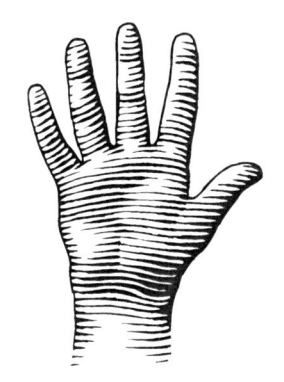

Debbi Dachinger: Interview with Psychic Tee

PSYCHIC TEE: Hi, Everybody, and welcome to the Psychic Tee Show. Today we brought back Debbi Dachinger. I received so many emails from everybody saying how much they loved Debbi, so of course I had to bring her back--because we all love some Debbi and everything she does. Now while we're on air and the chat is open, everybody--if you do happen to have a question that you'd like to ask Debbi about her business, or your dream or something, look at her website while we're talking. Just go to her website, its Deborah Dachinger with a "c,"--it's Austrian--Deborahdachinger.com. Right now I'm going to go ahead and put it in chat, and bring on Debbi. Hi, Debbi.

DEBBI DACHINGER: *Yoda-la-hey-hoo.* I'm so glad to be back. [LAUGHTER]

TEE: I love having you on, it's such a good time. [LAUGHTER]

DEBBI: Thank you Tee and thank you to your listeners who wrote wonderful things. I'm really glad they got a lot out of my first show with you. Tee and I aligned that we're going to do something else today with a lot of punch to it, so you should never be bored or disappointed. [LAUGHTER]

TEE: I know and I was just thinking about that. Because we do make an awesome little team. For anybody who doesn't know Debbi, she is the most awesome life coach that I know, and I am her biggest fan I have to say--possibly. [LAUGHTER] I probably stalk her, *"Debbi I'm stalking you,"* [LAUGHTER] but I'm one of her biggest fans. I love everything that she does. She has this awesome radio show called Dare to Dream Radio where she brings on remarkable guests that talk about how they go from start to finish--from having nothing, to creating something awe-inspiring with their lives. And you could just sit there and listen for hours to every single show. It is so cool. Debbi--so what's going on, Debbi, what's going on with you lately?

DEBBI: I've got to tell you I'm gearing up for a whole bunch of very cool things. It's off the hook. The first thing is this week I am teaching a global Teleclass. I'm so psyched. There are four hundred and forty people signed up so far.

TEE: Wow.

DEBBI: I know. Do people desire their dreams to come true right now or what?! Another upcoming event: I'm about to leave in a week for Canada where I'm doing a keynote speech for a women's red carpet event. I just bought my outfit today and I'm totally psyched.

TEE: Oh wow. That's amazing.

DEBBI: Yeah, and I get to be with wonderful women and hope to inspire them, and hopefully I won't come off too much like Suze Orman while I'm on stage. [LAUGHTER]

TEE: I know. [LAUGHTER] Everybody likes her and talks about her and I'm like, oh--okay. I guess she's good people, I don't know. [LAUGHTER]

DEBBI: She's really brilliant at what she does, and has a very strong point of view. Years ago when I did professional speaking as a motivational speaker, I was once coming off stage and someone—said with great honor-- "*Wow you remind me of Suze Orman.*" [LAUGHTER] I think that was a compliment. [LAUGHTER] Of course, I've changed drastically since then, I'm a lot more fun and free. I hope this audience will have different associations. They can call me Wayne Dyer now. I'll be happy.

TEE: Yeah. Suze to me, I don't know she's just so in your face. [LAUGHTER] I just can't grasp her.

DEBBI: Exactly.

TEE: I'd like to go. I would love to hear you when you're on stage. Now for anybody listening, and there are tons of you--and I'm so grateful for everyone listening and chatting with us today-- Debbi is what we call an expert in goal achievement. Now what does that mean Debbi?

DEBBI: What that means is most people have a dream or they have a goal and they don't really know how to make that come true, and that's where I come in. I'm an expert in how to achieve your dream and also in understanding obstacles that stop people--or what I call dream busters. Essentially I'm an expert at the method or recipe that one will follow to make a dream come true.

TEE: Now you were doing this sort of work before I met you, but I want to know since then and since your clairsentience has really come forward, and come to light, how has that helped you in the work that you've been doing?

DEBBI: Wow. That's a huge question, I love the question. The first thing I want to address-- when you and I first met, I just started doing the radio show, I had no idea that being in media in this fashion was my calling. That's the truth. I was just barely stepping into the possibility of where my radio show could take me. Never having liked radio, never having been interested in radio, I only got into radio because I figured it would promote my voiceover animation career. I began in radio and my first guest ever on my first program was a channel. It was a lovely experience and after our interview was complete before she left the radio station, she turned to me and said *"You know you're doing exactly what you're supposed to do, and you know you'll have a TV show, right"?* I looked at her like a horse with nine heads [LAUGHTER] and said *"No, I don't, but thank you for sharing, that's pretty cool."* As I kept pursuing radio, I discovered with clarity that I *was* doing what I was supposed to do. And then what happened is that, because I said yes to a lot of prospects-- and because I've been willing to keep expressing what's inside of me--so much has come to me and so even more clarity as well.

To address the other part of that question for your listeners, here is the deal. When I first met Tee, who you know is a psychic and medium, I was just in radio a year at the time. So I was pretty new. Tee came on my show to be interviewed. After our interview before we hung up Tee said to me, *"I want you to look up this word. This is a gift you have."* She told me to look up the word *"clairsentient."* And I did. For three days I read everything I could get my hands on regarding clairsentience and it freaking blew my mind because it spoke about things I'd experienced my whole life but never had a name for; I never understood this was something tangible in me. Therefore I never claimed it. Now I had an understanding that this *knowing* I'd always had was real--clairsentience became a phenomenal exploration along with rejoicing, really rejoicing, to have this gift. And so it's really--oh my goodness-it's a part of me now Tee, I can't imagine being where I am without having fully accepted that this is part of who I am. So when I work with people I have a greater understanding. I don't have to question when information comes to me--how do I know that, or how do I understand that--I just do. I think it's the same way I understand how to deal with people on a mass media level, and why I have the capacity to touch people. I was always told that's why I'm here; I feel I understand it now, I recognize clairsentience means I'm so-so-so extremely sensitive that I perceive things on a feeling level. I know things about people, I receive accurate messages, I can vibe locations, energy, smells and sometimes receive predictions.

TEE: Yes. I'm a firm believer that we are brought into people's lives for a purpose, and I believe we all have our path to walk. But sometimes--even though it's our path and we're made to walk it--sometimes, every now and then, a friend will walk with us just to point out the right direction. I believe that people come into our lives every day and do that to help us accomplish things that we need to accomplish, but are slow-moving about it.

DEBBI: Well, it was a great gift you gave me and I thank you. I gave you homage in my show recently when I interviewed you a second time and shared how you had gifted me and set me free. I gratefully, joyfully, again thank you for that. It was a life changing moment when you gave me that tremendous insight.

TEE: You're welcome. You changed my life too. You keep me motivated, girl. I tell you what. I listen to those shows. Especially after I had the surgery and had so much time to do nothing. I sat there and listened to those shows-- because there are times when I feel like, maybe this is not what I'm meant to do. I know that I'm good at it, I feel like this is my purpose, but maybe I'm burned out. And then I'll start to say, *"But what else could I see myself doing"?* Then I'll listen to one of your shows and I'm like,

"Okay, okay, I'm just going through a moment. I need to get back on board and quit acting crazy." And then I'm okay again. So it's very inspiring--your show is. For a lot of people who don't know Dare to Dream Radio—use the direct link to her show or go to Debbi's website.

DEBBI: Yes, the show is run out of a station in Southern California - I am the morning inspiration show five days a week. I'm also syndicated on many other networks throughout the country. You can listen live or stream it on your computer. I play it on my cell phone, and if you like to do what Tee just described--listen at your leisure from my website where everything's archived. Just sit back, relax and enjoy. Get a little inspiration bump anytime you need it.

TEE: Yes. It does inspire you to hear other people's stories. Some people went from nothing to an incredible something. They're very inspirational, so anytime you're feeling glum and you need some motivation, or a kick in the booty, run on over to her website, www.deborahdachinger.com, and listen to some of those archives. It is inspiring, it really is.

Now let's talk about your book because I didn't get to go into it like I wanted to the last time. We talked a little bit about how it would come out--how it was a bestseller. I want to dive into it. First, let's talk about the inspiration to even write this book.

DEBBI: It's such a crazy thing because I never saw myself as a writer. So the fact that I undertook something of that magnitude shows how unexpected life can be. Basically I just decided — first, from a business sense, operating at the level I'm at--I need product. Second of all, how can I reach more people than through my radio show? It was a way for me to get out the info on how to achieve one's dream. And that's where it started and the rest of it is I followed the goal achievement recipe that I teach on how to make a dream come true. That's exactly how I did my book. Every single step. I decided, I took action, I let go. I healed and I dealt with any kind of obstacle that tried to come between me and my dream of publishing the book. I didn't pretend the obstacle wasn't there, or run away from it. I stood there and I faced it down and I said *"All right, bring it.*

Whatever is going on, let's deal with it--because I'm going to publish a book." Then I would continue taking steps with faith and when I got to the end and I achieved, I made sure to enjoy getting the book out.

TEE: Yeah. A three-time best seller celebration I guess. [LAUGHTER] That's a lot of wine. [LAUGHTER] I'm telling you. That's awesome to be a best-seller. I mean it went best-seller the same day, didn't it?

DEBBI: Same day, yes. And here is something–when I was near the end of the process with the book, I had it written and was editing it and moving very slowly, I had no end game, no date I had decided to finish the process to publish. I was going quite slowly. A colleague of mine who is an expert at best-selling books, she teaches it, she has classes on it. She put a fire under me about the date I was thinking about releasing the book. She got me to realize that if I didn't publish the book immediately, I was going to be screwed because of the holidays: Thanksgiving, Christmas, Chanukah, New Year's: she explained to me--*forget it. You can't compete with the huge authors during holiday time.* And she was basically telling me it was impossible – because when we spoke, it was 1-1/2 weeks before Thanksgiving and my book was not even at a publisher! [LAUGHTER]. What a wake-up call. I had no launch date, nothing in place. No draft book version, nothing at the publisher. So here is an example of where clairsentience comes in and what's cool is that everybody out there can do this. Everybody. Hearing my colleague wake me up to the reality of the timeline, I went inside after our phone conversation and I asked, *"Based on what this book expert just told me--and I do believe her--I have a week--week and a half for this book to go out and that's it. That seems crazy. It's not even at a publisher yet. What should I do?"* And I added, *"....but ya'll let me know if I should wait until next year to release my book, then that's what I'll do."* And what I felt—I could say *"heard,"* but I don't hear voices it's more of a knowing—what I felt very strongly was a loving voice tell me, *"Do it now. We have your back."*

TEE: Yes. A lot of people would have ignored that Debbi. Would have talked themselves out of it.

DEBBI: That's correct, but I have learned, because it's a muscle like anything else in life, that the more we use our God connection, the more we use it positively, the more it works for us. And the more I trust and listen, God speaks more and I follow. That's the bottom line. So it spoke, and intellectually I felt bananas. It made no sense. How do you release a book--go to a publisher, have it be in print, proof it and put it on the market within six days? But loving Spirit of God/Goddess said to do it. [LAUGHTER] And the rest is history. The end story, of course, is that my book did release--and that day, it became a best-seller.

Also of note is that through that final week, during the short six days I had to release it, I surrounded myself with positive energy only. Occasionally if something came at me from someone or something and I felt the negativity, I knew that negativity was not my job to handle. All I knew was, in order to create a herculean experience like I had embarked on; I needed to have both my feet in, be one hundred percent committed to doing this, to executing, and be in the most constructive, positive space. That means every morning I woke up and listened to prayer-work that would immediately put me into the right head space. Anything that was positive I connected with. Anything that was not positive, I didn't even respond to, I just moved on--shelved it and moved on.

The day came and my book was released, and at eleven-thirty a.m. the phone rang and it was my colleague, the expert, Teresa. And she said, *"Oh, my god, are you sitting down? I don't understand how you did this; your book just rose above Sir Richard Branson. Your book just rose above Lisa Nichols from The Secret. It just rose above don Miguel Ruiz's book. It rose about Jack Canfield's Chicken Soup For the Soul. Debbi, you are a best-seller."* Then an hour later Teresa called me and said, *"Oh my god, you're now a best-seller in Self-Help. Who the heck does that right before Thanksgiving?"* Those calls meant everything. I was so bloody naïve that I didn't even know to be watching what was happening with the selling numbers on my book or that my book was rising. And it was humbling, it was really about this universe or --the All That Is....the event felt like love in action, and the message was the universe has our backs if we'll only listen. That knowing that told me to go forward with complete faith, that assured me this would work out? I asked, I listened, I followed, and they were right. They were right.

TEE: Wow. Wow. Now that's inspiration for me to finish my book. See? See what I mean everybody? She just motivates you, it's crazy. [LAUGHTER]

DEBBI: Yes, finish your book.

TEE: Now in your book you have exercises that people can actually do for themselves.

DEBBI: I did that on purpose because I want everyone to have an experience. I basically am saying in the book, if you'll take the dream that you have through this book, and read this book from beginning to end, and do the exercises you'll create your dream. That's why the exercises are purposely in the book--not for my health. I've done them already. [LAUGHTER] I'm teaching, I'm literally teaching. If you'll take the time--out of love for yourself and care for yourself--to do those exercises, they're all simple, and fun, and they're meant to illustrate, and show, and guide you. What's going to happen is you will either achieve your dream, by the end of the book—or I mean I don't know how huge a dream you're going to take on, but depending on the size of it-- it will either be accomplished, or you'll be well on your way. Either way you'll understand how to set yourself up to achieve a dream, so you can do it on your own at any time. That was the point. The book offers teachings and also exercises so you have the exact experience. There's also inspiration throughout with stories from people who share the marvelous things they've achieved, and how they've gone through hurdles to become who they did. Lots of points of view.

TEE: Wow. Definitely. Go buy her book. What are ya'll doing? You need to buy it for goodness sakes. That's awesome, awesome, awesome.

DEBBI: The book's name is *"Dare to Dream, This Life Counts."* You can purchase it on my website or on Amazon, also Barnes&Noble.com, or go to any local bookstore and request it.

TEE: I've put it in chat for everybody so you'll be able to have it there. I'm really interested–and I've never asked you this question, but here's the funny thing: Every time we get off the air with each other, I go, "*Oh my gosh. I didn't ask her that question.*" But you know what? Today I'm asking the question I never asked you - how on earth you even got in the radio business for all of this to even happen. I've always wondered that.

DEBBI: Oh my goodness, a miracle of events. Here's the deal. I had been married – I was with someone for eight and a half years--and when I was completely ready to leave something that wasn't right for me–I did so. And for anyone who knows what it's like to go through a separation or divorce, you really go into this crazy space. Have a lot of compassion for any friend going through that, because it's emotionally a lot to go through, and you have to go through the emotional muck to get to the other side. So I was in that space. What preceded that separation right before the divorce is that I had done animation. I had been booked to do a cartoon. I sang in the cartoon, I did the voice in the cartoon. It was a really popular cartoon and I freaking loved it. Like, *oh my god, there is a place for somebody like me who does voices all the time--and who's totally animated anyway.* I was trying to get more voice over work but the work I was getting was a PSA, a film narration, not to diss any of that, it's all good work. But my soul really longed for--I guess--the theatrics and the fun voices of animation work. I had an agent and everything and it wasn't going towards cartoons. So I left the marriage and while looking for ways to get my voice out there more I happened to see an ad for a radio job. And I thought, *"Oh, if I get on the radio more people will hear my voice."* [LAUGHTER] It honestly doesn't make any sense when you want to do animation, but it did for me in that moment. I went for the job, and I got it. I did a music show for about 2 months. I would show up at the station, and I would think, *"Why am I here? I don't like radio."* I made the show as interesting as I could; it was a music show where I played different genres of music and tell the audience trivia they wouldn't typically know about the artist or the type of music. But still I would sit there and wonder, *"What am I doing here"?* Then I would tell myself, *"Don't worry honey you can leave any time you want."*

After 2 months the people who ran that particular station--several stations ago-- came to me and said, *"We want to offer you your own show."* And in that moment I just—I don't know—I had no clue what was going on, and it just sort of flowed out of me. *I'm going to do a talk show, it's going to be Dare to Dream, I want to interview people who are wildly successful and great achievers and find out what they did.* And I think I desired to cover the subject of dreams come true because that had been my wound in my life. I think I was built to be a big achiever but because of what I experienced early on in my life—I had a lot going on in my earlier years that was debilitating.

I don't know if ya'll are watching the Olympics on TV right now. I am and I love it. Think about those times, when the world class gymnasts--that you know are the best--sometimes get out there to perform and you're just sitting at home thinking, *"Oh my god, they're a beast. They're just super-human. Whoa – look what they can do."* And then sometimes you see the greatest athlete go out to compete and they choke. And that was my experience. I was so inconsistent I would sometimes be fierce in achieving dreams and sometimes not be able to show up and deliver. I got really tired of the pain it caused me, and I really desired fulfillment. I wanted to be able to give myself the dreams I dreamed of. I wanted to give myself the life I believed I deserved but yet, somehow didn't believe I deserved. And because of that, I moved into the place where I had the biggest wound, which was I wanted to dare to make my dreams come true. So that's what I predicated my radio show on.

Like I said, the very first show the woman who channeled came on and turned around and made a prediction for me --and I didn't understand it--but as I kept on the path it started to become abundantly clear. *Oh my, there is something going on here and it's much bigger than me. I feel like I'm just showing up for something to unfold that's supposed to happen.* The show went from zero listeners, to now I have close to a million. Like today I was even reading on our special Facebook page for the hosts at my radio station--and it was saying we're having trouble with the servers. So many people are listening to the shows on the station that it's knocking out servers and they have to buy bigger servers. Which is a great problem to have! And here I am-- within the six years I've been on air-- I've done all the things I've set out to do, and said yes to everything I have.

Long explanation but the bottom line is— my life is one thousand percent different. It's so clear what I'm meant to do.

TEE: Wow. And I never would have thought *"voiceover."* I never would have put that together had you not told me. [LAUGHTER] I never would have even thought it. I would have thought they were looking for some great person to do this great radio show, she applied and got it. I never would have put that together. And I'm psychic and [LAUGHTER] I still would have sat here and said, *"Wait a minute--voiceover? What was she--voiceover"?* That's fabulous. The weirdest things come into our lives and we never think that they'll be anything, and then that's the thing that puts us where we needed to be. That still floors me how things like that happen in our lives. The littlest things end up being the biggest. It's crazy. I can't even go there, it's so big.

DEBBI: It's a huge point that you're making, Tee, because that is a lot of what has been the thrust of my success. It's when things came along and I said yes to them. I don't mean things that ate up my time like hanging out with a person I don't particularly like, or getting into a relationship I didn't really want to be in. [LAUGHTER] I don't mean like that. I mean a real opportunity. Even though it didn't quite make sense I often would say yes to things and then all of a sudden it would lead me down a totally different path. And I urge people—to be open to doing that. When you're taking action toward a dream, part of the process is, you've got to let go. You have to just let go and let the winds of the universe flow around and between your dream and intention because that's where the magic and the miracles take place.

TEE: Yes, that is so true. Coming out of the psychic closet I feel I never would have done that ever. Here's a funny story, this girl--I was buying something from her on eBay, and she was psychic herself. But she wasn't advertising psychic readings; I think it was jewelry because back then I was buying a lot of jewelry supplies and stuff. Her name was Tracy, and I found out through talking to her--there was something wrong with my order and I ended up talking to her--she was a psychic. Then she told me I was psychic, and I thought, *"That's really weird."* That, right there, buying that little piece of jewelry that the order was messed up on, ended up bringing me here. That's crazy. Isn't that crazy?

DEBBI: Bringing you here to the radio show?

TEE: Bringing me here, period. Out of the psychic closet. Where I am today. It's crazy. It's just crazy.

DEBBI: Yeah, they're like little markers those events. It's so funny, Tee--I realize I always call them my unseen friends— you know, those that guide me? When people say, *"Why do you call it The Universe? What are you referring to"?* I say, *"Well, it's God, it's All That Is. It's Source, that's what The Universe is. Whatever you believe in--your unseen friends."* And I just realized, Oh, with people like Tee it's not an unseen friend. You *see* all those friends! [LAUGHTER]

TEE: Yes.

DEBBI: For me they're unseen. For many of us, they are. For some people—you actually see what's on the other side of the veil. And that's what I mean. I think those that love and look out for us (The Universe) puts markers there for us, and each is like a little pebble--and we get to pick it up. It completely changes the trajectory of our lives.

TEE: Yes. And even now, in seminars and everything, I try to explain that to people, because a lot of people will say, "*My life's horrible, I don't like what's going on with my life--I don't like what I see in my life and I have these problems.*" And I think well, maybe—sometimes--it's these small things that take us to the bigger picture. You there Deb?

DEBBI: Yes, honey. I'm here.

TEE: I don't know what happened. [LAUGHTER]

DEBBI: I think we had so much going on we just shut the station down. [LAUGHTER]

TEE: We shut it down, girl. We shut it down.

DEBBI: I would love to know what's going on with the listeners. I always like it when you tell me what they're saying, and what the energy is out there.

TEE: Does anybody in chat want to send me a private message I would be happy to ask Debbi a question, or tell me what's going on in your life? My radio show gets messages on Facebook and is slammed. [LAUGHTER]

DEBBI: Wow.

TEE: Oh, I have something from somebody. People, please don't write me a book. I don't have time to read a book. [LAUGHTER] Just a few sentences would be great. Basically what this person is saying is they know their passion in life, but it's going on five years and they still feel like they're in a rut. Do you have any advice for someone who has basically given up on their passion to try to figure out something else they can do to try and make money?

DEBBI: I need a few more details. Like did they happen to mention what their passion is? Here's the bottom line: Because I understand what that's like, by the way. When I was an actress I had a very inconsistent financial life and like I said, because of what was between my ears I booked jobs, I didn't book jobs, and that makes a whole issue with the kind of money you can make, what kind of vacations you can take, and all of that. So here's what's important. It's always good to figure out where you are right now. It's good to comprehend what the obstacles are going on for you. Just for one moment, let's address what could be happening from the outside. First fill in the <u>blank</u> with your dream career or passion. This is what I know: To try and do something from scratch without having the means, and without having financial support, is a big thing to take on. Most often, what I've witnessed is that people do not do well. It's way too much pressure to try to establish yourself in a passion--brand new--get it rolling, because you know sometimes it takes years to actually make enough money to call it a "living" you can rely on. So the first thing from the outside I suggest is, don't let go of your daytime job. Keep some kind of job that's going to give you finances--a 401K, health and sick time, vacation time--consistently. And bless that day job for what it allows you. Then on the outside you go after what it is you dearly love. Then when the balance switches and the passion-job you've pursued on the outside is flowing with abundance, is bringing you the money, the clientele, when you get to the point where you can securely leave your day job — that's when you make the shift. But you don't leave before then. So what you do is build it up on the outside.

What could be happening for you on

the inside--the internal work that needs to be handled--things like doubt. You don't have certainty that it's going to happen and so doubt plagues you. It's a tape that plays over and over in our head and becomes a reality.

The next thing is others. We often feel beholden to others. It can either be that we feel that people have influence over us, and somehow we have to be something other than who we are. Whether that's your sexuality and you deny what's really going on--whether that's what you really want to be because, let's say, your family said, *"Oh you can never be an artist. You'll never make a living."* There are a lot of beliefs around that. Whatever it is that you experienced that made you step out of your authentic self and shift into something you're really not --because that's very painful. And the other thing about others is, we look at the outside and say, *I can't do this because my husband, wife children, fill in the blank, depend on me.* So we pretend to blame them while we sabotage ourselves.

The next one is trust. That we trust ourselves that if anything happens we have our own back, or that the universe has our back. That there is something greater than ourselves that loves us and cares for us and is there for us.

The next one is playing small. Because if we're breathing on this planet now, we're here for greater good, and we're here to play a big game in whatever element we've come here for using our gifts and talents. Most people, many people, are trying to put a lid on it. It's like you've got this beautiful light from within and you're trying so hard to put a rock over it so no one can possibly see. Because if they see you, you'll be visible. And if they see, you'll be responsible. It really is about stepping out into new and big arenas.

And the final thing that could be stopping you is fear. I want you to get this image for a second. Picture a playground, and there is a bully and the bully is picking on a little kid. And the bully is saying terrible things to this child, demeaning things, vile things, they're terrorizing them so much that the kid doesn't even want to go to school, doesn't want to go outside, the kid is losing all self-esteem and all motivation. Well, that's what *we* do to *ourselves*. We are the victim and we're the bully. We're the person inside saying *I want this, I have a dream of this, I desire this, my soul speaks to this.* And we are also the bully; we come after ourselves with *"Who are you to think like that? What, are you kidding me? I mean look at you. You're a mess, you don't have any talent. Who do you think will hire you? You're a loser, a failure. Your dreams are a joke and will never happen."* Everybody in the gathered crowd starts laughing and guess what? They're all you. They are all you: desiring the dream, ridiculing who you inherently are, and denying the possibility of the dream. You are the victim, you are the bully, and you are jeering crowd. It's *you* holding you back. It's you sabotaging you. It's you demeaning and bullying yourself. And we use fear to hold ourselves back from that which we desire the most.

Once you can start to see through this smorgasbord of emotions, beliefs, and experiences, the patterns come up, over and over again in your life that hold you back, you figure out the issue that screws you up, and that's the work you have cut out. Take it on as a project. Face your dream-buster and tell it: *"You've been holding me back my whole life. No more. Bring it. We're going to deal with this right here right now because I am worth having my dreams come true.*

And fear, thank you so much for sharing. You know what? You've done nothing for me my whole life except really bully me and I'm not taking it anymore. I'm so much bigger that, and I was put here for great purpose. I'm going to step into my dream because I am loved. I am a beloved child of this universe and I deserve, yes I do."

TEE: You know, you hit on some really good points there because some of that could even remind me of myself. Living in the Bible Belt town that I do. Scared to come out of the psychic closet where I am, for fear of what people will think of me, my family, what they will say. And then on another note, I have my family--my husband and kids, of course they're supportive, my brother and sister--very supportive, but then you have to look over here at the rest of my family going, *"Oh my god, I hope nobody finds out that she's related."* You know, things like that just because of where I live. That's a big fear too. So when you talk about other people--letting them influence us--that is so true because it can keep you from what you really want to achieve just because of the fear of what you think they'll think of you, and you may lose them in your life. Awesome. [LAUGHTER] Also, when you talk about the fear--for years everybody hears people, and life coaches, talk about fear of success. People always laugh and go, *"Are they crazy? Why would I have a fear of being successful? Everybody wants to be successful."* But right then and there, you probably gave one of the best explanations of that--right there--that I've ever heard. It's not that we have a fear of success; we fear what we have to do to get there.

DEBBI: Yes. I will paraphrase what Marianne Williamson once said, *"What we fear is often how great we are: how powerful we truly are."* Our greatest fear is our own magnificence.

TEE: Right. It's so true because even now, out of the psychic closet only four years and I went from a two to a ten and like *"blam,"* that quick. [LAUGHTER] Whoa. Hold on. But even now I want more. I want to do this, I want to do that, and even now that fear still gets me. The thought of what the rest of my family thinks, and how far can I take it. So it's not so much of us looking at ourselves but we look at our children. But then, you have to think that you're teaching your kids that that's how you do it. So you're basically telling them I don't want you to be successful and follow your passion because Mommy's not going to do it.

DEBBI: Exactly. What you said is so rich, and thank you for that-- I want to address a couple of them. The first thing you said is that you went from a two to a ten and then you keep wanting higher and better. Exactly! When you start shifting into who you are, and allowing yourself to live from your authenticity that is precisely what happens. You do achieve goals and what happens is, then you desire higher goals. Do you hang out for a while and enjoy where you are? Of course. That's part of it. And then yes, it's about higher, loftier, bigger goals. It's just what happens. The other thing you brought up is the fact that when you do that--when you step into the next bigger aspect of yourself, or experience of yourself, those patterns about others, those patterns about fear, those doubts creep in. So here is a little secret: It doesn't go away. *Wah wah wah wah.* It is energy and that's the bottom line. It's energy. When you consistently approach and complete goals it does however dissipate over time.

Anything stopping you from your

success and passion is a pattern--it's like a movie, like a script, right? So Tee, you're operating here and you're thinking, *"Oh this isn't so bad, I have a radio show I'm writing my book everything's cool. Yeah, it was weird at first but now I know I can do it."* Then suddenly you get this new idea. *"Oh, I'm going to produce a magazine."* [LAUGHTER] And you step into pursuing that and you think, *"What the heck am I doing? What are people going to think about me"?* See every time you step into the next, grander version, your sabotage script is going to start running. The others--the children, your family, the small town mentality, the fear, the doubt. The pattern may not change, but it's what you do with it when it starts to run that's significant. In my experience when you manage the inner script and choose to take steps to your dream anyway, the pattern pointedly decreases over time, because it no longer holds power over you.

So when it happens, it'll feel real. And then, what I suggest you do is create a new default. If it comes up for you, let a new muscle kick in that says, *"Oh. That's my dream buster trying to stop me. Got it. Trying to control me. Got it. Have you ever worked in the past? Have you ever encouraged me or taught me anything* beneficial? Have you ever brought anything very fruitful to my life? No, okay, got all no's on that. Well you haven't ever helped me and I know achieving my goal is where I'm supposed to be because I feel it. My soul is inspired to do it, and that's enough. So thank you for sharing, I'm going to do it, and we'll all be okay." You can also speak very compassionately because there is a little person element to the pattern. Speak to that energy, and say, "I really hear you. I really hear that you feel like the family will hate me and I'm very sensitive to that. I really hear you say that my kids will go without if I take on one more darn thing, and thank you for caring so much about them. And I really hear you say you have tons of doubt I'll ever finish this book or be able to manage everything and that I'm even a good psychic or that I'm supposed to be doing that. All right. Thanks I got it. I hear ya'. But you know what? With great love I'm going to create my dream anyway, because I believe that's where I'm supposed to be." Once you manage debilitating patterns like that--with that level of compassion, and love towards the energy attempting to stop you--that voice is going to weaken. You can meet it with compassion and firm determination so you can move forward quickly. Does that make sense?

TEE: Tons of sense. Tons and tons and tons of sense. And I know people are like-- well, easier-said-than-done, and I saw a couple of people saying that and they're right. It's easy to want things but it's harder to put it into manifestation.

DEBBI: I disagree.

TEE: And I was getting ready to say I do, too. [LAUGHTER] A lot of times when people say easier-said-than-done, sometimes I think those are the people who listen but then turn around and go, *"But I'm not ready to do that."* So it's not that it's easier-said-than-done, it's just-- you feel like you're not ready. It's easier to say that than to put your own wheels into motion.

DEBBI: That's for sure. Because you have to understand, I'm not like Zeus coming down from the mountain spouting this stuff and going back up to some mountain. I'm flesh and blood. I'm as human, and as feeling, as any of you. You also have to understand, from where I came from--the kind of experiences I had growing up-- my brother and I still look at each other and go, *"Wow. We are miracles."* Of all the choices we could have made: being out on the streets doing drugs and--go from there. We always look at each other and say, *"I can't believe the positive, life-affirming choices we made instead."* And that's the bottom line. It came down to choices. I want to address that, because when somebody goes to *"it's easier-said-than-done...."* [LAUGHTER] my sweet love.... Hear me and open your heart to this: Is it any easier to live held back from what you really love and have been called to do?

TEE: No.

DEBBI: Is it easier to have a dream and deny it? Is it easier to have a goal that's wanting to be birthed inside of you, and not allow that to happen? I can only speak from my experience, from when I was younger – it was painful. To deny my dream expression was soul killing. It is much easier for me to deal with any emotion when it comes up and handle it--or go see a healer or a coach to help manage it when I can't alone--and then walk through to the other side as a free person. I adore all of you and desire the best for you so I hope you can hear that.

TEE: You are so dead-on. When I was—and everyone of course knows my story about foster homes, blah, blah, blah. It was harder for me to keep living these lies and pretending to be something that I wasn't to please everybody else, than now, *"I'm Psychic Tee,"* that's just who I am. It's so much easier for me to keep taking these steps in my truth of who I am, than sit there and deny who I am. It's like when you tell a lie and you have to tell another lie, and another lie, and then you dig a hole deeper, and then you forget the first lie, and now it's just devastating. It feels like, *"Now what do I have to say? But what did I say before? Well, now I can't remember what I said I did before."* It's so much easier just to live in my truth, be proud of who I am, and just keep going forward. Someone is always going to have something to say about what you do. But if you let them hold you back then you won't ever become what you were meant to be. If I was worried about that I never would have done this. I never would have come out of the closet, I wouldn't be doing shows, I wouldn't be talking to Debbi now, I wouldn't have met all these wonderful people, and I wouldn't be living in my truth. The bottom line is if *"These people who are so negative about you, are they* *living your life for you? Are they paying your bills? But you're living your life to please them."* [LAUGHTER]

DEBBI: May I ask you a question?

TEE: Sure.

DEBBI: I was thinking about this today. With clairsentience I started doing something and I want to ask you about it Tee, since you're the expert here and everybody will benefit from this. What I started doing is--when I get information about somebody, I have been realizing if I don't do something with what I hear it becomes like a hamster in a wheel. It's almost like it keeps ringing a doorbell inside of me and telling me the same thing over and over again. I was on a walk, and I heard something about my coach and I finally called her and said, *"Look, this happens now and then and I don't understand why, but can I tell you what I heard in relation to you. It's a message for you?"* She was open; I shared it and she was very grateful. And then it happened again. I heard that I'm supposed to be doing work with somebody--I don't completely understand the realm it's going to take. It was telling me, over and over and I was like, "*Okay.*" [LAUGHTER] So I picked up the phone and called this person and I said *look I just want to share this information so it will get released.* And once I did it freed me up. It's not in there pulling my attention anymore. What do you think about that? Do you understand that?

TEE: Yes. Girl look, that's one of the things I teach in my seminar. Girl, it is so true. Let me tell you, I do that now. I'm going to tell you a story—I went to the grocery store the other day, and I'm always picking up people's energy. So I went to the store and I usually keep my head down but for some reason I looked up, because I had a spirit bothering me. I'm in the Bible Belt now, everyone. I don't do this like Teresa Caputo. I don't just walk into stores sharing about spirits. So it kept bothering me, and I told my husband, "*Oh my god, this woman's dead husband won't leave me alone. I'm going to go sit in the car.*" He said, "*Just go tell her.*" I said, "*No.*" So, I go sit in the car and it kept going, kept going, and kept going until I was getting ready to have a migraine. I couldn't get rid of the energy. I couldn't let it go. No matter what I did it was still there. So what did I do? I walked into the grocery store and I told the woman. I said, "*I know you don't know me. Your husband's been driving me nuts. He wants me to tell you that underneath the staircase in the basement there is a loose board, and he put two bonds in there and he needs you to go find them.*" And she was like, "*I've been looking for those for seven years.*"

DEBBI: Oh, my god.

TEE: [LAUGHTER] And I said, "*I was supposed to tell you that.*" And she thanked me and I took off. It's true, Debbi. It happens. They will bother you until you do what you are supposed to do. And the stronger your gift gets, the more it will happen, and happen, and happen. The only way you can release it is to share the information.

DEBBI: I love that story. Next time you do that, give someone a business card. [LAUGHTER] That's so wonderful that you told her. I know--that is a quandary--like, "*What's going to happen if I share this*"? I just got to the point recently where I'm like, "*Let me just share. At least it's been set free.*" Because it's really difficult to keep inside.

TEE: I told you guys, Debbi was awesome.

Didn't I tell you Debbi was awesome? She's wonderful. This energy cannot be contained, everyone. Cannot be contained and needs to get out there. Definitely.

DEBBI: Definitely. I'm happy about how we facilitate this, and also have a really good time--keep laughing and sharing personal stuff.

TEE: Right. Definitely, definitely. Everybody thank you so much for tuning in tonight. We had a great time as always with Debbi. And thank you so much Debbi, for being on the show. [LAUGHTER]

DEBBI: Oh, yes it was such a pleasure. I appreciate all of you. And Tee [KISS SOUND], you're the greatest.

TEE: Love you, Deb. Night everybody.

END

Debbi Dachinger:
Interview with Deb Scott

DEB SCOTT: Hello, all the best people I know. That's you, and welcome to a special evening show with Deborah Dachinger--Los Angeles, Hollywood, award winning television radio personality. She is dynamite. I love this lady. She is so cool. She's all about making your dreams come true. I know she's all about making my dreams come true, and I'm privileged to be able to say she is my friend. Another Deborah, she spells it the same way too, so, I'm excited to bring her on. We're at a great point in the year when we're looking at life and we're thinking, *"Okay, I'm this many months into the year. What's my dream, where am I at, what do I want to have happen,"* and Deb is the shining star to help us accomplish just that. Deborah

Dachinger is an award-winning radio and television talent. She's host of Dare to Dream. Since she was a child, Deborah's background has been in talent and entertainment. She attended U.S.C., the University of Southern California, as a performing arts graduate, then went on to act and sing in Europe and throughout the United States. Deborah received a Los Angeles Drama Desk Award acting nomination and was in the cast of *Follies* which won the Fringe First award. She also became a successful motivational speaker--you'll see why tonight--leading workshops on balance and life goals. Her professional voiceover work includes the lead in the popular cartoon movie *"Life At The Pond: The Big Mouth Bass,"* corporate training animations, PSA and film narration. Deborah's radio career has spanned several years through *Dare to Dream* where she has interviewed successful people who have made their dreams and goals come true, manifesting their passion into their reality. She's interviewed some of the best of the best around the globe. *Dare to Dream* is a metaphysically-based talk show driven by fascinating conversations with a large audience following Deborah. She's also been published in All Access Sports, and she's contributed to inspirational books. Many of you are familiar with her work and she's been heard on the circuit singing big band and jazz with various combos. Deborah came to Live Out Loud to share her zeal for helping people make their dreams come true. She's here tonight to do just that with us. Hello, Deborah. How are you in L.A.?

DEBBI DACHINGER: [LAUGHTER] I'm doing terrific. I gotta tell you, that was fun. It's great to be on this end of things for once. Thank you for having me.

DS: I'm a little intimidated interviewing Deborah. You have won so many awards for interviewing, television, radio, acting and all these things and now I'm interviewing you. Whoa. [LAUGHTER].

DEBBI: I actually understand that. I tell you, Deb that sometimes I have world experts come on my show and my heart can beat a little faster too. And really, they're just another human being with the same infinitesimal energy running through them. All I know is that every show I do on the radio is like a master class. So if I can sit back, connect, energize, synergize with the person, all is well. It flows. I learn a ton and so do the listeners. I'd like to do that tonight with you too.

DS: I love it. I know. I have to say that this is so much fun. I always learn something. You are so about happiness and dreams and prosperity, and taking all that energy and making it positive. You've always been creative and you've always been able to express yourself. I'm just pondering--for somebody listening right now who's wondering—*wow, how could I do that?* How could you show where that creativity and talent has led you to be where you are today?

DEBBI: How has my creativity and talent led me? Very interesting question. I have been--I feel like—at the effect of my talents and abilities and what it draws in. So even though sometimes I feel as though I really want "x," it's interesting that while pursuing "x" that "y" comes along. I have a tendency when presented with a very positive opportunity; I've learned to say respond positively to it. When I say yes to the "y" opportunity that was originally an "x," all of a sudden a whole new vista opens up to me. That's really been my life: If I let go, if I just let it flow, it all happens beautifully. I've been an actress since I was a very little girl. That's the only thing I knew how to do was act and sing—loved it, loved it. Did that most of my life. At a certain point I started to make jewelry—to tell the truth, I was actually going through fertility treatments while married, in order to become pregnant. And when you go in for fertility treatments you sort of have to stop everything. You can't really exercise; must avoid stress and not do much activity. My whole life took a big change. The fertility treatments lasted three years, and during that time I tried to find more sedentary things to do, so making jewelry became my outlet. Once I made one piece I was on fire. I started making and selling jewelry across the country in stores after three months. I went a bit stir crazy during those years. I was like a volcano that hadn't been able to express herself; I had to put a lid on it. At the end of three unsuccessful years of fertility treatments, I was singing at a Christmas party and entertaining, one of the party goers approached me and said, *we have a band looking for a singer, will you audition?*-- I ended up singing with big bands and performing jazz and blues which opened up a whole new experience for me. At some point I started motivational speaking just because I always wanted to experience it. I was speaking across Los Angeles, and out of the blue got a call from somebody about doing animation. That was unexpected; I had never done voiceover work. I agreed to audition, which was a huge prospect for a first timer. I got the gig. Beautiful job, beautiful pay. I wanted to pursue voiceovers. I said, *gee how can I do this?* I saw a job for radio and went after that. Now mind you, I didn't even like radio, I wasn't even interested in radio. I only did it for voiceovers, but the universe had bigger plans. And I started a radio show.

DS: Wow.

DEBBI: That's how *Dare to Dream* was born. I tell that story because it's remarkable to see the meandering path that my life has taken. I've never been a mutually exclusive person because at some point I may start singing again. I may start acting again. I may do animation voice over work again. I'm open to all of that because they're all joyful expressive outlets for who I am.

DS: You know what I love about your story--I think anyone listening can hear the hunger and fire in your voice, and the happiness and the joy coming through the airwaves. I love that you're so creative. You're open. Who would have thought fertility treatments—jewelry making—taking you to one creative area. And then the voiceovers, and then the speaking, and the radio show. And it wasn't as though you said, *okay this is what I'm going to do, and I must accomplish x-y and z to achieve my goal to create my definition of success.* It seems as though you're just being open to God, open to the universe, to be open to use your talents wherever you were being led to express them. And then things just started to happen for you. Just the way you were describing your radio show and someone just happened to be listening, happened to be saying, why don't you do this? It seems as though people were there at the right time for the right reason while you were going about doing your business of living with the most zeal and passion that you knew how.

DEBBI: Yes, there's also been frustration along the road. I wanted "x" to manifest and found, *"oh, this isn't quite happening how I want it to," and* then—surprise—eventually something even better came along. So there's been a bit of that. Also what you say is true and I think it's actually key because what I experience on the inside is reflected on the outside. So when I'm feeling joy, when I'm in my groove doing what I love to do, it's amazing how much opens up for me. It's like that joy is exuded out to the world and beyond and reflected back. That's why we want people to accomplish their dreams and goals—to go after them one step at a time, because it makes us all happy and able to even create much more.

DS: Speaking of happy, I think that's something that people achieve or experience. People experience happiness when they're living their dreams. I think the dreams do keep us alive. We have to have dreams; the human condition is that we all yearn to be something better tomorrow than we are today. We all want to reach a full capacity for love, for connection and purpose. Unless you're a sociopath I think that's what most of us want to experience. [LAUGHTER] To that end, happiness is something that people define in a lot of different ways and I'm wondering if you can share what your definition of happiness has been, or become.

DEBBI: Happiness is our destiny. If anyone out there doesn't feel happy--it's time to check in because it's your birthright. My definition of happiness is positive or pleasant emotions ranging from contentment to intense joy. There is no one way to bring that about, happiness is contingent on each person and should be experienced from within and exuded without, rather than having something external be the cause or demise of your happiness.

The point is, if you want to be a writer, then write. If you want to be a painter, paint. Dancer, dance. Fit and healthy, then be fit and healthy. If you dream of travelling then travel. Just decide to do it, understand there's brevity to our time here; the time to be happy is now. No matter if you're eighteen or eighty—*tic, tic, tic.* If you've ever lost anyone significant in your life, you appreciate in a whole new way that every breath, every moment we're alive is a great gift. Losing someone you love teaches the immediacy of life. The quickness of life, and how not to waste it. Now is the time.

And by the way, happiness changes. One thing can make you happy now and then, as you go along, that may fade. It may become something else that causes pleasure or well-being, and that's okay. [LAUGHTER]

DS: [LAUGHTER] That may make some people happy to hear. That is so exhilarating, what you said. Happiness can change, but it is in the now. That's bittersweet because death is part of life. None of us are staying, as much as we feel like we're going to be here forever. There really is no reason to put off the things that are those desires in our heart. That's one of those things that you talk about and teach and what you're about. It's living in that now moment and making sure that you do those things today that your heart desires. In that there is happiness and there is peace. Sometimes thinking about 'now' can motivate us to know what we really need to do. It's ironic, isn't it? Anybody can die but not everybody can live. Not everybody does it. Why is that irony there in life? Why don't we step into the dreams we most want to achieve? What's blocking us from making those goals come true?

DEBBI: I don't think most of us know our own magnificence. I think we were born with an inner-illumination that is so bright that if we were to let it fully shine we would light up the darkest place on the planet and the darkest souls as well. Many of us weren't taught—from birth--how wonderful we are. That's the irony isn't it? We are alive, yet not fully living. We are magnificent, yet hiding our brilliance.

Success is a certain *je ne sais quoi*. Anyone can have it, anyone can do it. Another irony – but do they? Success and goal achievement is really a "do-it-yourself" situation. I don't care where you come from. I don't care how tough your background is. I didn't come from a planet of love or parents who had all their ducks in a row. There was turmoil in our household. But at some point you've just got to decide.

And the word: Live? You talk about living? I noticed one day out of nowhere that live spelled backwards spells evil. Isn't that interesting? Evil? That's exactly what it feels like to not live in happiness, to not live our dreams, to squelch that desire and longing. To put yourself down, hold yourself back. It's shattering. It takes more energy to hold back expressing your dreams, than to let it out. On the flip side, you can live your life out loud--then *woo-hoo*! Keep putting it out there because it's a beautiful thing to experience.

For people who desire to achieve something and feel they lack the support necessary here is a suggestion. Gather together a group of friends or colleagues, and become a mastermind group, where everyone connects each week and shares what they want to create in their life. Use the group to get support to realize your goals. I'm in a mastermind group. That was something I put on my bucket list that I wanted to create this year, and it came to me like, *bam*. I got a phone call, connected to some influential people and they invited me to join their group. When they invited me I thought, *"Well, the universe took care of that goal within two weeks of my writing it down. I can scratch that off."* [LAUGHTER] Being part of the Evolutionary Business

Council is really helpful. Participation in the EBC has taught me business with love.

DS: I want to pause. If somebody doesn't really know what a mastermind group is, can you define that? And what happens in them, and why someone would want to be part of one?

DEBBI: The beauty of Mastermind Groups is that participants raise the bar by challenging each other to create and implement goals, brainstorm ideas, and support each other with respect and honesty. The concept of the Mastermind Group was officially introduced by Napoleon Hill in the early 1900's. In his classic book, "Think And Grow Rich" Napoleon wrote about the Mastermind principle as: *"The coordination of knowledge and effort of two or more people, who work toward a definite purpose, in the spirit of harmony. No two minds ever come together without thereby creating a third, invisible intangible force, which may be likened to a third mind."*

Mastermind in general is not a group of advisors. It's a sense of companionship and reciprocity, where everybody is showing up in support

Wisdom To Success | *Debbi Dachinger*

for the other, whenever they can. Of course what you give out you get back tenfold. You create amazing friends. Mastermind groups make the going easier, if you have people you trust who will show up and do their best to champion you.

DS: Oh, wow.

DEBBI: Here is a really cool idea. It's called the FedEx project, where people create a party with their friends or family. Everyone sits around in a circle and shares a dream that they desire to create and just like FedEx each person has twenty-four hours after the group disbands to create it. The idea is to get your project underway within twenty-four hours and most important is to then follow up at the end of twenty-four hours and share with your group what you did. It's potent and gets the juices going.

DS: Yes. Because it really is that action that leads to more action, and you have to begin where you are. Sometimes the hardest part is just getting started. But with these types of likeminded enthusiasts, you really have no excuse to not do it. And that is such a great way to help other people achieve happiness. You're going to become happier seeing your influence helping somebody else achieve their dream. Anyone can join a mastermind group. That would be a great take-away from today's call. Or put it on your Bucket List and maybe they'll find you. [LAUGHTER]

DEBBI: [LAUGHTER] Find a mastermind group to participate in. Do a FedEx party; keep the energy and the dream alive and moving.

DS: Perfect. So that gives us a lot of enthusiasm and there are a lot of mastermind groups out there that we could join. The point is it's a great way to begin—to get with likeminded people. I did want to ask you to tell us about: Soul goals. What is that all about, and how does that help us dare to dream and achieve dreams?

DEBBI: Soul goals are internally inspired and they bring about internal transformation. They're worthy goals. We all know that change is inevitable. For those of us who hate change, *"wah, wah, wah, wah."* [LAUGHTER]. That's what life is: its change, constant change. Change we like, change we don't like, change we foresee, change we had no idea was coming around the corner. Change is inevitable, but growth can be intentional, and life is a do-it-yourself project. So a soul goal is something that always changes. At one point in my life I dreamt of doing a marathon. And now I've completed two marathons; it's out of my system completely. [LAUGHTER] At the time it was so soul-inspired, and I got several things out of Soul Goal experience. One of which was overcoming everything I thought going into it—*"You'll never do it: 26.2 miles, are you nuts? You're not even a runner."* My head had a million reasons why not, but all I knew was that I yearned to do a marathon. And I did two. I did everything right: I signed up for the training; I trained for months and months. I followed the expert's protocol that I had aligned with because they knew better, and the end result was I completed a marathon and it was joyous. It showed me there isn't anything I can't do if I put my mind to it. That was a big lesson. The experience is 50% physical, and 50% mental and I got both to work 100%. [LAUGHTER] A Soul Goal is internally inspired. Maybe you love to create woodwork. [LAUGHTER] For some people it's golf. For some it's about animals. There are so many things to love on this planet. So many passions and ways to express one's self. I want to share with everybody: stop playing small. Stop it now, now, now. Just start really living. Live. Be who you were meant to be. Be weird, and quirky and fabulous. Today's the day to be all of that. I think that's why we love Lady Ga-Ga. Here is a woman who was beat up in school, bullied. Didn't have a friend to speak of. I think her real name is Stephanie. *"Crazy Stephanie."* She's nuts, they're throwing stuff at her. The girl had a passion. She had a soul-inspired goal, and she had talent. Whoa. Talent to back it up. And look at her now. Now who's laughing? You think about the show TV "Glee." It's all about misfits. The fabulous, talented, well-intentioned, misfits. And who cares what they look like, sound like, you know? That's who we really all are anyway. We're all awkward, quirky, insecure, beautiful ... misfits. [LAUGHTER] Just let your dreams become real, baby. Go do your soul goals.

DS: I love that. Soul Goal. That is just such

a great catchphrase, I just love it. I was just thinking with it being summer, finally—you're originally from New York—and finally we had summer up here, Deb. It's just unbelievable. I thought it would never arrive after this past winter. People were down at the beach making sand castles and sea turtles. Kids are creating all these magnificent things in the sand. And the waves are going to come up and high tide is going to take it all away, but they do it anyway. You know? They're enjoying making it, they're enjoying the process of being together and it was all worthwhile even though everyone knows the ocean is going to come and carry it all away when the high tide arrives. But it's all of that that's happening in the process of the creation that makes it worthwhile. Those memories, those feelings, just like you're sharing with us—your running, your marathon. Nobody can ever take that away. And just because it isn't the same top goal ten years from now or twenty years past, doesn't mean that it wasn't the exact right-on-time thing for that specific moment. So you're really telling us that it's okay for those things to change and to just celebrate our uniqueness right now.

DEBBI: Absolutely. My bucket list right now is really one of the most interesting. It was a list written from the space of *I-don't-want-to-wait-anymore-for-this-to-happen*. [LAUGHTER] Here's an example of one: Every year my boyfriend asks, *"What do you want for your birthday."* And every year I say, *"I want to sit at a table with monkeys, with them all wearing birthday hats."* That's who I want at my birthday party, a ton of chimpanzees. I have—since I'm a little girl—just been, well—I've been bananas about monkeys since I was a little girl. [LAUGHTER]

DS: [LAUGHTER] That's very cute and clever.

DEBBI: I'll say that to Ed and Ed will say, *"Okay, Honey. Now really what do you want?"* Because he's like, *"How am I going to give a table of monkeys to you"?* So I realized this year—it's *my* passion. I gotta figure this out. Well, wouldn't you know it? [LAUGHTER] As soon as I decided—and deciding is what happens before anything manifests—you just decide. You step into the creation of that. *This is going to happen—I intend.* And I did. I remembered someone who is an animal intuitive; a lovely person. She happened to mention last year, something about a monkey. I contacted her, we had some back and forth emails, and it ended up that I drove up to Northern California last weekend as a guest in her house — I spent the night, we became friends. Robynn had llamas, goats and dogs where she lived, which was fantastic. She also took me somewhere special — a wild animal refuge where the owner opened the doors to this sanctuary just for me and her. I spent the whole morning there with Cookie the monkey, and with Izod the crocodile and with bears and with raccoons, I kissed a kangaroo and the kangaroo kissed me, and spent the day with twenty-five wild animals I never would have had the opportunity to experience, up close and personal, if I hadn't gotten off my pretty bum and made this happen. It was such a blessing and a grace that came to me through Robynn and the refuge owner and I can actually say now, I've had that experience. I think it was Jack Canfield who said we should write at least 101 things on our bucket list. Spend your lives making each of them come true. That's happiness, those are soul goals. How exciting. I did white water rafting twice – in the U.S and in

Costa Rica. I have literally gone disbursed camping all over the western mountains. And I've hiked pretty much all the Southern California trails. I wrote a book. I danced on stage with the Bella Lewitzky dance company. Just sense that energy, feel how exciting that is?

DS: I'm telling you, I'm feeling it. The thing about your website is you have pictures. There you are with the monkey, and you with the crocodile. [LAUGHTER]. I go to your website and I just think it's hysterical and it's great. And the smile on your face is just terrific. I love that you share that with all of us because I think you achieving your dreams and doing those things, sharing the story, and seeing the picture with the crocodile and the monkey. I think those really are catalysts to energize us to try to make our own list and that's what this show is about. That's what you're doing. You said at the very beginning. Stop thinking small. It's a big, bold world out there, with a big universe, a big god, that power that's greater than us, who cares about us. We really need to share ourselves in that way and be open. Just the stories you've talked about—it's a great place to come from. I'm wondering if we could, get into intuition because you do listen to your intuition when it comes to making your bucket list or making your soul goals. All of these dreams that you have in that wonderful definition of happiness. Somebody listening may not feel like they can tap into their intuition or they don't know how to. What do you say to them to help them get started?

DEBBI: Listen to your intuition. The word intuition is Latin for "in-to-you." What that means is the truth lives inside of you. We can all access what's already there. Have you ever been in a relationship that was crappy and your intuition was screaming to get the heck out now? But you know, we decided to stay, or felt we weren't worthy, or lied to ourselves that it was the best we were ever going to have, *blah, blah, blah.* But our guts knew. Intuition was clearly communicating: *Take care of me, get me out of here.* But the rest of us said, *No, I'm going to stay and see this drama through to the end."* [LAUGHTER] We know. When we use our intuition we make wise right-for-us decisions. We also cut to the chase quicker, right? If we would only listen to our intuition instead of thinking so much or attempting logic, our lives would be much more peaceful and successful. The information is already in us. Intuition is our inner GPS. It's our God Positioning System. If we just tune in to our inner Radio Clarity, we will know. [LAUGHTER]. We all dream, and we all have intuition. If you feel disconnected just develop it like you would a muscle – it will get stronger with use. I used to play with intuition. For instance, if logic told me I shouldn't get on the 405 freeway because it's generally full of traffic, because L.A. is notorious at this time for having the worst traffic flow. But still I'd ask my intuitive self what to do. This happened recently where the knowing was that it was okay for me to drive on the freeway and although it seemed nuts to me, I trusted what I'd heard. And wouldn't you know, I got on the freeway and it was open and clear. Hot damn, this works. You start using intuition in various places. Some of us feel a buzz when we come around certain people. I do. I know someone to *not* spend time with, and I know someone who is good to the core. You start developing your intuition by listening and following what you hear. You can meditate. Have a little bit of quiet so that you create still space inside of you for truth to come up. It really is how our angels, our guides, our loved ones who are unseen, and our highest self, our source of power, our best self, speaks to us, if you take time to listen. Ask questions and see what comes up. And don't play the doubting game. You're just going to have to believe. Allow yourself to ask the questions. It's incredible what we all really know in the collective consciousness.

DS: I really do believe that some people are given a real gift when it comes to that. Super sharp intuition or psychic ability, and we all have it. It's like anything else--and I love your analogy--it's not going to get any better if you don't use it. Just asking questions will help us with answers. But if we don't start asking questions we can't possibly get answers. You make it so easy when you give the examples that you do. Just talking about, what's this person's name or how do I feel around this particular individual? Or even when you're on the highway. These are all practical things we can apply. That being said, for a final thought—

Deb, you'll have to come back and continue on the dream theme--and I want to make sure that you're leaving us with a final thought about how to step away from fear and move forward into making those dreams come true. You've already said so much, but just letting go of fear and moving forward into making those dreams come true. What take-away do you want to leave us with?

DEBBI: If you remember him, Glenn Ford, the actor said *"If you don't do the thing you fear, then fear controls your life."* That's the thing about unfounded fear – it's senseless. On your way toward your dream when fear suddenly steps in and warns you: *"Don't go for that job opportunity, you can't handle it." "Don't have that dream. It'll never happen for you."* If you let it fear will control you. You might as well put fear on a chair and genuflect to it, because if you listen to it, fear is your god. Now, here's the good news: you can choose your god. So you can replace unfounded fear with courage. Do you know what the meaning of courage is? Courage is to do something in *spite* of fear. So we may have fear but we go forward anyway. The subconscious is like a computer, so if we put in great information, positive pictures, good choices, make dream boards--see our life as the movie we would like to experience, it will start preparing you. I know sometimes the hardest thing is just starting, but dare to dream, dare to do it, dare to be different, dare to put it out there. Life is short and while we are here, we are the masters of our universe. Isn't it beautiful to have the life you prefer? You deserve it. That's what I know. We deserve it. We all have our kinks along the way, but don't give into fear. You can acknowledge fear and think, *wow that was really interesting, that drama Fear put forward, telling me why I shouldn't do this, or have this experience, or have that person in my life. Wow--thanks for sharing.* [LAUGHTER] Whenever fear tries to create obstacles, the bottom line is: you don't have to align with a naysayer like that. Right? It's just like people. You don't want negative individuals in your life. You don't want to engage with people who say you can't do it. You do want people who will cheer you on, who will encourage and support you. And so it is with fear since it comes from within, be your own cheerleader and tell yourself that you can and will do it. Just forge ahead, let people root for you. We want you to walk the path so we believe we can too. Steven Richards said *"When your back is to the wall and you're facing fear head on, the only way is forward and through it."* When we create our dreams we inspire and inform each other.

DS: Well, I tell you what, you've inspired me, and I know that people listening, recording live, they've been inspired. You just have such a great presence. I love how you make those dreams come true in your life and you help so many other people make their dreams come true.

DEBBI: Thank you, Deb Scott. Thank you for the opportunity to connect with you and your wonderful listeners. I really have enjoyed myself. Allow yourself to grow and achieve what you desire.

DS: I'm telling you, Debbi Dachinger, you rock. You are amazing and I am so excited. We've waited a long time to get you on the show, and it's just so inspirational having you and sharing your dreams, because that is your gift. It's helping people make their dreams come true. And the energy, the enthusiasm and the sincerity and all the things you have done. I know in my personal life how much you've changed and inspired me to grow and to make those dreams come true and I know for everybody listening that you're going to do that and so much more. I will say, one of my favorite things that I love that you do, are those YouTube videos. If I ever need a little dose of inspiration I can always get those mind vitamins on your page because you have them posted. They're just great. It's so available and really appreciated. I know you'll come back and share your shine with us again, I hope. We won't wait so long next time.

DEBBI: I would love to. Kudos to you for an awesome show.

DS: Best People We Know Club. That has to be us, Deb and Deb. Awesome. Everybody, I'm getting choked up, I'm so emotional. You are so cool with so much wisdom. Eleanor Roosevelt said, *"You cannot make all the mistakes yourself."* You have to learn from other people. The great thing about Deb is-- don't make anything a mistake. Everything is good and getting better. Just learn how to think big and dare to dream. Set your dreams free because your dreams are free.

DEBBI: Yes. Dreams are free so free your dreams.

DS: Alright. Great tagline. I tell you, I'm going to be posting on Twitter too. I love that: *"Live spelled backwards is evil."* You've got to live to avoid the evil, so get out there and live, and live large. Thank you so much for helping us do that Debbi for sharing your shine and helping us to dare to dream and step into those things that make us the unique diamond that we all are. Be a blessing and have a great evening. I'm grateful for you, Debbi Dachinger.

END

Quotable

"I've spent a lifetime making mistakes, messing up, falling apart, and falling on my face. Even though I've been taught by masters and smudged by shamans and prayed till many dawns, time and again I've learned the same lesson: When bad things happens, the seminal question is not "Why me?" but "What am I going to do now?"

"Seeing yourself as the victim is like being punched in the face and, while you're sprawled on the ground, hauling off and whacking yourself again to make sure you stay down. Feeling sorry for yourself and looking for someone to blame takes away your power.

"By this time, I had rejection chops; I had experience enough to realize that this was not the end of the world. Which is not to say I didn't cry, a lot, but I was soon on the phone hunting down copyediting work. Then I called an agent's office and landed a deal to write *Riding in Cars with Boys*.

"To recount I got pregnant in high school, became a convicted felon, almost killed myself, and ended up in college. I graduated from college, was hit by a car, then went to graduate school. My thesis was flunked, so I quit writing, found a full-time job, and was finally published. Fired from the job, I got a book contract.

"Again and again, pain and disappointment launched me in a different direction, opened doors, and seasoned me.

"I've learned that the important question is not "Why me?" but "What now?" Then one morning, years later, I was struck by a lightning bolt of insight: Why on Earth wouldn't I want to be changed by a powerful experience?

"Is there ever change without loss? Is there ever pain before recovery? I find life infinitely more interesting -and tolerable- when I believe I may find some gift in tragedy. As theologian Richard Rohr says, "Faith is not for overcoming obstacles; it is for experiencing them." Pain may provide the incentive to grow, and perhaps picking ourselves up, moving on, and learning is what we're called to do with our lives."

■ **Beverly Donofrio**

For Parents and Teachers:

~Children, Students and Their Dreams

Debbi Dachinger: Interview with Margaret Ashley

MARGARET ASHLEY: I'm honored to have Debbi Dachinger joining us today. Debbi, thank you so much for taking time out of your busy schedule to be with us.

DEBBI DACHINGER: It's my pleasure, Margaret. We're going to discuss what I consider to be an important topic: the beings to whom we are bequeathing this planet to - our children. I'm very grateful that you're having me on your show today.

MARGARET: Well, thank you. Folks, I'm honored to introduce you to my guest, Debbi Dachinger. Imagine how different the world would be if everyone was taught how to get what they want out of life. To not only dream of what they want, but the steps to actually make those dreams a reality. Now, imagine what you and your children would do with your lives if you knew you couldn't fail. This is what our guest Debbi Dachinger will be sharing with us today. What I'm most excited to talk to Debbi about, is exactly what process we can teach our kids to help them dare to dream crazy big dreams, and create lives without limits that are full of happiness, success and fulfillment. Debbi, I know our audience is going to get so much out of the information you share with us today, so again than you for taking time out of your day to be with us.

DEBBI: Yes. Absolutely I'm delighted to be here.

MARGARET: Debbi, give us a bit of background. I'm curious, what led you to focus your work on goal setting and on turning your dreams into reality?

DEBBI: You know, what led me here is really — I wasn't so good at it myself. [LAUGHTER]. I think that the greatest teachers have done the work to manage and handle a debilitating life issue. The compelling thing that causes them to become a healer or instructor is that they take the time to reconcile their obstacle or inner wound. That's certainly my story. I always had big dreams and huge desires and I continued to get in my own way. I had no education on how to achieve a goal. I know I'm not alone in that because it's not taught in our schools, it's often not taught or modeled at home; it's usually not modeled by our peers. Often we end up in our twenties and thirties and we have all these dreams and goals and they keep falling by the wayside. I experienced plenty of dreams not coming to fruition, until it was no longer acceptable for me to live life like that, so changing my inner my world became a project I took on. I started to harness my desire, overrode whatever was going on, and I did what it took to get through. A lot of inner work. The beauty of my journey is, as I was realizing my dreams and they started to come true, I started to achieve some very lofty goals. I then entered into conversations with masters and transformational leaders. I would hang out with them and ask all kinds of questions. I saw patterns in them that distinguished them – made them successful and different. And now I utilize those same patterns in my life today. Everything I teach, I also use. Every time I use it, I see the end result is that my dream is made into reality. So I went from somebody who couldn't create my desires with consistency to somebody who now knows the formula and uses that method with excellent results each time.

MARGARET: Awesome. Now was there a moment that was a pivotal point of transformation for you that led you down this path?

DEBBI: You know, what comes up is around weight loss. I had tried to lose weight and I just couldn't do it because my head was set to a larger size and larger weight-number than my body preferred, which caused me to do behaviors that kept re-creating that number—that weight. That pivotally changed when I was processing some inner healing work with a partner, my friend and I were not even working on my weight. He was someone I deeply trusted. And unexpectedly, in the middle of working with this man I realized that since I was a child I'd held the belief that *I was broken*. As soon as I felt the power of what that means—to be a broken person, unwanted, discarded—I could feel the tentacles that went out from that belief into multiple areas of my life, and how they had impacted my body and weight, and also most of my living. I felt the feelings. I grieved what I had never grieved as a child when I had decided that about myself. And once I was purged of all those tears I had a beautiful empty space. I believe that empty space is where magic lives. And into that empty space I placed a new belief that I really liked and that worked for me. I basically implanted and birthed within myself an amazing new idea that was proactive and self-loving. A new belief that I was whole and complete and perfect. I came back out from that deep inner healing experience and I then lived my life from that moment on with the belief of being whole, perfect, loved, and complete. My life became proof of it and I was on fire. First thing I did was lose the weight. It was really pivotal in changing things.

MARGARET: That it was. Now there is a lot of information out there about setting goals. Your book which is over two hundred pages, hits on some key points that aren't generally talked about with regards to this topic. I would like to focus on that. What do you think holds people back from getting the goals they set, or going after their dreams in the first place?

DEBBI: I am going to gear a lot of this to young people. Our youth can really go big and have fun with goals, ideas and dreams. They can get very excited. They generally aren't as limited-thinking as adults. What we know is that any time we endeavor to achieve anything, we may experience setbacks. But it's what we do about the setback is what makes the difference. So those who throw in the towel and say, *"that's it for me,"* clearly their dream is not going to come true. What holds young people back is they can become easily distracted by their friendships, social activities, technology, and peer pressure; these are things that can cause an achievement to take a backseat in their lives. Often our youth have not been taught to be motivated by hard work and find when pursuing a dream that they go into a sense of overwhelm, and what do they do? They abandon the dream and in letting go of the dream they feel their anxiety go down and they conclude: *"Ah. I let go of the dream, this feels so much better."* But really what happens in the background, in their guts, in their deepest soul, is that dream and goal still is crying out for life. *Give me life. Give birth to me.* Succeeding is all about how to deal with blockages to our goals and still get through to the other side, and it can be done.

MARGARET: With that in mind, what is the biggest obstacle and how can we overcome it?

DEBBI: The mother lode is not learning how to deal with an issue and how to keep moving ahead. Let's break it down - the biggest obstacles are, a) gifting ourselves by doing what it takes to make it happen, and b) not knowing what we don't know. So if we haven't been taught how to achieve a goal, if we don't work with a coach and learn, or we don't get the right book or the right information, how do we learn how? That's what it's all about: how. It's about learning the steps and the process.

MARGARET: Got it. What I really liked about your book "DARE TO DREAM: *This Life Counts!*" is, it not only outlines the process and obstacles but it gives exercises to move people through everything from helping them plan to healing aspects that might otherwise stop them from going after what they want in life. What made you decide to include exercises?

DEBBI: I included exercises because I wanted to engage readers so they had their own journey. It's very easy for me to say *"I did this and that person did that,"* but if I don't engage the audience I'm not giving them the information they need to jump-start their life. My suggestion to readers was, take one dream through this book, I'll teach you how to do it, and by the time you're done with this book, your dream will be made real, if you do the exercises.

It's about involving people so they know how to do it, so they can go out and replicate this successful dream system over and over again.

MARGARET: Exactly. I really, really appreciated that because—as you said—there are so many books out there that tell you what to do but they don't outline it in step one, step two, step three, this is exactly what you need to do in order to get there. I found that just extraordinary about your book. They say that if you want to learn something, learn it from someone who's mastered it. What have you determined are the patterns for achieving goals to get phenomenal results?

DEBBI: The first thing is balance. Creating an ebb and flow in your life, which isn't always easy, right? [LAUGHTER] We have a lot pulling at our attention. The irony is we all bought into promises from brilliant technicians who continue to create new technology and swear it will make our lives easier. First there were computers, then fax machines. Later there were cell phones. In the beginning, we purchased cell phones for emergencies. But times have changed and we walk around with a cell phone twenty-four-seven and they're constantly pulling at our attention. Then there's email—which was supposed to take away paper and green our planet. It has not. What it has done is add another feature that we need to handle every day, and in fact, when we disengage from our lives and go on vacation it's often very hard to fully detach because of the demand technology has on us. Sometimes texting, checking email and cell phones can be an addiction. We open our email browser and find there is tons to read and deal with—and then if you have children, you take them on play dates or their sports or after school clubs—it's a lot! So it's about looking at your entire spread of to-do's that's calling your attention and instead of allowing it to lead you around, you make a conscious choice. That's one of the first success principles. Technology can pull at us and we can be its beck and call, or we can self-empower to decide, "I want this, I want this, I want that—and that, not so much." How do you decide? When you write down your goals and know what you really desire to achieve in your life—then it's clear what should have your attention, and what to-do's and invitations should not. You start to know where to say yes, and when to say no. The next thing that successful people focus on is doing what they love. Seems simple right? But when many of us look at our lives we notice the percentage of activities that eat up our lives are activities that are not bringing us joy. We can focus much more on what we love, put our energy there. Another important element is resilience. It is a fact that at some point we will get knocked down. I have. Listen, I've met with people over time that were very interested in my work and were in a position to make big career-changing promises. But they didn't always come through. Was it personal? Not really. Was it disappointing? You bet. Could I have thrown in the towel? Sure, it's an option. I could have said, *"Oh, wow. They didn't want me. I worked so hard; I got all the way here. It didn't work out."* But I did not go that route; I believe in what I do. I believe in my goals and my work so I kept moving forward knowing the right persons will align themselves with me and me with them. It's all about having a pliable and hearty spirit to keep going. And another pattern of successful people is they invest in themselves. The cool thing is, all of the listeners, right now, they're all investing in themselves by taking the time to listen to this show and learn about making dreams come true.

MARGARET: Absolutely.

DEBBI: Successful people invest in their growth. They take classes, they work with coaches, and they go to workshops. These individuals are hungry to grow. And last, successful people express gratitude. They take time to be grateful; they give back to their community. They are of service. They use tools like meditation and maintain a strong spiritual connection. Those are the patterns.

MARGARET: What great, great patterns. In your book you break the goal setting process down into five steps. Would you share with our audience what those steps are?

DEBBI: The first thing is writing. Right? You want to take the time to write what your goals are. For example, *I want to take a trip to so-and-so. I want to improve my grades. I want to apply to such-and-such schools. I want to get healthy. I want to create a relationship. I want to learn* *how to love and appreciate myself and heal inside. I want to buy a new car. I want to be of service and start a charity.* Anything and everything that appeals to you should be written down. Things that create a sense of passion in you. Now if I told you that there was a treasure and a pot of gold somewhere, you'd be pretty interested in getting it, wouldn't you?

MARGARET: Oh, yeah.

DEBBI: If that's all I told you, would you know where to go to get it?

MARGARET: You wouldn't. It would be like looking for a needle in a haystack. [LAUGHTER]

DEBBI: Exactly! That's just how it is with a dream. If you don't know how to get there then you can't locate the treasure. So instead, you create a treasure map and literally write down the steps of how to get there. How to get from here to your dream -- what particular steps do you need to take? You write it down. It has to be written. They've done studies on students who graduated from Harvard. Twenty years later, only three percent of the students were still writing down their goals and their percent of success was extremely high - off the charts. The action steps need to be written down, otherwise, how do you know what to do or if you're getting to the goal? So that's the third step. Now that you've written down your treasure map, then you refer to it each day. For example, let's say your dream is to travel and take a specific trip. You've written down the necessary action steps and each day you take out your sheet and read the steps still to do and decide which one to execute. You look at your sheet and say, *The first thing is to call a travel agent and inquire about airlines and prices.* So you take care of that and once complete, cross it off your list, put a line through it. That's your daily action step. The next day you address whatever step is not yet completed. Such as: *I need to call Sally because she took a group on this trip and I want to find out more about specific places she recommends where I go.* Then you handle that. You see you follow these steps. Acton steps are the bread crumbs to get you where you desire to be. Now, sometimes things go wrong. That's okay because it happens. We may have in good faith written down something but someone didn't show up, or an event didn't quite happen, or we didn't get what we desired. Or maybe that country suddenly isn't a good place to travel to. Whatever it is, it's perfectly fine. We make adjustments as we go along in executing our steps. We can't know what we don't know. We learn as we go along, be accepting and patient with the process. What happens when we do this journey of the action steps is the dream starts to come alive; it starts to activate and it says, *"I am your dream."* [LAUGHTER] *"And I am going to come true because you're taking steps."* It's palpable and it is the most exciting thing; you will come alive.

So first you decide your dream, second -you write down necessary steps to achieve the dream and third -- you start taking the steps. It's helpful to have some kind of system to check in on yourself. I have a computer calendar and I type in my action steps there, or you can put daily reminders on your phone. Just keep tabs on where you're at, and what's happening. Another suggestion is to create some kind of victory board. A victory board — have fun with it! Every time you have a win, no matter how small or large, the win is put it on your Victory Board. Such as, *"I called a travel agent,"* or *"My neighbors will take care of* my dog while I'm gone," or attaching your plane ticket to the board with a thumb tack. It can be photos, words, objects, tickets—whatever it is, you paste it on your victory board and the more you put there the more you start to see that activated dream (your goal) is becoming real. It's happening. It's coming true.

MARGARET: Great. Do you find that people don't even know what they want?

DEBBI: Uh-hmm.

MARGARET: How do you get them on track thinking in terms of dreams again?

DEBBI: Well, it's interesting; you just have to get out of your own way. Spend quiet time alone. I think if we're not quiet we can't connect with our soul and hear our soul's song. To gain clarity become quiet and go inside of you, and let whatever is inside you bubble out. I received emails from a woman named Linda who purchased my products. She's interesting because she was a registered nurse and she was sort of meandering along life when she started doing the processes I taught, and taking on my suggestions in earnest. Months later she wrote to me and said,

"You know what's amazing? Since I was a kid all I ever wanted to do was be an artist. And everybody told me you can't make a living as an artist. So I gave it up and I went into medicine. I've never been happy there." She started to follow the steps I described—she went out and bought art supplies and started painting again. She's an amazing artist by the way. Still working as an RN, Linda began painting at the same time. Then she was able to start selling what she created, and then others started to notice her talent. Then the city where she lives commissioned her to paint murals and then galleries became interested, and businesses also, in her work. Now art is what she does all the time, she is an artist and also teaches art. It happened by virtue of her becoming quiet, going inside and asking, *"Who am I? What do I love? What might I have been put here for? What are the things I'm attracted to? What makes me happy? What are the things that if you said to me, you can do anything you want today over this next hour, what would I choose to do?"* And even if there isn't a huge hit after asking those questions, take what you hear, follow that energy and start to do that. Because often when we do things, other things reveal themselves to us and then we follow those leads. It can

be a fun journey to follow energy like that.

MARGARET: Yes. It sounds like a lot of us have kind of lost touch with the dreams we had as children because of what someone might have said to us. That is a really good way to get back in touch with those dreams and aspirations that we've put aside.

DEBBI: The mantra should be: *"I can do it."* [LAUGHTER] On the subject of success and achieving goals, yes you can.

MARGARET: I really want to thank you for your generosity Debbi. We're here because we're passionate about empowering children with life skills. We've all set goals at one point or another, and somehow for the majority of us they seem to fall by the wayside after a short period of time. What tips would you offer that would help people stay on track?

DEBBI: Here's what I suggest for any parents out there, or if you're an aunt or an uncle, or god-parent, or grandparent to a young child or student. Talk to your child or student about a goal they desire. Your first time out make the goal reasonable as we want to ramp up the ratio of success as you get started. Starting with a smaller, simpler dream raises the bar on the feeling of success and helps in understanding the method. Once your child shares their dream, in return, you offer to share a goal with them that you desire to accomplish. Then strike a deal and make a pact between you to both support each other to pursue and achieve your goals. When you and the child (or teenager) each take on one dream then the onus is not on either one of you, and it's a shared, fun experience; be sure to have regular times set to check in with each other. It's an exciting journey to teach your child how to make a dream come true. In order that you both keep moving forward this is what I suggest: First thing is always believe in their dreams so they believe in their dreams. Never deny their goal. Children dream big, right? That's what's amazing about them. Remember that your child's dreams are not about you. They came here with their own design, you know? They're their own beings even though they may have some of your genetic makeup, or maybe they were adopted. It doesn't matter. They came here with their own purpose, and that's how it should be. We can teach them to make decisions based on probability. The next thing is get out of the way. We can assist children and teenagers when we believe in how capable and limitless they truly are, through supporting their dreams. Kids say: *"I want to go to the moon one day." "I want to be an actress-ballerina."* [LAUGHTER] Yay!

MARGARET: Yes, absolutely.

DEBBI: Next I recommend releasing control. This isn't about control. This is about having fun. Learning and using proper dream and goal setting. The reason I recommend *let's all do the dreams and goals together* is that you'll get to cheer each other on, and get to model a positive view on goal achievement. The next thing is to set a good example. You've heard that saying, *"Children learn what they live, and live what they learn."* Children (and even teenagers though they may get a little ornery) really do look up to us. They are noticing what we do all the time. It's important we take on a goal along with them — whatever you want to achieve, so they can see us in action modeling what we say, walking the walk. For example perhaps your goal is to get healthy and specifically you want to start small and work your way up to walking three miles a day - share that with them, and let your child know how you plan to make it happen, write it down. Then every day at five o'clock when you're leaving the house with your sneakers on—you're taking steps toward your goal—and you leave for that walk, they know, they see you have aligned to make your dream your reality. *Wow mom, or dad, is going on that walk. They're doing it.* Set a time each week to check in together to see how it's going and where you're each at with your goals. You want to create success together and you'll establish a successful family sharing in the process together. The next thing is help them take action. When they develop interest in different things, awesome. You want to support that. You want to see them achieve their dreams. And just like I shared the "treasure map" steps earlier, once you've both decided on the goal you'd like to attain, follow the steps. You're each going to write down your dreams, research your dreams, set a timeline for achievement, and develop a plan of action. You both will learn about focus and perseverance. And the last thing is support, support, support. Check in together. How's it going? How does it feel? Share what's going on, how the steps and goals are unfolding. For example: "*Everything's great. I'm going to take the dog on my walks from now on. And also, my neighbor wants to join me. I've desired a good friend and now I have a neighbor to share things with. And can you believe I've actually lost five pounds?*" All from committing to taking a walk every day! When you start to share with each other you acknowledge what's new, positive and changing. Kids should put down the electronic games and release the distractions. There's a purpose, and you will develop the muscle that wasn't there before. That's a muscle you can keep working out, which is how to take on bigger dreams, and bigger ideas, and execute those too. Make your dreams a family event.

MARGARET: Right. That sounds like a great plan. Do you find that worthiness or lack of worthiness plays a role in whether people can attain the success they want?

DEBBI: What goes on in our head can stop us. A person can be incredibly talented and yet not attain success because they view themselves as lacking. I have met people like that, where you look at them and think, *"Wow. You're so attractive."* Or, *"My goodness, you were given so many gifts and talents."* And people sometimes throw their lives away because what you know about their brilliance doesn't compute for them of how magnificent they are. There were students, when I majored in performing arts in college, I would look at and think that compared to some of the other students they weren't as talented. But lord knows, they must have had a positive idea about themselves, a real drive, because after we finished college I saw some I had underestimated go out there and become the more successful people amongst our graduating class. So yes, our own worthiness can be very powerful. Here's the bottom line: We decide our worthiness. Nobody gave us worth and nobody takes away our worth. Our circumstances as children do not determine our worth. Our circumstances in life do not determine our worth. We determine it. And if we're breathing, if we're here, if we're alive, then we have great worth. Our role is to choose that we deserve, to decide we are worthy.

MARGARET: True. That's very true. How important is the language used when setting goals and going after dreams?

DEBBI: Well, that's interesting. I think that imagination is important. Rather than *"languaging"* our dream, if we can feel our dream, sense our dream, envision our dream, that's where it becomes alive and rich. If we can access our dream in our imagination, we have an idea how superb it will be when it becomes real. Imagining can drive us forward and bring the dream towards us. So I would say it's more about what we can feel and imagine than how we language it.

MARGARET: Because when people are writing down their dreams they're using specific language. I don't know that they would necessarily interpret that into writing down what they see and what they feel. I think that's a really important point to bring forward, that when they're writing down their goals to use their imagination in what they see and feel and put all of that down as part of it.

DEBBI: What a great point. I appreciate you bringing that up, the writing of the goals. The writing of the goals is literally just having something on a sheet of paper so we can check it off once the task is done. So the words are not necessarily paragraphs of information, the writing is bullet points, the action steps that are going to take you to the finish line of the dream completed. The question is *"What do I need to do to make this happen?"* Often when I write down goals I already have a deep feeling about it. That's the most exciting part. I'll just bullet point what the action steps are and then I start implementing the action steps. I don't write out the action steps in great depth. Again, it's bullet points of what I need to do in order to get there. That's our checklist to help us move forward, and that's the "languaging."

MARGARET: You refer to affirmations in your book. What is the purpose of affirmations and how do they aid in goal achievement?

DEBBI: What we tell ourselves is everything. So if we say — *"I can't amount to much, I'll never have what I want, I'll always be a failure, no one ever believes in me, things never work out for me"* — it's powerful. There are those who have spent time saying affirmation after affirmation. Sometimes it works, and often it doesn't. And that can be disappointing. It's like, "*Ah – there you go. Even that doesn't work.*" [LAUGHTER] Much more important than affirmations are our BELIEFS. A BELIEF is something we say a lot to ourselves or to our friends, or in our own heads over and over again—it's a belief. Beliefs are the filter through which we live and encounter our life. Our beliefs are the glasses that we put on our eyes and see out of every single day. The belief is the filter through which we experience the entire world. And until a negative belief is recognized, unearthed, and then changed, it will continue to control us. It is our job to permanently change a debilitating belief to a positive belief we prefer. For instance, someone who looks in the mirror and tells himself— "*I'm fat. God I'm so fat. I have the biggest thighs. I can't even stand to look at myself in the mirror. I don't know what I'm going to wear. Nothing in my closet fits. I look awful. I don't want to go to this event because I'm so fat.*" When we repeat cruel statements like that to ourselves over and over again—we are creating a set point, an internal thermostat for being overweight, and certainly for viewing ourselves as such, no matter what is really occurring on the outside. We are powerful beings in regards to image, weight and everything else in our lives. And until you take the time to allow yourself to experience: *what does that feel like, to believe that you're fat? That you were put here to be fat? That there's no hope for you because you're fat?* Experience fully that pain—truthfully we have to stop resisting and just go to the pain. That's why a belief becomes solid—it's been a repeated and resisted perception -- at the same time -- and we become certain is real. So we repeat and resist the belief and live out the struggle. I promise you'll make it to the other side if you'll feel it once and for all. Once that's done you will comprehend the tsunami of what that belief has been doing to your life, and you can then choose not to live like that anymore. No one else is going to come into your sphere and love you and change your insides but you. You have that ability. You are capable of caring for yourself at that level. So, what new belief can you now adopt? How about I'm healthy? *I am healthy. I'm magnificent and I'm healthy. I eat well because it is a loving kindness to me. I am excited to get together with people as they support my idea of the new healthy me. I am beautiful and unique.* And you'll see it's a whole different paradigm to live from. So affirmations are lovely, and we need to bump it way up to figure out the core belief bugaboos that get in our way. What are those? What's stopping us in life? Make a decision to feel the truth of what comes up. To hit the pause button in your life and finally feel the power of what the belief is doing to you and then make a new choice.

MARGARET: Right. Good point. Let's talk about visualization. Why is visualization an important part of the process for manifesting goals and making dreams a reality?

DEBBI: I'd like to give you a quick process to use since we're specifically talking about children, students, teenagers, and parents. We can all use this. What's different in teaching children goals is that they often have varieties of options that come up and they like quick gratification and may not always think through what a choice will create. We want them to make conscious decisions, so they're actually the regulator of their situation and can govern the movement towards their dream and make good decisions. Let me offer an interesting, simple process with visualization to assist kids in aligning with their values. Let's say the example is that your child's goal is to write a book report. They share with you, *"I'm going to write a book report for this class, and I'm going to do it on X subject. It's got to be twenty-five pages long."* Next they write down what action steps need to occur in order to get to the completion of a twenty-five page book report. For example, *STEP ONE: I will write five pages a night in order to finish my paper on time.* Now let's say everything went great the first night, your child wrote five pages. But on the second night the phone rang, and their friends called to ask: *"Hi – we're hanging out at Joe's house. We are all together, can you join us?"* And your child is saying: *"I want to go. Can I go? Can I go?"* I suggest returning the decision back to them and offer, *"You have choices. You can go out with your friends, or you cannot go out with your friends, or you can sit and write and come up with a time to meet your friends after you finish your writing."* Have them use visualization to look at each choice and its potential consequences. They can visualize each option, *"If I go out with my friends I could enjoy it. What are the consequences?"* They will see that outcome. Perhaps they'll realize *My concentration will be interrupted if I try to write later when I'm tired. I might not write at all if I keep allowing distractions like this into my life. I may stay out too late and then I'll be late for school tomorrow. Oh, once I miss this deadline then I'm going to set myself back.* After having viewed their choices and consequences then they decide which choice is right and best for them and for the achievement of their goal? Again–what are the consequences, what are the choices? Visualization is rich since it allows us to virtually experience a situation as though it's real time. Initially kids may perceive themselves having fun with their friends, they'll also clearly see the clock going *tic-tic-tic* and the twenty-five page report they need to write building up and the goal possibly not being reached. After they imagine their potential choices they can make an informed decision about what's going to work best. This is how we can help them achieve goals and make good decisions. This allows them to be accountable and it's a win-win for everybody. That's one way to use visualization.

MARGARET: That's an awesome example. Today's kids are very technologically oriented. Do you have any wisdom to share on how they can use technology to help them achieve their dreams?

DEBBI: I'm so glad you asked me because, back to the distractions—we all experience this—social and professional media. Need I say more? [LAUGHTER] It's constant. You know I make videos. I have a YouTube channel and I create weekly inspiring videos. Sometimes I do them on my iPhone, and while videotaping suddenly a tiny bar with Facebook messages starts scrolling by. *"So-and-so said this, so-and-so posted that."* I'm like *"please."* [LAUGHTER] Depending on how it's used, media can be marvelous or media can be disruptive. It comes down to consequences and choices. Properly managing our attention is time management, which is attention management. We don't want technology to become a big black hole that takes our dreams down. We all know that feeling of losing precious time. The first thing I suggest is boundaries. Don't be at the beck and call of technology, rather you be in the deciding seat and with intention only read email three times a day (or whatever limits you set). And outside of that, email is off limits. Next thing— only go on media sites—Facebook,

Twitter, LinkedIn, etc., for thirty minutes two or three times a day. Get in and out. Do what you need to do and be done; operating efficiently in that way has a positive effect. Next recommendation: We all use passwords and passwords can be overwhelming since there's a ton of them to remember. What happens with passwords is it's a lot of goobley-gob to remember and trying to retain those extra numbers and symbols in our head? Instead create a password that promotes your dream and your goal. Write a sentence down that incorporates your dream and then make that into an acronym. Let's say your dream is to publish a book. The sentence might be, *"I have written and launched my new book and it is a best seller."* Now-take the first initial from each of those words and write it out – you're creating an acronym. What you have is: Ihw&lmnbaiiabs. And that's what you type in as your password every day. And guess what; while you're typing it you don't think Ihw&lmnbaiiabs in your mind. Because you have to remember the password, as you're tying your mind is repeating, *"I have written and launched my new book and it is a best seller."* Over and over throughout the day. Each time you type out the acronym the suggestion gets implanted. How many times a day do you type in your password? I type passwords 20 plus times a day. When using the acronym message - you're putting a potent belief into your head over and over again. I've been using that one for quite some time.

MARGARET: Great suggestions. Now how old does a child have to be before they would get this process and be able to work with it?

DEBBI: They can be quite young. We often hear children—the younger ones will come up with more fantastic things. *"Mommy, I want to build a little house for my dolls to live in."* [LAUGHTER] Or, *"I want to go camping in my bedroom."* Awesome. What would it take for us to have a campsite in your bedroom? *"I would need a tent, a flashlight, I need music and I need to know you're close."* [LAUGHTER] Whatever the dream is, you can start all the way from when they're young in supporting their goals and finding ways to start implementing the steps. Pay attention. Kids can come up with amazing ways of going after goals as well as making a dream to be of service to another family or the community. Take steps. Work with them on that. And perhaps they're not doing well in school and you're going help them raise their grades and what would that take; what do those steps look like? I would say as early as you start seeing an indication of their interest, run with it.

MARGARET: Right. I noticed an interesting strategy you recommend for moving forward in goal attainment that you refer to as the 3-2-1 technique. Would you explain that technique to our audience and how it can help them towards their goal?

DEBBI: I love that you read my book. [LAUGHTER] I have so many techniques in the book.

MARGARET You have seventy-seven chapters in this book. [LAUGHTER] It was a very interesting read and I found it extremely insightful in the exercises, and it really got me thinking about exactly how to go about doing different things that I haven't been doing and how to share that with my child, for sure.

DEBBI: Excellent, that's why I wrote it! [LAUGHTER] The 3-2-1 technique helps to accomplish your To-Do list. The 3-2-1 list will get you through a holiday, can build your business, anything that you want to create, this is a workable method with simple writing. To do this technique you're going to do three different things. So the first thing is to write down THREE: Tweaks. If there's anything in your life that you need to tweak so you can move towards your goal? So in other words let's say: *I want to go into horticulture and what can I tweak that will help me?* Well, one of things I can tweak is I can replace the gardening tools I have. They're quite old and rusty. That's a little tweak. What else can I do? I can set aside every Saturday morning to work in the garden. So write three little tweaks that will move you towards your goal. Next write down TWO: Celebrations. This is important because we can keep moving forward, right? We can be warriors on the path to our dreams. But what does it matter if we don't ever take the time to acknowledge our achievements and relish what we've done. Enjoy the journey and the accomplishment. Whatever it is for you, make some merry. [LAUGHTER]

Start right now. Write down two things that you'll celebrate. And last write ONE: Stop. What is the one thing you'll stop today? Perhaps it's one of the beliefs that may have been obstructing your dreams like I discussed earlier. Or anything that you promise to stop doing because it gets in the way of your goals. Stop it. Stop it now. So the 3-2-1 technique basically keeps you on track and it fashions simple and profound adjustments along the way to your goal. You can look at your goal and written action steps once a month, and ask yourself — what three things can I tweak, what two things can I celebrate, and what one thing can I commit to stopping today?

MARGARET Yes. Its simplicity attracted me to that strategy so I wanted to make sure we shared that with the audience. I feel that's an extremely helpful technique they can use anywhere, anytime and get results from. Now we also have a lot of teachers in our audience. Are there any specific exercises you would recommend that they can put into practice in the classroom with groups of students, to get their students moving in the direction of learning and implementing this in their lives so they can do more in school and out?

DEBBI: Yes. I come from a family of teachers and love teachers. Teachers are important. Bless you for the work you do and for your calling. I have a specific technique to share. We've heard a lot about list-writing. There's the *Bucket List*, right? If you don't know what that means it's *"Let me write and execute this list of things I desire to have, be and experience before I kick the bucket."* [LAUGHTER] Then there is a *Birthday List*. Before your birthday write down your goals for the next year — *what do I want to create during my calendar birthday year?* There's a *New Year's List* – what we'll create in the New Year. And something fun you can do in your classroom is called the *Ripped Sheet Technique*. It's a playful way to start to incorporate intuition into your student's everyday life. Have your students take a piece of paper that they will cut it into pieces big enough to write on so they can put one-two sentences on each small piece of paper. Ask them to write random things they desire to do on the paper — anything. Such as: *I want to check out that train shop. I want to go roller skating.* It's random, as long as it feels exciting to them. The next thing is places they want to go. *I want to go to Mount Shasta. I want to visit the town's museum.* Then have them write down three--people they want to see. Anyone in their lives they want to see or spend time with. Four--things they always say they're going to do when they have time, but haven't. And five—is any experiences they've always wanted to have. This is a rich way to tap into dreams waiting to be born. Now as they write this, this sort of *"why am I still not doing these things,"* on small cut-up sheets of paper, the idea is to keep it local, do it low cost, and to keep it easy. This is a non-stress exercise to get them in touch with dreams and goals. When they're done writing they will put the pieces of paper into a jar or a box and it's theirs to keep. They fold each piece of paper and put it into the Intuitive Jar. Teachers, set a time frame for how often they will do this process. Perhaps you'll agree the students will do this once a week every Friday for instance, or Saturday. On that day a week, the student will put their hand in the Intuitive box or jar, and because the papers are folded they ask their intuition to guide them to choose a ripped piece of paper just for them, they'll pick a piece of paper, take it out; unfold it, and read it. What does it say? For example: *"Take a guitar lesson." "Send someone I love flowers just because." "Take a painting class." "Go to this part of town to explore." "Check out this local museum." "Rollerblade on the beach." "Visit my relatives."* Whatever it is, they commit to doing what is on that piece of paper that day. Potentially and probably they will have a magical time. I call this the *Ripped Paper Technique*—because it's basically writing a list, ripping the papers, trusting the intuition, letting go of all thoughts to immerse ourselves in the process of whatever intuitive goal we pull out, and that's what we go out and experience.

MARGARET: That's a great technique. I think it would get kids in touch with what they want, first of all. And get them motivated to take some action.

Folks, thank you for listening to this interview, and Debbi, I am so grateful that you were able to join me today. Thank you for taking the time to share your insights and expertise with our listeners.

DEBBI: It was my pleasure.

MARGARET: It was my honor to talk to you today. That concludes our interview. On behalf of Debbi and myself, I wish you an empowered and fabulous day. Take care.

END

If It Scares You, Do it!

Do you know how blessed I am to be here? It's so important that we have something that we can pour our soul into that is meaningful to us. This is it for me and it is a joy to keep expanding and stepping into more of who I am. I want to give you a message; I desire to speak to your soul. I often speak to your more action-oriented side, but I feel like specifically speaking to your soul and to your heart. Here you are reading this book; I am so fortunate. How did I get so lucky? You're divine. I want you to know that whatever life experience you've got going on, or whatever issues you feel that you're dealing with—I hope you know that you're precious. You're full of joy. You're full of greatness just waiting to be executed into beautiful, positive ripples through the world. You have tremendous freedom. You are here because of your unique contribution to people, our planet and beyond.

It was Dennis Waitley the author and speaker who

said, *"Learn from the past. Set vivid detailed goals for the future and live in the only moment of time of which you have any control, now."* Live in the now. Yes. You are given this lifetime to step up and fully express who you are. So many people are experiencing right now the incredible vastness and fastness of time, how much is expected of us. How much we have to do, and be. It seems so cram-jammed. Don't try to figure it out. Just keep moving forward because it is up to you, it is up to me. I can't wait for anything from the outside to handle how my life is led and experienced.

Just know that you make good decisions in your life. And you are choosing your life just as it is. If you want to experience joy, and delight, and love and prosperity and adventure then choose it. If you're not experiencing that then change your thinking. Change your direction, right? Take contrary action. Because if you're getting a result that you're not happy with, know that you're the one taking the action that's creating that. So if you will switch the path that you're on now — make a different choice — it's all about choice and decision. Your choice, your direction. You change what you think and when you do, that is a start.

Treat yourself well. Treat yourself with health, with love. It's key. It's possible to have everything good. Love is everything so be it — receive it. Become it. Embrace it. Many people in the spiritual community are very good at giving. But how many of us actually receive? [BREATH] Just allow and receive, right? Allow yourself to receive at least as much you give.

True power comes from your heart, it's essential to completing your goals. I know that deep in your heart; you're really and truly confident. I know you have the power to move mountains. I know how positive you are and how much you enjoy living in ease and simplicity. It's time now to focus your thinking, and I want you to think about this: First of all, in Los Angeles, California, it's one hundred plus degrees outside today. Very, very, very hot. Yes? So if I were to go outside and put crumpled papers on the sidewalk and bring with me a magnifying glass to hold over the papers—but I kept moving the glass around and around and moving and moving—nothing would happen to that paper and I would have spent a lot of energy. And that's what it's like. Here you are. You have tons of inspired goals and dreams you want to manifest like the paper down there. Right? The crumpled paper on the sidewalk is the dream just waiting to happen. In between you are the steps you need to take but you're not taking those steps. Why? Because you're so busy moving around, not managing your time, giving so much to people, sabotaging yourself, living from fear, doubts, lack of trust, playing small. Playing small on this planet right now is not going to cut it. Truly, we're called to step into our greatness. So if you're moving around nothing is going to happen. Now I propose to take contrary action. So there's the paper on the sidewalk. Here I am. In between me and that goal is the magnifying glass. Above me is the energy of the sun. What if instead I hold still? I hold that magnifying glass so that the sunbeam energy goes through the glass onto the paper. What will happen if I take concentrated action like that, focus, focus to get to my dream come true—action, action. Just stay still and allow it to explode into flames. That's right. Wildfire. The best kind of fire. You will have your dreams burning in front of your eyes and you ignited them to come alive. That's what you want to do. Start a fire in your own life. Use your focus. Use your attention on the dream and take action to make it your reality.

And if you are experiencing any level of dissatisfaction in your life in any aspect, get excited. Huh? Get excited—why did she say that? Because it means you now know what you *don't* want. So determine what conversely you *do* want instead. Decide what you desire, clarify what it is, write down the steps you need to take in order for it to become a reality. Review your goals. It's essential to look over what your goals are and what your steps are so you know what's working, and what is not. This is how we make modifications and adjustments along the way.

The time to change your life is now. It's not tomorrow. It's not the next day. It's now, now, now. Now is the only time there is. So invest in the future you want. You already have the power to align with your destiny.

It was Bob Proctor, the author and speaker who said, *"Set a goal to achieve something that is so big so exhilarating that it excites you and scares you at the same time. It must be a goal that is so appealing, so in line with your spiritual core, that you can't get it out of your mind. If you do not get chills when you set a goal, you're not setting big enough goals."* Whoa. Beautiful, yes? Set a goal that's exhilarating that excites you and scares you. I can relate to that. Every time I step into the next version of me when an opportunity comes along and it's big and it's new and it's juicy and I say yes. I believe in my heart it would not be presented if I didn't have the skills and power to make it come true.

I read something recently about the actress Connie Britton, who used to be on the TV show *Friday Night Lights* and then was on *American Horror Story* — she's a cool actress. I read that Connie's agent called her to say *there is a new series starting up and they want you to star in it, it's about a Nashville singer on her way out.* And *oh, by the way, you'll have to sing on the show.* Connie said she was terrified — and so she accepted the work. She said, *"It scared me so much I knew I had to do the job. I knew that job was for me."* That's what it's about. Look at her. She's on that TV show now singing, doing it. It's on fire, folks. That's what I'm talking about.

So I see you. I feel each and every one of you out there, listening, reading and participating. You are an amazing piece of this weird and wonderful puzzle we call humanity. You're needed in this world as a leader and a chief. You're gifted beyond measure, and whatever your passions and proclivities are they're there because you're meant to be utilizing those inclinations in this life. I see you and your brilliance and all those things you were taught about you that weren't right or that were weird about you, or different, or awkward or unlovable—they're actually your most wonderful presents to us all. So every awkward, weird, bizarre thing that's different about you, embrace it. Because you're unique and so needed. It's so essential – for you to be all of what you were born to be – fabulous and so potent because you are unlike any other. There's nothing you need to do differently, you're already divine and that is my message to you. That you being you is a gift to all of us.

Don't just dare to dream, dare to make your dreams your reality.

Transcript

Debbi Dachinger: Interview with Allana Pratt

ALLANA PRATT:	Debbi! How the hell are you? How is your day?
DEBBI DACHINGER:	Oh, fantastic. Really fantastic. I attended a party today for someone who is retiring. And as a testament to her personality, four hundred people showed up to send her off and wish her well. That says so much about what one person can do in the world and how we each can affect others. So today I celebrated somebody and saw them into another segment of their lives.
ALLANA:	And it's kind of Interesting too. The title for our show today is, *Showing You How Far You Can Go*. There are different journeys, different phases. From being young, and then in our middle-age, and then in retirement. We still can benefit from having a

dream and having a goal.

DEBBI: I am so full of dreams and goals that I'm going to have to live a long time. That I can tell you. Because I have a lot I want to experience while I'm here. This is a juicy life.

ALLANA: Tell me about how you became a goal-setting coach. How do you define goals as opposed to dreams?

DEBBI: The words goals and dreams have a different vibration for some people. It's about what catches your attention and makes sense. For me they are dreams; for others it's, *"I want to achieve that goal."* I became a goal-setting coach because this is my passion. Besides having fun in this life and other wonderful things, I feel like my soul, in this incarnation, came with a blueprint of living out loud. Being very visible and achieving in a big way, and being in contact with lots of people in a mass way. Those are the internal clues and messages I've received, so I'm honoring the call. The call of the wild. [LAUGHTER] It also means that I've had my share of disappointments early on in life in this area. So with the wisdom I have been so fortunate to gain, I hope it makes me a good teacher. Thus far, that's been my path.

ALLANA: Can you give us an example of a challenge you had in such a way that we can see how you turned it, or learned from it, or allowed that energy to fuel you into clarity with your priorities now and your dreams now? Does that make sense?

DEBBI: Yes, it does. I think a benchmark for me when I first was coming out of the idea of "I can't," and starting to engage inside that I possibly could, was when I wanted to do a marathon. I actually left a relationship where I had shelved all my dreams and goals. I don't know why I did it. Clearly that was a pattern for me, and nobody asked me to do it but I just did. But when I left the relationship and I was on my own it suddenly struck me what I had denied myself all those years. I sat down with a piece of paper and wrote and I was amazed at the list of dreams I longed to experience but had suppressed, like whitewater rafting, like travel outside of the country and take an adventure, I desired to experience shooting a gun, I wanted to complete a marathon, I wanted to take a workshop but had stopped myself because I thought it was too much money. I looked at the entire list and thought *wow. I'm going to do this. This is my next year right here on this paper.* One of the big goals right up front was to do a marathon, however I thought, *twenty-two point six miles. How does someone do that?* So the first thing that came up for me was fear and doubt and what if. I couldn't trust my body to do a mile, much less twenty-two. How does someone do that? Thankfully, I picked up the phone and called the L.A. Marathon office to inquire. As it turns out, they told me about existing training groups. Where I would go and when and how to show up. There are dedicated groups that put on entire training régimes for marathon-wanna-bees. Sure enough, for eight months I showed up on Tuesday nights and on Saturday mornings. I did exactly what the training groups prescribed. I'm very good with formulas. You give me the instruction for something; I follow it and will have success. And that's what I did. They told me what to do. I listened, and what happened was I saw myself go from like a Don Knotts type of character [LAUGHTER] – I can't put one foot in front of the other, to someone who became stronger and more confident. I still didn't know until the day of the race that it was possible. I knew the desire lived in me but I didn't know for sure if I could and I knew I was willing to do whatever it took because it meant that much to me. The day of my first marathon, I crossed the finish line. I got the medal. The second year I went back and did it again and set a much higher goal for myself. I would say that was a huge turning point because while crossing the finish line it became clear that I am capable of much more than I previously knew. If I put my mind to it, I can do this stuff.

ALLANA: Without that recipe, that structure, I kind of doubt you would have done it. Would you agree? Is that a key to achieving our goals?

DEBBI: I think so. I do think so. With all honesty—I've been going after goals for some time. Having a structure and formula to rely on is the way to do it, and each dream fills in the structure in a unique way. Most goals have a feeling of being challenging. Like, really stepping outside of our comfort zone. We haven't had the experience yet, we don't know what it's like.

We're not always sure how it'll look getting there. So it will seem challenging and I would say with the marathon because I was just starting, the one thing I knew how to do was research. Make a call, ask questions, and learn things that I didn't know that would help me to take the next right step.

ALLANA: It seems there are many magic bullets in order to hit our goals. Go into some of the other ones you think are really key in addition to this recipe that will help us actually attain what we say we choose to have.

DEBBI: The first thing is the desire. We know from growing up that if our parents said do one thing, and we really didn't want to, like go play sports but you would rather be an artist, well it isn't going to work for you. [LAUGHTER] But no matter what you desire — whether you say I want to lose weight, I want to quit smoking, I want to have this adventure, I want to take these classes — desire is the very first thing.

ALLANA: Over twenty years ago I said I wanted to be married, but really I just wanted to feel safe. It wasn't a desire that was good for my soul, I was just scared but unwilling to admit it. Is there a way that we can check in with our desires to be sure they're pure or in alignment with our soul?

DEBBI: I did the same thing. And what powerful creators are we? [LAUGHTER] We both got married for the wrong reasons ultimately, and what's so cool is to know you have that level of power inside you, that you can say, *I want this*, and it manifested. It happened. It created. I think a good question, when concern for alignment with our soul comes up, especially around relationships is, *why*? For me, I know I was so focused on--I just wanted to have kids. That baby thing kicked in, I wanted kids so badly that I wasn't looking at all the information there that would have informed me otherwise. I went ahead and was married for eight and a half years. On the flip side, no regrets. I learned so much. When I came out the other side my connection with myself, with men, and where I was willing to go, and how I was willing to do it—I was a new woman. Completely new slate. I've never gone back to that misalignment. I think "*why*," is a good question to really understand our motives.

ALLANA: We build fuel for our dream as we do these deep inquiries.

DEBBI: Yes, absolutely. And embrace failure one hundred percent. Failure is actually something that we're going to experience. Just like how we have one guarantee in life and that is change. We also have another guarantee, and that is we are going to bomb from time to time. What failure does if we use it for the fuel for our dreams, is offer the potential to teach us. We can learn so much from something that didn't work out quite like we hoped it would. The data informs us so when we carry on we can opt to do things completely different. We alter our path and our course, and perhaps transform ourselves.

ALLANA: You say embrace failure—I think there is a tenderness with ourselves that needs to be present when we do these alchemizing of experiences into wisdom.

DEBBI: It's amazing how we lose sight of ourselves, as well as that ultimate connection, with Source, God,

Goddess—All That Is—Buddha, Allah. That's the ultimate connection because that's the connection right back to ourselves in a cycle—and when we step out of ourselves and say, *I so want this*—and it's wonderful to desire a love relationship. A significant person in our lives. And from that space it's amazing how that desire can shift into enormous desperation. *Where is it? When is it coming? Why is it not showing up? I'm not quite satisfied.* And our way of pushing to create a relationship often is to see something in front of us and suddenly our values go out the door. We convince ourselves: *Well, this won't be so bad. I can be with this person, and if I compromise here look at what I am getting.* What happens is there are some really big ticket items that are red flags, *wink-wink, nudge-nudge.* [LAUGHTER] Red flags that are saying: *Pay attention to me. This person's not going to work for me.* [LAUGHTER] But we pretend the truth isn't calling to us. Of course, six months, one year, five years-- down the road, guess what comes a'calling. The truth! I remember a great process for this, Allana. I used it a long time ago when I was going through a breakup and I did a process that was revolutionary. Here I am crying at a dining room table because

I'm heartbroken. I had just broken up with somebody, and I'm writing my response to this process which was: Answer this question—*when you first met this person you just broke up with what was it about them that you knew immediately would not work for you?* The idea is that in actuality we know everything the instant we meet another person– what we like about them and are drawn to and what immediately pops up as an issue that we choose to turn a blind eye to. I was fascinated by this because the truth for me in that break up was that the moment I met this particular man I was not attracted to him. He was probably one of the most phenomenal men I've known. He had a million fabulous qualities, however the chemistry was never there for me and three years into our relationship it was an issue. I blamed myself and I went to therapy and tried this, and I did that. I did everything I knew to fix it. And after the break-up, when I sat down to answer that question—I remembered as he and I were first introduced, I saw how he looked at me and my first thought was, *"I'm not attracted to him."* Three years later what broke us up was ultimately that aspect. Chemistry is chemistry is chemistry. It was not there and I could not falsely manufacture it. So it was powerful for me to concede that what I had always known and pretended not to know became the demise of my relationship with him. I have used that question after any love relationship I've had ended—no matter what beautiful, luminous qualities were in the other, there was something that spoke clearly to me and that I already knew right at the beginning. [LAUGHTER] We truly know everything, we just make-believe that we don't. It's interesting because a lot of the questions Allana, that you ask on your show are about relationship sabotage, what we desire and value, what contributes to lack of fulfillment in relationships, or how to be healthy — as I was looking over the questions something emerged that I know to be true for me. It's about brutal honesty both with myself and with my partner and it's about not losing myself. Never, never losing myself. I've done it. Even in my marriage how I started extricating myself and even how I existed in it, and ultimately how I found myself again. Now when it comes to dating, when it comes to relationships or the relationship I'm in right now — I choose to be and express myself one hundred percent. Even when I went on dating sites I posted a photo that looked exactly like me, I wrote my bio blurb to honestly represent myself. Let's face it – anyone who looks at my photo and my by-line and is not interested, perfect, that is one big step out of the way, I only desire to be with someone who really sees me, who gets me and who likes it. That's important. Just like living out loud has fueled who I am in my career by being a big dreamer and achiever, it also fuels my relationship. It has to be that I show up, that I am genuine. That means maintaining my friendships outside of the relationship. That means me engaging in projects and activities that fill me with joy. I won't play small for anyone, and my life path is to be loved for who I am and all that I bring, which I think is quite good. I am fiercely independent and I am also a very good companion; I like being in a relationship, I like being part of a couple. I'm not sure that's a very popular point of view today; however that is mine and it works for me! [LAUGHTER]

ALLANA: Am I going to instill all of this in my son now and he's never going to have to go through the pain that I did, or is that just part of the pressure of the piece of coal in order to turn it into a diamond?

DEBBI: Yes and no. I think there is perfection in everything, and there is no judgment that you have arrived where you did, how you did, and how you're continuing to arrive. At the same time the answer is yes. Your son's journey is his journey, and he did choose his parents; his soul had reason for that.

I recently had a colleague ask, *"Can I have thirty minutes of your time? I need to ask five people some questions and you're one of them."* I'm said, *"Sure."* And our conversation was riveting. She asked me to share my perception of her by answering, *What are my strengths? What are my weaknesses? What don't I know about myself that you know that I need to know?* I was honest in my responses; I love this person and have great respect for her. I was lovingly real and shared from my heart all the beauty of who she is and also those weaknesses I saw that were holding her back and some of the things she had done out in the world, I don't think she was aware of. Imagine if we each went to the significant people in our lives to ask them reflective questions about ourselves, people who could respond honestly like that. Even people we've been in relationship with and ask, *What do you know about me in relationships? What don't you know? What do I need to know about myself?* And asked a list of questions and were willing to sit still and hear this person's truth about you. What would you learn? You could even add to that to spend quiet time if you meditate or in silence and just inquire, *"What do I need to know, Beloveds who watch over me and care for me? What is it I'm not seeing that will inform me and change me from this moment forward, because I want to be magnificent during this short time I have here. And if it is your will I want to do it in partnership. Right now I'm not doing such a great job. What would you have me know that will change me from this moment forward?"* and be still and listen. So will your son be spared your pain or will he become a diamond? Perhaps you can ask him. Ask what you are instilling and what his pain is? Ask what his joys and pleasure is?

ALLANA: What would you say would be next, taking us along the path to reaching our goals every time?

DEBBI: Desire is it. The next thing is decide. And deciding means you do what it takes. You really align yourself energetically and stepwise to do what it takes. You have to write up what little steps are needed to take you from right here to that goal. If you do one thing at a time a day, trust me it will happen. Now here is something else. What I'm talking about is taking action. Here's a little secret. Besides taking action, we also need to let go. And the same thing by the way with dating. We have to take action in dating, whether you put yourself on a website or you're working with a coach, you take the action. And you must let go. Why? Because we are co-creators. And if we want to get there quickly, trust me. Get out of the way. [LAUGHTER] The universe has magnificent things in mind for us that we couldn't possibly conceive of. The universe is like a giant restaurant. We say what we want, it's like a waitress writing it up and sticking it on the little silver turnstile that spins around to the chef in the kitchen. The universe, the chef, is the source. They're back there cooking up our dream! [LAUGHTER] So take action and let go.

ALLANA: So just get out of your way, Allana.

DEBBI: Exactly. Now this addresses what you are talking about, Allana. It sounds like procrastination. You get in your own way by getting in your head and wondering *"where do I start,"* and thinking about it rather than doing it. [LAUGHTER] People have patterns that stop them.

ALLANA: Mine is, if I do all this and fail, I won't want to live. That's kind of bizarre, isn't it?

DEBBI: Allana, It's interesting to me. I think I'm a high achiever, and I play a visible game, and I can pull back from the intensity and remember — this is a journey. Just enjoy the journey. Because along the journey we change. When we manage the failure issues or being a perfectionist, or procrastination. When we start working toward a dream, it's going to come up. Now we can do what we've always done and say, *"Augh. There it is again. Forget it, it's not worth it. I hate this dream thing."* [LAUGHTER] Or realize it's not coming up to harass you, it's really thinking it's doing a job. Start to transmute these things into what they're intended to be.

ALLANA: My awareness from what you're sharing right now is to get over yourself and have some excitement and fun with it.

DEBBI: So much for our best thinking and figuring it all out. We don't always know. We just have to know the next right step. Trust it, because you can always adjust your path.

ALLANA: Right. It's sort of like you're a ship in this ocean. You think you're steering, and maybe a little bit you're steering. But really the ocean and the wind are just taking you where you're meant to be. But we do have to show up and take action. Reflecting on my life, the universe is on our side. Look how good it's gotten.

DEBBI: I like what you're saying about the ship and the water—let's be honest. We have to operate the sails, okay? [LAUGHTER] Yes, you're the captain of your ship and there is a force of nature and the ship is going to take you places. The deal with the letting go aspect is that we can release trying to figure it all out. We can let go of the discomfort with changing directions. Just be willing—you don't have to know it all. We can let go of worrying our dream into being, because it's totally contrary, right? Dreams — yummy, juicy dreams — are really about relaxing and playing. That's what brings in the greatest opportunities: lightening up. You have to also let go of thinking you need to be anybody else to succeed. You do not need to be or look like anyone else. Period.

You know, I'm a curvy girl. Think Kim Kardashian, think Sophia Vergara — the actress on TV's *Modern Family* — that's me. Boobs, bum and a small waist. I'm *baboom*. It took me a lot of life to accept the body that God gave me and [LAUGHTER] to really get that a lot of men like my type of body and to understand that those who don't love curves like mine are not for me. I learned to fully appreciate my curves and the strong, healthy body I was given. So whatever story you tell yourself — *I can't because of this, I couldn't because of that. This will never happen because of "x." I'm not enough.* People get so married to their story and their made-up limitations. Do you want to know if you have a story? [LAUGHTER] You know you have a story because you tell it to everybody.

[LAUGHTER] Tell me about you. And it's the same story over and over about your limitations. Stop the story. Give it a rest. It's not working. Instead, what contribution and value did you come here to be? Ask the universe if you dare: *"Show me the divine design of my life."*

ALLANA: Divine design, which we don't need to be anything other than exactly who we are.

DEBBI: Right.

ALLANA: Yeah. When I say fall madly in love with exactly who you are, it's that. Madly in love with the divine design. *"Hi, perfect me."*

DEBBI: I know a lot of your audience tunes in for talk on relationships. I was out there doing it wrong for the early years of my life. I approached the whole dating thing incorrectly; I was kind of a relationship idiot. Because I kept operating from the idea, if someone likes *me* I ended up in a relationship with them -- I had no discernment. And I had a desire to get it right. I decided to acquire a relationship education. Boy, did I learn. I was a good student and I researched, read and ingested new ideas on the subject.

I was following information that made total sense and had many light bulb moments. I started to see why what I was previously doing wasn't working and why other people would succeed. And when I learned better I went out and did better and I did everything differently. I immediately saw the results. My attraction rate went out the ceiling. And the men I was pulling in were very high level people. I became the chooser. And in dating I could see that my sense of value about myself was reflected in the people I was interested in and who were interested in me. When I fell madly in love with exactly who I was and my divine design it was easy for others to come into my life to express love for that too.

ALLANA: And now you're living it, and enjoying it.

DEBBI: Yep. I am.

ALLANA: I want everyone to have your book. It's like twenty books in one book. You open an entire new reality with every chapter of your book. You're so amazing. What are your parting thoughts?

DEBBI: Maybe it is—*maybe*—time to do

something differently. And if it is that time, you can change your story. There is greatness in everyone, and each of your decisions creates your destiny now. I urge you—participate in your own evolution. Call forth a new story and in this story, be here for good; you can live your dreams and goals from that new story.

ALLANA: Choose it. Absolutely choose it. Thank you, Debbi Dachinger. Thank you.

DEBBI: Yes, thank you for the great venue you offer here.

END

Quotable

"Throughout the centuries there were men who took first steps down new roads armed with nothing but their own vision. Their goals differed, but they all had this in common: that the step was first, the road new, the vision unborrowed, and the response they received--hatred. The great creators--the thinkers, the artists, the scientists, the inventors--stood alone against the men of their time. Every great new thought was opposed. Every great new invention was denounced. The first motor was considered foolish. The first airplane was considered impossible. The power loom was considered vicious. Anesthesia was considered sinful. But the men of unborrowed vision went ahead. They fought, they suffered and they paid. But they won."

- **Ayn Rand,** The Fountainhead

On Abundance and Creating Wealth

Transcript

Debbi Dachinger: Interview with Daniel Gutierrez

DANIEL GUTIERREZ: Hi, this is your host Daniel Gutierrez with Awakening To Abundance. I would like to welcome you to our call and introduce you to today's guest: Debbi Dachinger. Debbi's abundant career is in using her voice to live out loud while her passion is to dare people to dream out loud. Today you will discover how fulfilling your dreams and goals can lead to creating abundance in life and how to use the law of abundance to make your dreams a reality. Debbi says *"If you were given the dream, then you were given the power to make it come true."* Debbi, thank you for joining us. Welcome to the call.

DEBBI DACHINGER: Hey Daniel, you are one of my favorite people, where else would I be?

DANIEL: Can you do me a favor; can you spend a few minutes and share how you got to the level of success you are at today?

DEBBI DACHINGER: The turning points have really all been internal. By virtue of internal, it is acknowledging what is happening externally. It is also about me agreeing to accept; agreeing to own and represent the gifts and talents I was given. We are all given gifts and talents. But the real ability: I was given an inner light, and given this light to shine, as we all are, and that light for us is part of our soul blueprint. So for me, especially with my background, I feel like a miracle. I definitely did not (even though I always had the ability) feel worthy of much; certainly not of abundance; certainly not of all my dreams coming true. It took getting tired of holding myself back. I was tired of sabotaging myself. So, I had to go on a healing journey and say, *Heck, No. I am not going to live like that anymore. I am going to figure things out. I am going to stop being tethered and now fly.* It has been amazing: lot of twists and turns. Thinking I was here; then something else showing up there; noticing openings and good breaks. Then seeing what is next: so it's been an internal and external journey.

DANIEL: And we are going to talk about that within the next hour. So, for those of you who are listening, can you tell where she gets her radio voice?

DEBBI DACHINGER: Thank you.

DANIEL: Deja Vue. [LAUGHTER] Listen, I

am really excited about our call. What is your definition of abundance as you perceive in your world?

DEBBI DACHINGER: A lot of us think of abundance as prosperity. Yummy: money; cars; that's cool; that is true to some extent. Abundance is so much more; it really is an indication of who we are; and how we feel about ourselves. It is our seat of power. I saw a picture this morning of a goddess sitting on a throne; she was a beautiful being sitting on the throne of power. The message is: we don't *step* into our power; we *sit* on the seat of our power; on our throne of influence, authority and command.

For me, abundance is about flow; where the flow is or the lack of flow is in our life. Abundance is an energetic term for the flow; a breath in and a breath out; a yin and a yang. It is an action and a surrender. If you want to make a dream and goal come true, you must take action. You must also let it go. It is the same thing with abundance; like gently moving water. And when we are in flow with the All That Is and with life; then our dreams will come true in life. Then abundance can flow to us.

DANIEL: Are fulfilling dreams and goals and creating abundance similar or the same? Many people get that confused. Is there a reason?

DEBBI DACHINGER: Yes, they are the same in that they are both our willingness to receive. They are the same in that they are about acceptance. They are the same in that they are about creation. In both dreams fulfilled and abundance created, it is about acquiring something, making something new happen, right? Maybe you want to climb a mountain. Maybe you want to be a dancer. Maybe you want to change careers. They are things that make us joyful and are our passion. There is a flow principle for abundance. Again about our power: I want to be clear that we don't ever have to be fully in something to make it happen. We don't have to be completely confident. Some think the process is: *I have my stuff together. And I got it all figured out.* Not so. We only need to personify some of these principles; and more than anything we need to have an incredible willingness to live out our dream, to reside in our innate potency. The glory of what we were created to be. The rest will happen. The lessons will come. The journey will unfold.

DANIEL: What holds people back then? There are probably people listening here now saying *"Gosh: I tried that all my life. Enough is enough. What do I need to do internally to get what I want?"* What holds people back from obtaining their dreams or obtaining their goals?

DEBBI DACHINGER: There are a lot of specific things; however, I will give you the umbrella answer. Fear or doubt creates overwhelm.

DANIEL: Interesting.

DEBBI DACHINGER: People fail because they get overwhelmed by issues blocking their goals. They manufacture lots of explanations of why it can't be done. *I can't possibly make this dream happen because…* and fill in the blank _____. Successful people, on the other hand, find a way to do it anyway.

DANIEL: I had a thought when you are speaking a minute ago that came to mind. I have always been fascinated by people who climbed Mount Everest. Right, I always watched the movies about Mount Everest. There is a part of me that said *wouldn't it be great to climb Mount Everest?* There is another part of me that says, *you are crazy; you're not really going to climb that mountain.* This year in September, I will be in Kathmandu in Nepal. I will have scheduled a morning flight over Mount Everest as the sun comes up. As far as I'm concerned, I will have met my goal. Maybe later in life, I will continue and climb it. It's the tallest mountain in the world. Throughout your life, did you always feel like you were on the path to living or to getting your dream?

DEBBI DACHINGER: Wow, I love what you shared. It is perfection: that there will be a fulfillment there for you. You will know after flying over the mountain if you have succeeded in experiencing Mount Everest in the way that is meaningful and fulfilling to you. Kudos to you for desiring to experience Mount Everest and for making that dream realized in spite of any reservations you had about your goal. That darn mountain elicits the same response in me too! But only through watching documentaries about it - I don't desire to climb it! [LAUGHTER]

As far as my being on the path my whole life, no, not at all. Mama Mia. My being an expert in goals is a phenomenon. You know, I come from a very interesting place. I come from a broken home. My father was not even there when I was born. He stayed on in Israel where I was conceived; my mom flew back to New York in her ninth month of pregnancy with me and we then lived with my grandparents. My grandparents were my saving grace. My immediate family was dysfunctional. There were problems: but I believe that everyone has someone there for them, an angel of sorts who is there as a constant in their life: pastors, ministers, a teacher…. In my life the angels were my grandparents. So my father was not around. He was a holocaust survivor. What happened to his family was so traumatic that his response to the horror he experienced as a child and teenager caused him to choose to not be available, physically or emotionally. My mother was present but had to carry the load of two parents, including earning a living. And I had an older brother who was also impacted by our environment. I was lonely most of the time. When I was born I was essentially a joyous, animated little thing bouncing around with curls on her head. Yup, I had hair with curls and a face with freckles! [LAUGHTER] I was joyous however my home life was dark and chaotic; it was tough. What I desperately wanted was to be seen. My wound was: please acknowledge me – please listen to me. Let tell me I am special and cared for. I got great love and care from my grandparents, not necessarily in my home. I grew up with so many neuroses about even being on this planet: being worthy to be here.

One place that I found that I could excel was on the stage. For whatever reason, I could confidently get up on the stage. That was my place of potency in the best way. I could express myself and be free. Something great and magical happened there, and people, audiences responded well to me. It took a long time for me and my history to work itself out. I was an actress and singer for a long time. I had success in several mediums. There were also times when I should have been amazing but because I lacked self-assurance at the time, I screwed up. I took a class in Los Angeles at the well-known Los Angeles Music Center with a big casting director. He'd watch my performances and he'd tell me after every enactment: *"Debbi you are so talented."* And there I was, in a theatrical mecca, with a very important, connected casting director who adored me and found me talented - I had a shoe-in, you know what I mean: I had *two* shoes in [LAUGHTER] – it should have been easy. This casting director knew I could star in various roles, and that I was gifted. He'd request that I audition at the Music Center for various plays and oh! I'd get there – to that level and start sabotaging myself. Inside me was a ton of talent and possibilities, there's a casting director who adores and believes in me and has asked me to audition, and I am letting all my internal issues get in my way. Ouch. I had dreams, yes, as well as poor beliefs about myself that blunted those dreams.

At one point I sat down to write. I created a list of all my dreams, I looked at this list and I thought: *wow. Who has been holding me back, here? Me! Money, uh! Relationships, experiences, health and body, full on career? Uh, uh, uh!* I was looking at all this lack I had created. I was amazed at what that lack was costing me in interest. That was a huge turning point. I decided at that moment, that I was going to make every one of my dreams come true. From that moment on, my whole life changed. It was a brilliant choice. I started to have a good feeling along the journey of: *I am doing this. I am capable. I am getting there and experiencing it.* It was so exhilarating to turn my life around like that. So I can tell you it can be done.

DANIEL: For the listeners who are having challenges in their life: how did you come to believe in abundance and prosperity? Does it work, is it real? Having been through the challenges or opportunities that helped you grow (I believe that you believe in this), how did you come to believe in this? Even when it was something that was not apparent in your younger life?

DEBBI DACHINGER: Well, can it happen? Just remember that the word impossible, has the word possible in it. Abundance exists. If abundance and prosperity are not currently a reality then there is some kind of inequity there. The common denominator in my life was me. The work had to happen in my realm. I think these things really got me through to the other side: first of all to keep it simple. Remember that there is enough right now. In fact, there is more than enough right now. It was starting to focus. What is here right now? Is it enough? Allow it to be enough. And by virtue of that: allow it to be enough for myself. The biggest place for me to start with abundance was with love: an abundance of love. How do I show up in love for me? How do I love others; and how do I love humanity? When I am going through my day and my life: What kind of love do I give out to this planet? If I am at a stop sign do I let other people go first or am I aggressive? Am I flipping people off?

DANIEL: You must live in L.A.

DEBBI DACHINGER: Yes I do. Why, have you seen me on the road? [LAUGHTER] So it is a big task in how you are showing up for yourself and everyone else. I started to have an abundance of love for myself. And what came from that was: *I do know what I desire; and I love myself enough this moment to take action and do it.* That was enough for my journey to start.

DANIEL: I love it. Now, You say that there is enough. There really is more than enough. You have said that more than once in this conversation. I believe that you have some kind of process or experience to take the listeners through? It seems to me that we did not have the right kind of tool. Because it seems to me that it felt that there was not enough. If there is enough what can you teach our listeners about that? You said you had to deal with an inward and outward experience for you. Maybe listeners lost a job or a home. What do we do from that perspective?

DEBBI DACHINGER: Fantastic, my pleasure. The first place is to know: the filters that we look at our world through; is the world we experience. If we change the glasses we wear, or the filter we look at things, we can shift. I invite everyone to have a willingness to shift. Be willing to go on a small journey.

Close your eyes. Allow yourself to go within. And breathe. Allow yourself an abundance of breath, in and out. Take your breath back in again and let it out. In the stillness that you are creating inside, whatever it is that you feel that you desire in your life; that feels like abundance but that you feel like you cannot have; just feel into that; just for this moment; in that space where you have that desire; hear your objections; just accept it; accept those feelings; and also accept that desire. Can you accept it just a little more? And now just embrace and accept it just a little more. And now, find a still state of peace in your body; inside of you. Let your consciousness drift into that state of peace. Just be there; be peace. And from there; expand out with peace; expand your energy out with serenity emanating up, down, all ways moving out ad infinitum. Expand out past your body; and fill the entire room that you are in. Now fill the building that you are in. Now expand, and fill the city that you are in. Expand out into the state that you are in. Expand out into the country that you are in. Allow your energy to keep expanding so that you are now the entire earth; go deep into the core of the hot earth and back up to its oceans and lands and mountains and all its' people, connected to all humanity. And now continue to expand out into the universe as you know it. And once you think you have reached the limits there; keep expanding out; and as you expand out; you realize that energy; matter; particles; all you are, All That Is; there is no separation; separation is an illusion; we are connected to all life; to all our dreams and aims; and all our abundance, and all that is there is – just is. And while in that state, let me share that when we are given the dream, we are also given the power to make it come true. A comfort zone is an illusion. You are expanded everywhere. You are comfortable everywhere; because truly you are everything. Remember: every time an opportunity comes to you; it is just like a door. All you have to do is put your hand on the knob and turn it and walk through the door. Allow the abundance to overflow. Overflowing around you in a beautiful wave; an abundance of plenty. Breathe it in; invite it in; welcome it; accept it; encourage abundance; appreciate abundance; and surrender to abundance. Abundance is always there by virtue of your vibration. You need do nothing for it to follow you wherever you go. Now invite prosperity into your body; your physical body; your physical world. Accept it. Encourage it. Have fun with it. Appreciate it. Release it. And you continue to prosper and abound with plenty, because you are a beloved part of the All That Is; the Source that already knows it is enough; connected with All That Is and with ultimate pure love. And with a deep breath, bring in the plenty; and come back; grounded; choose to be here; wiggle your toes; and allow yourself to be in the now; come back with all, plenty and all abundance.

DANIEL: Wow, that was nice, Debbi. I am comfortable. Thank you. I am sure that this beautiful meditation that you just took us through, you were asking them to expand their mind; to expand themselves beyond their current place; their current state; beyond their country. What are these dream busters that keep coming up and plaguing us, and how do we get rid of them?

DEBBI DACHINGER: Good, let's take on doubts. We doubt that we can ever handle the dream. Oh my God, I had that one.

DANIEL: What are you going to do? I love that.

DEBBI DACHINGER: We say: *What if I am not able; what if I am not capable? What if I'm not likeable?* That is what we think in our heads. Understand that the opposite of doubt is certainty. We have to create a sense of certainty in our lives. In order to create certainty, we need to generate the opposite of doubt. We need to internally craft something different -- champion ourselves and not allow doubt to take us down. You can create a new voice that speaks to you and believes in you. So if doubt were stopping my dreams, the new voice might say: (Spoken with an accent): *"Excuse me a minute; I have to tell you; you are talking to a winner here. I have seen this girl; and she is victorious. She's got a big V over her head. I'm telling you: Not only can she; she will. When you come back to this playground; you are going to have to deal with me."* [LAUGHTER]

DANIEL: Oh, Boy. Were you ready for that? [LAUGHTER]

DEBBI DACHINGER: Oh my God! You never know what voices or accents are going to come out of me!! [LAUGHTER] Also you can create your own alter ego. You don't have to have an accent like me. [LAUGHTER] The alter ego's mission is: to be your own cheerleader. The cheerleader loves you, nurtures you. Create a new loving, certainty when you are in a good space. And then when you pull out the "certainty" voice nothing can stop you. Another thing about healing doubt is to use courage. Courage acknowledges fear but moves forward anyway. Courage knows it can overcome doubt. I really enjoy the etymology of words; I think their meanings are very telling. Old French corage from 1300, meant "heart, innermost feelings; temper," and was a common metaphor for inner strength. From Latin, *'Cor'* means heart, and so the original definition of courage was to share all of yourself, share your whole story, share your whole heart. An act of courage was an act of storytelling. Can we acknowledge that heart is something we all have right now? Acknowledge and appreciate your big heart. Have a heart for yourself and for your dreams. I *have heart to give myself what I so richly deserve.* That means you are already halfway there.

Another dream saboteur is fear. Just acknowledge the weird things you do when you are fearful of failing; fearful of succeeding, and are fearful of being seen. We are afraid of screwing up and being seen. We are fearful and create so much anxiety and stress that we will crack. You can't let fear win. We have to harness fear and make it work for us. The other side of fear is real excitement. That is the truth. Usually it is just a skewing of energy. Ultimately you are in control so do it anyways.

Here's the deal. Remember when you were a kid; some people thought there was a monster in their closet? I was afraid there was a witch under my bed; she would kill and eat me, and that would be the end of me. [LAUGHTER] People love horror movies, right? The whole idea of a horror movie is that you are horrified; you are terrified. You're watching the actors on the screen thinking: *Don't go down the stairs; don't go in the closet.* You suspend the idea that it is an illusion when you are watching a horror movie. Fear is the same way: it is an illusion. It is saying to us: *Just suspend the idea of safety. You are going to believe me; and do whatever I want you to do. I am fear, so big and bad.* So-- we give fearful thoughts all our power. Fear is an illusion. To stay calm we have to keep our eye on the ball. That's the bottom line. Let fear do its thing and realize what it is: it is an illusion.

Then for some people: it is about others. *What will others think? I can't do this; because everyone depends on me; I can't let them down. People need me to be a particular way so I will live my life to please them. I am beholden to others.*

Another dream saboteur is: We believe that someone else has to do something for us to afford it. Someone else has to do it *for me* to make it happen. We think that other people determine our fate. Or we think that we come from the wrong side of the track. Not true. Not true. I am going to tell you the solution right now. I think this is a statement for our time. We are being called right now to step into who we are. You have great persistence. You are here for a reason. You are a light worker; meant to do what you are supposed to do on this planet. To get to who you were meant to be, to who you are supposed to be; even with your perceived awkwardness; and quirkiness; and brilliance; and funniness; and strangeness; and fabulosity; the whole good-funky of the package of who you are. And when you take down the walls to please *yourself*, to be authentic, the Universe shouts: *Hallelujah; you have now arrived.* It is like Lady Gaga who was teased terribly as a kid because she was different. Baby, look at her now. *I was born this way.* Now that is a song of the times. We are meant to be who we are. When you are on this dream journey, the Universe will support you.

DANIEL: Wow. I love what you just shared with us. What I would like to do; is talk a little about Science. Quantum Physics as it relates to the laws of abundance. Let's jump into the keys of what we can use to get to an abundant life. Can we go down that rabbit hole, so to speak? If you can share about the Laws of Quantum Physics; how it works with the law of abundance?

DEBBI There are a lot of laws in Quantum

DACHINGER: Physics: Law of Vibration; Law of Attraction; Law of Cause and Effects. One is the Law of Growth. Quite simply the Law of Growth states that for EVERY seed planted a harvest will be received. It isn't the Law of Growth in and of itself that determines your life experience but rather it is that "something" MUST grow based on the kind and quality of seed planted. Once the seed, meaning idea or dream, is planted the Law of Growth in its absolute perfect timing guarantees with 100% absolute certainty combined with the unfailing interconnected certainty of all the Universal Laws that new life is inevitable. Let's look at the Law of Growth as it pertains to your life and how it is that the events, conditions and circumstances that you experience in your life come into being. Based on the kind and quality of the seed planted the harvest will produce a harvest in kind. EVERYTHING produces in kind 100% of the time. The Law of Growth doesn't judge or make determinations as to *what* is grown and can only operate within the parameters of its intended purpose. It only insures that *something* grows unfailingly and with unwavering perfection. All that can grow is based on the seeds that are provided to grow. The Law of Growth is constant. Intention. Visualization. Willingness. We become conscious and purposeful in what we project or plan. The Law of Growth, or Law of Production, says we choose our wealth. Love brings love, health brings health. Like produces like, an effect resembles its cause… A smile brings a smile, peace brings peace; and never will this spiral cease. As you sow, so shall you reap. Carefully choose which seeds you keep. [LAUGHTER]

Then the Law Of Polarity allows us to experience life to the fullest. You know? If poverty did not exist; how would you know what it is like to experience abundance? Death vs. Life. The events or conditions or circumstances; they all work together for good. And when we can allow all of life: this is just pure acceptance. This is what I was telling you from the beginning. Then we can receive all that is ours.

There is a Law Of Reciprocity which is universally connected to reciprocity in this unfailing process that reciprocates. Return in kind. What we see a lot today is the best business models that are thriving and succeeding in doing so because of reciprocity. Can you imagine a planet where countries operate under the laws of positive reciprocity? A law of universal good?

The Law Of Reversibility: Everything has a way to operate in reverse. How do you figure out your dream? Do it in reverse. How do we go about this with the Law Of Attraction? You decide what you want; and envision yourself as you are already having that or doing that. The feelings are so important. Smell it; see it; touch it. And from there you come backwards to where you are now. And that is where the energy comes.

So to get where you desire to be, first Awaken, because your life is created from the inside out. Then Embrace Personal Responsibility. Empower yourself. Know that you can change your circumstances and learn to be happy by intentionally and intelligently making better choices, by consciously choosing your thoughts. And last, Choose. Choose and Take Action.

Quantum physics proves that there are always infinite possibilities for everything and we, the observer, decide on which possibility becomes our reality. Therefore, we are creating our reality moment by moment by what we think or believe will be there. The "waves" of possibility becomes an experience in our reality because we expect it to be a certain way, and our expectations become the solid atom. Whatever you think about and believe to be true regardless if those beliefs are based on "real truth" or "perceived truth" are what determines how your life will unfold. The Quantum Field is an "Infinite" field of potential. Anything and everything that has, does or will exist, begins as a wave in this field and is transformed into the physical realm, limited only by what can be conceived as truth by the observer! Who is this observer? YOU! If you believe, think, feel at some level, whether consciously or subconsciously, that money is difficult to come by, the energy emitted and broadcast will harmonize with energy of a harmonious frequency and your life will reflect that of money being difficult to come by. By the same token, if you believe that money flows to you effortlessly and you maintain the conscious and subconscious beliefs regarding that, you will find that money becomes easy to acquire. Taken a step further, if you can conceive and believe in the materialization of your biggest hopes, dreams and desires, they already exist as a wave in the quantum field as a probability of existence only awaiting you to make them real. As Quantum Physics has proven it is you who is responsible for whatever is occurring and being experienced in your life right now. This includes your partner, your work, whatever difficult situation you have around you, this difficulty is reflecting what you have put there. If you don't like it then change it. And that my dear, is science.

DANIEL: Wow, I am glad you said that because there is a science to all this. There is a science to this. I do know that if scientists are the most pragmatic on earth; in terms of showing before we believe it. What are the keys to abundant life? Can you take us through an exercise?

DEBBI DACHINGER: Yes. I will take you through the Law Of Abundance. In the etymology of words, the word abundance is an adjective of the verb abound. From the Latin: it means overflowing. An accurate definition of abundance is to overflow. It multiplies effortlessly. I love that image. So, again, we plant a seed; for an energy that we want to project. If you're not experiencing abundance in your world look around. The coolest thing is that we are not at the mercy of anything. You can change and heal. If something is taking place that is creating some lack, just acknowledge that simple abundance surrounds us everywhere now. You can look at fruit; trees; water; air; life.

It is a spiritual law and I will take you on a spiritual journey: a small adventure to visualize abundance.

Whatever you are doing right now;

put it down. If you are multitasking: stop. And start to breathe deeply. Whatever is inside: stress; anxiety; the day; whatever you are listening in to this interview for; whatever you feel that you got or didn't get: let it go. Just for this moment, accept all of who you are this moment; no limitations; complete understanding; let's unlock your abundance; let's unlock your divine nature; let's step into your direct relationship with Source; and from that space; be grateful for everything you have now; feel thankful; for whatever you need to learn; be compassionate; empty your subconscious; clear it from agendas, ideas, pressure; commit to making your life into a treasure; and from that place; commit to making a treasure map; where you can imagine the dreams; the goals; the abundance and how you will get there; later write it down; right now; feel into what that is for you; know what you deserve; every day have a time of stillness to meditate; be still; that is how you nurture and refill yourself; in this moment; in this space; forgive yourself; forgive yourself for all of who you wanted to be; for the commitments that you made but did not see through; for the promises that you made to yourself and others that did not happen; for any perceived failure: forgive yourself now; abandon all anxiety; release all stress now; [PAUSE.....] visualize your dreams; one at a time; see your dreams coming true; experience your dreams as being in your life right now, big and juicy in this moment; put yourself there in that dream, you are already there; fire up your faith; let your faith prevail; and imagine yourself and your life with the dream real, say: *I am open to the flow of abundance in all areas of my life; I always have more than enough of abundance; thank you universe for my great abundance; today I expand my awareness to the abundance already around me; I allow the universe to bless me with great abundance now.* [PAUSE.....] Within you beats the message of your heart and the universal heart; you have a unique path with a unique reason; you are a beloved piece of Source, of All That Is; feel the flow now. And allow a message to come to you from the Universe of what your next step is to bring that dream into your life. Listen, it's important and it's a message just for you. [PAUSE…..] And breathe it in. What a beautiful creation you are. [PAUSE…..] Come back having received information, knowing this abundance is just the beginning. For anyone that is feeling lightheaded: picture your feet with roots growing out into the earth; feel the energy. Breathe. Come back. Be here now; fully present.

DANIEL: Thank you Debbi. Wow. I feel great! Can you take a minute to explain the turnarounds of people who you teach?

DEBBI DACHINGER: The turnarounds that I have been experiencing are through people I have helped: this is my passion. I really want people's dreams and goals to happen. It is good to start reaching kids and teenagers to begin having their dreams come true, especially during these interesting times. Some coaches have made my book a required reading for their clients, which is humbling. I have an award winning actress who wrote to me that through using my dream achievement method she finished writing her book and it's about to become a movie. I have got a fan in Spain, who has become my friend,

Warie, who writes to me periodically. And I am moved deeply as he continues to share with me all the magnificent changes he is making in his life, I am proud. I receive letters and emails of thanks, some use my coaching tools for attaining their goals. I have clients who are of service to people with special needs and were having trouble getting their foundation funded. They have been implementing what I teach and finally influential companies have come forward to financially assist them. I also heard from people with troubles in life. A fellow in Florida wrote me that his friend, a lawyer in L.A. has been depressed. The L.A. lawyer used my books and my products, and his life made a positive turnaround. The friend in Florida was so impressed he purchased my products as well. And a very meaningful email: I heard from a man in Minnesota: a young dad. He was scared of getting in front of people and doing a presentation and talk. It was holding him back in life. What impressed him in my teachings was hearing me say he should not be afraid to fail. He got it; like he totally got it. He said: *even though I hate business meetings because I'm terrified of giving speeches; for the first time in my life; I am going to do it; I am going to talk at a meeting; I am going to attend social experiences and go up to people and just talk, stop being so afraid, and I am going to get a job in public speaking.* A woman from Transylvania, after 50 years old, said she is daring to make her dreams a reality. On and on: from Scotland; from England. But mostly I want you to know is that I can give you the secret to success, the 1-2-3-4 punch. Once you do it; and you understand how it works; you can replicate it in any area of your life, for any dream. I want to offer you that; so every day of your life is rich, and you can have the fun and enjoyment of life that's available.

DANIEL: I get really excited about helping people to take control their lives. There is so much more we can learn from Debbi. I encourage you to go to Debbi's web site.

DEBBI DACHINGER: It is important to surround yourself with the right thinking. Use all your senses to allow your dream to come true.

DANIEL: That is beautiful. What are some of the benefits that people can expect to experience right away or over time by applying your program?

DEBBI DACHINGER: What dreams are percolating inside you? If you could do anything and be anything – what would you do and be? What do the dreams feel like? How will you start the process? How to keep it going? How to finish the goal? Hang in there. Complete your goals. Don't let anything knock you off your path. Use your conviction to keep you going. You have all you need to make your dreams become a reality. Generate an abundant life. Shift into your dreams and start your passage; you can bring your goal to success.

DANIEL: Thank you so much for sharing that with us Debbi. I look forward to spending time with you again.

END

Transcript

Debbi Dachinger: Interview with Kris Britton

KRIS BRITTON: All of the experts here on *Your Wealth Building Summit* can relate to one thing, they all had to overcome their own personal broke beliefs and the fear behind taking the necessary steps to live their purpose and touch as many people as they are today with their greatness.....

Retrospectively, Debbi, what do you remember as being your biggest fear or broke belief that used to hold you back from creating a business around your purpose and making money doing what you love?

DEBBI First of all, if I may, when we talk

DACHINGER: about a broke belief, I'd like to explain from my perspective, what a belief is. Beliefs are thoughts that we think over and over until they become solid and when they become solid they are the filter through which we experience our reality. Beliefs are also indoctrinations. They're ideas that have been passed down to us through our religion, ethnicity, society and our families. Negative beliefs are governors or gates that hold us back. And the good news: *Beliefs can be changed.* What held me back personally? 1) First the belief of: *"I can't."* 2) And next the belief in the wrongness of who I perceived myself to be. I turned around the belief of *"I can't"* by taking the *I cant's* and making *I can* out of them. I moved forward towards my purpose anyway and proved that belief was unfounded. I proved that voice wrong time and again. And it became clear that really, *I can.* Not only *I can*, but also *"I will."* Next, I embraced what is unique and different about me and rather than seeing it as a "wrongness," accepted that my unique qualities are actually my best and greatest assets. It's what separates me from others in that I can make money from my distinctive personality. If I try to blend and be like others – then who will notice or desire what I have? BUT if I come from who I truly am then I am irreplaceable. No one can conceive quite like me. No one can create or express quite like me. And the same is true of you. Who you are is your greatest strength.

KRIS: When did you get the internal nudge, that "ah-ha", that made you look at your beliefs around money to know you had to change them so you could allow the abundance to appear and how did you go about changing your "story"?

DEBBI DACHINGER: My ah-ha came when I grew tired of living in lack. Tired of working very hard and not creating enough money. There were tons of output and very little input. Lack creates suffering. I turned it around when I put everything down on paper. I wrote down what actual money I made, what really was coming in. Then I wrote down every single thing I was paying for each month. Then I wrote a new column which listed how I preferred to live. If my life could look anyway I chose to, what were the specific things and experiences I desired and what finances did it take to live like that? Then I crunched all the numbers so I could see what I was making compared to what I truly desired to live from. I then knew how much more money I needed to make each month.

When seeking to create more money it's important to not spend everything that comes in, not overspend. For example, if I am impacting you and you say you want to buy the bestselling book I wrote or my products because you sense they will help transform your life, but instead you go out and buy a new shirt and take everyone out to dinner, then where did your money just go? How are you aligning with what you just said you desired to create? What sabotage did you set yourself up for instead of aligning with your intention to buy the book and products? If you desire to buy my book and products, then make that your priority and live financially, like that, from your true intention. The same is true of any place you decide to appropriate your funds, don't get side-tracked by the cool things that glitter and catch your eye and take you off course. Stay the course.

KRIS: We know change is uncomfortable and reworking our broke beliefs can allow some resistance to pop up, so how do you suggest one deals with the resistance against the change and continue with the commitment they have made with themselves?

DEBBI DACHINGER: The only person who likes Change is a wet baby!! *[LAUGHTER]*

People say they live in a "comfort zone," but it's actually a *dis*comfort zone; it's an uncomfortable place they've squeezed themselves into. The only time we're truly happy is when we are growing and expanding and changing. Everything in nature is predicated on change, and we are as much a part of nature as anything else. The cells in our bodies constantly change, the seasons and the weather change, there is life and there is death, energy is mutable and constantly changing. We are energy, so anything that is not in change in us is therefore in resistance. If we resist anything in our life it means we are fighting what is and struggling against life and others. Anyone living from that place can attest – it is exhausting. It gets you nowhere fast and lands you in frustration, where you generally attempt some control. And life and circumstances will never be controlled.

To deal with resistance one must surrender. One must let go. How that is done? By breathing deeply and by choosing to be present, to be here now. To accept all that is, just as it is. To allow what's around us and in us to transform and amend, and flow with it just as it is. A much easier way to live. Having a mantra can be helpful. Or a paragraph you repeat each time you realize you're resisting by saying: *"I let go and I know that everything is as it is supposed to be right now. All my needs are met and everything works out. I let go and I let God. I surrender now and appreciate the peace of this moment."* Now commitment is the act of committing, pledging, or engaging oneself. Commitment is what transforms potential into reality. It is the words that speak boldly of your intentions. And the actions which speak louder than the words. It is the making of time when there is none. Coming through day after day, week after month after year. Commitment is the stuff character is made of: the command to change the face of things.

KRIS: What would be your biggest tip for everyone on this call today to take with them and apply to see more abundance in their business and in their life?

DEBBI DACHINGER: Once you understand that all things are made up of energy, you begin to see money through a different perspective. Money is currency and currency is energy. Energy flows! Stay in a state of receiving – all things. Pay little attention to poverty, scarcity, and lack. Focus instead on abundance, gratitude, generosity, and appreciation. If we want to experience abundance, we must experience what abundance feels like. What would it feel like to have all our needs met, and to, in fact have more than enough, to live from the overflow? What would it feel like to have so much money that we'd easily enjoy more freedom? Freedom to do what we desire, freedom to contribute to society? Freedom to give from abundance? Allow yourself to feel that. Be in the vibration of abundance, and you'll find yourself having a new creative idea or insight. You'll begin to notice opportunities. When that occurs, follow through and take action on the insights and opportunities. Physical action feels good. It will feel like moving in the right direction, because we're in alignment with what we're seeking to bring into our lives. And when we're in alignment, always and without exception, we feel good. We can learn to live from the inside out. We first embody in consciousness the essence of what we wish to experience. And then take action on the ideas and inspirations that come. Abundance in my life and my business is so much 'richer' and deeper than that. It's about time. How much time I give and have for me. It's about relationships. How much love and friendship and partnership and connection I have in my life. It's about gratitude. How much there is for me to be grateful for, recognize, acknowledge and celebrate. It's about actions and behaviors and getting to do what I desire.

KRIS: Do you have anything else to add to the conversation that you would like to share?

DEBBI DACHINGER: Abundance is everywhere. Abundance is an innate quality of the Infinite. God, in its nature knows only abundance. Lack, limitation, and scarcity are conditions that exist only in the human mind. In and of themselves, these conditions have no reality, they are a mistaken perception. Source, God Goddess, or the Mind of the Infinite could not demonstrate lack, since then it would no longer be infinite. Lack means finite and limited. Yet God is not finite or limited. So if there is no such thing as lack, limitation, and scarcity, then why are individuals experiencing these conditions? The answer is that we live in a belief-driven universe. We live in a universe in which our every thought, belief, and expectation is constantly being mirrored back to us. The physical universe is our spiritual mirror, and it reflects back to us our internal state of being.

To summarize ~ change your state of being. Change your beliefs. Have new faith and certainty about what will come your way, and then take physical action steps that align with these new thoughts and ideas – go out and prove your new abundance. Come from a place of lavish, plenty, over flowing wealth. Feel wealthy in who you are, what your unique gifts are, as well as your exceptional personality and be in grateful encouragement that anything can change if you desire it to be so.

END

❧ Quotable ❧

"The spiritual stimulus package, as I've indicated, begins with this type of inner broadcast, an awareness that nothing about you needs to be fixed, and nothing needs to be added. We are all here to download and reveal our gifts on this planet with ease, grace, and powerful spiritual dignity. It takes strength to lean on the invisible, because the surface mind wants you to lean on your quantifiable strengths and your intellect. It wants you to lean on all the things that you've been told you can depend on. But to mature spiritually, sometimes you just have to do things that appear crazy to others. Leaning on the infinite invisible elicits a sense of joy that is like nothing else.

"Human beings are primed to begin again, leaving behind beliefs which separate and divide humanity. Having a spiritual realization of our oneness with God opens us up to the revelation of the ever-expanding good – the kingdom of God on Earth as it is in the mind of God. I'm sure the surface mind is asking, "How do we do this?" First, you want to stay away from dangerous people. And the most dangerous people on the planet right now are those without a dream, without a vision for their lives. Why are they a danger to themselves and everyone around them? Because they're operating under the aegis of the status quo. They're seeking to be anti-bored until they die. A person mired in such a limited state of mind is constantly being run by things that have already happened in the past, or by thought forms of society. They're not stretching to become ever more of their true selves. They've forgotten they have an inner calling, a call to which has nothing to do with convenience or comfort. Rather, it's a call for us to constantly progress, evolve, and share more of the light that's within us.

"Choose to be free right now. The surface mind may be describing the prison that you're in: I don't have enough money. I don't have enough time. No one likes me. They said something about me. They didn't do it right. Your description of circumstances may feel accurate, but you don't have to remain imprisoned in it. What happens next in your life all depends on what happens next in your mind. Harboring negative thoughts coagulates them into experiences, But you can be free right now. Consciously choose this day to whom you will serve, what you will serve, and how you will serve. Choose. Ask yourself at any given moment, "Where am I coming from?"

"There's something about us that comes directly from divine presence. When we attune our inner ear to hear the inaudible and our inner eye to see the invisible, we are able to do what the world calls impossible. We're up for the challenge and the transformation that comes with it.
"A noted scientist once said that human beings are the star system becoming conscious of itself. Think about that for a moment. All the power of the cosmos, all the power that is producing millions and millions of galaxies at millions of miles a minute—all that power is within you, right now. Perhaps you've been swayed by popular opinion that star power has something to do with celebrity. But real star power is what you are. You have the power of psychogenesis. At any given point in time, you have within you everything required to begin your whole life all over again. When you remove your attention from the external world, when you pull your mind out of the sea of mental garbage, you can begin your life anew.

"We're speaking in terms of being an individual light that has the same

magnitude as the stars, the same magnitude as the light and life of God, because there's only one light, only one life, which is our individual life.
"Take a breath and allow yourself to become aware of the field of infinite possibilities surrounding you. See through the façade of your life, through the baggage of history, to the freedom of your infinite potential. Give yourself permission to live the true purpose of your incarnation. Feel yourself grounded in the energy of high potential. Embrace yourself in a consciousness of unconditional love. As you do this, know that you're also embracing your entire community, even the entire world."

- **Reverend Michael Bernard Beckwith,** from "*Transcendence Expanding*"

Transcript

Debbi Dachinger: Interview with CINDY BRIOLOTTA and LINDA CASSELL

CINDY BRIOLOTTA LINDA CASSEL: Welcome to the Art of Joyful Living. Thank you for joining us. We really are so delighted to have Debbi Dachinger with us today. What is it that we most want to accomplish before the year ends, and how do we do it? Well, guess what? [LAUGHTER] Debbi knows. Debbi is someone who knows how to achieve a lot. Many of us, however, remain frustrated that our dreams reside somewhere out on the horizon. Today, Debbi is going to discuss how to start the dream process, how to execute your dream, how to keep it going, and most important, how to finish and complete it. Debbi, thank you so much for joining us.

DEBBI Thank you Cindy and Linda. It is a

DACHINGER: pleasure to be here with you, I'm an ex-New Yorker myself, so we're all in good company. [LAUGHTER]

CINDY/LINDA: [LAUGHTER] Debbi, you've had such a great career throughout Europe and the U.S., so can tell us a little bit about your own personal journey and how you came to be doing the work you're doing right now?

DEBBI: Oh, pleasure. That's a good question because it is my opinion that we now teach what we needed to learn. That the wounds we had, if we take the time to handle those wounds and heal them, they actually become the gift that we're put on this planet at this time to share. So, with that said, my wound was about, first of all, achieving my goals successfully. Second of all, being worthy of them. Really getting past all that stuff that was in my way, in my head. And the other thing was about creating some consistency because I was on and off, on and off. I basically suffered from it. I mean I'm starting quite young because I was an actress when I was a little girl. Then I went to college for acting and performing. It's all I ever wanted to do. And was I talented? Yes. Big time — pouring out of me. I was definitely put here to express myself. But sometimes it would show up, and sometimes it wouldn't--in auditions, which meant sometimes I got the job and sometimes the one that I really wanted, that would have propelled me forward in a huge way, I bombed at. And that was all because of, first of all, what was between my ears was stopping me and sabotaging me, and second of all, it was because I didn't have the recipe. Nobody taught me how to have a goal or a dream carried it through to fruition. So because of that, and because of the journey I've taken, I learned how to fulfill my dreams over decades of research with masters and some of the great leaders today, and through my own journey. I've been able to replicate what I call a recipe to wonderful benefit over and over again. I've seen the success in several careers, even becoming an author which frankly I never thought I would do. [LAUGHTER]. I didn't have too much interest and then I wrote a book. I thought, *"Okay, I teach how to be successful, I teach how to reach a goal, so I think I would like to be a best-seller."* And six days later that's what happened. And that's been my journey. It was about using my method to achieve goals over and over again over long periods of time—well-tested so that now I'm known as a goal achievement expert which is pretty cool.

CINDY/LINDA: Wow. That is very cool. I'm intrigued Debbi when you said that yes, you were talented. Sometimes that's a hard thing for us to say because we believe we should be modest about it, so good for you for owning that and being proud of it. I'm intrigued when you say sometimes it would show up in auditions and sometimes it wouldn't. That's such a great metaphor for life, right? Sometimes we're on, sometimes we're not. So what's the formula for making sure that when you need it to show up, it shows up?

DEBBI: There are five steps to goal achievement every time. I'll tell you the steps and of course, there is detail that goes with each one, but the five steps are: Number one, decide and to choose. You have to decide to completely step in with commitment. Number two is write. We must take paper and pen. [LAUGHTER]. Or it could be a crayon. You do have to write it down because you'll often refer to that sheet. It is your guide. The third thing is, we must take action. Taking action means we wake up each day, we look at our list and commit — today I'm going to handle this action step. There is something that goes along with taking action as number three. That's letting go. Because we co-create with the Universe. The Universe is like a 401K plan. As we put in, they put in. We take action every day. We let go. We take action every day. We let go. The fourth thing is we must heal and deal. That harkens back to the story of my life and the lives of most leaders doing noticeably good work today, work you admire, is that you have to effort through your obstacles--your internal obstacles and your dream busters. The fifth step is to achieve, and when you arrive you must celebrate.

CINDY/LINDA: In your experience, what is it that holds people back from achieving their dreams and goals?

DEBBI: Well, doubt is one big dream buster. Others, is another. Isn't that an interesting one? But truthfully, people let other people hold them back. I know that one. [LAUGHTER]. I can tell you that for me it was in my mind. I would get into relationships with men. I would think, *"Oh, I can't do that anymore. I'm in a relationship."* It was amazing to me because nobody asked me to put my dreams on hold. So it's really a self-sabotage, but it looks like it's others. The other piece of Others is that sometimes we feel beholden to either our family or friends, or society that we have to be a certain person that we're not. Or we feel that *"I can't do this because my family depends on me."* Another one is Clarity. Some people don't have clarity and they don't take the time to be still enough to start hearing what's happening in their soul and what they desire. Another one is Trust. To trust that the Universe has our back. To trust life will work out for us. To trust that we're capable. Another one is Playing Small. This is pretty prevalent, that people don't want to show up as large as they were created to be. They don't want to play in a big arena. They keep themselves small and invisible because they believe somehow it's safe. Another one — and this is an issue of our times is — time management. People allow the minutia of life to get into the way and then they say they have no time. *"I couldn't possibly go after my dreams and goals. Take action steps? What are you, crazy?"* [LAUGHTER] No time.

But truthfully, we have to dream a big dream and create the space for it. And the last one is fear. Fear shows up in so many different ways for people and essentially fear is a bully. We talk a lot about bullying today. Get an image of that—like the bully on the playground who's going after someone, who makes the one victimized so scared, who makes that person not want to go to school, who takes away all their friends, who hurts them over and over again, says horrible things to them, demeans them. That's what we do to ourselves. We create fear as our own personal bully to push us around and hold ourselves back. The truth is, fear doesn't exist. It's just an energy we connected with and chose. We can unchoose it. And we can choose something different. That's mostly the dream busters and people experience either one or sometimes a combo platter that holds them back. But they can all be dealt with to move forward.

CINDY/LINDA: You said *"no one asked me to put my dreams on hold."* So it sounds like what you're saying is other people don't hold us back unless we allow them to hold us back.

DEBBI: I would say almost one hundred

percent of the time, even if we blame it somewhere on the outside; it's really all about us. We just make it look like it's the outside so we don't take responsibility for not being happy, for not being accountable for our lives and our soul. Because when we step into who we were intended to be—the greatness of who we are intended to be—it is inspiring to everyone around us. It literally is a ripple that starts changing what's happening on the planet. It's no joke. We're really needed right now. And no matter where the gifts are —in any realm, in any career, in any hobby—in anything that gives us great pleasure. As you go after your dream, when you're in that vibration you will change the vibration of everything around you.

CINDY/LINDA: What are some of your favorite fear busters?

DEBBI: I like to think of fear as though it's a baby bird. There are a couple of analogies I use that help me get through. One of them is the idea of a baby bird. When you think about a bird, right? It's born, it hangs out with other chicks, it's high up in a tree, it's in a nest, and mama comes and feeds it. Suddenly one day Mama says *alright kids, it's time to fly.* The kids look out over the nest and they go whoa. *It's pretty far — what do you mean? Why do you want to push me out I'm going to fall and crash and die.* And Mama's like *no, trust me. You were built to do this.* And the baby says, *I've seen you do it but I've never done it — that's pretty scary.* They get to the edge and they go back. They get to the edge, and they go back. Because it's like *if I jump, I will die.* At some point they have to. They may get pushed out and off they go, and it may be awkward and uncomfortable, and they may not fly very well the first time but all of a sudden their DNA kicks in and those wings take over, and off they go. By the tenth or fifteenth time, they know they can fly. It's very much like that with dreams. We have to step out in great faith, knowing that we're going to be caught, we'll be supported. We have our back, the Universe has our back. We will not fall and crash and burn, and it works. Once you've flexed that goal-muscle — that muscle is the same as any other muscle, you just have to use it. And once you do you start to see, *Oh. I can do this. I am good at this. I can succeed. I can move out into bigger arenas.* So that's one buster of fear. And the other one is growing up and we think there is a monster in the closet—or in my case, I thought there was a witch under my bed. [LAUGHTER] I really did. I thought if I fell asleep and my hand fell over the bed witch would snatch that hand and pull me under. It was so scary and so real. And that's how we create our fear. And to bust it you've gotta open the closet and shed light in there and realize, *my god. It's empty. What am I doing to myself?* Look under the bed. *There is no witch there. What am I doing? It's just dust bunnies. Clean that out and get going here.* [LAUGHTER]. There are many things we can do for balance and for investment. The balance comes when we take time for stillness. I'm about as busy as anyone could be. However, I meditate every day. I take time to do my lists every day to know where I'm headed and what dream path I'm on. Period. Because if I don't keep my eye on the ball nobody will do it for me. That is so important. And another thing is investment. I invest in myself. I have a coach. I have a mastermind group. I have people who I work with, who are operating at much higher levels than I at all times and I need that. When something is going on and it's not something I can address, I work with amazing healers. There are wonderful people in my life. I basically have a team that helps me keep going. I'm a well-oiled machine. [LAUGHTER]. What is vital to remember is, whether it's fear or any other emotion, it's just manufactured and you can use any of those illustrations—the bird, the closet monster or the bully. Then you have to take action in spite of the fear. It's like, okay—*that's really interesting fear, thanks for sharing but really? I know you. You hold me back all the time and that's your purpose. So thanks because your words are powerful and thus far, fear, I've allowed you to rule my life. But now I'm going to do this differently. I'm going to keep moving along here and do what I desire to do, because that's what makes me feel happy, and I love myself. And being happy is important to me so, here I go. Watch my back.* [LAUGHTER] *because I'm leaving.* [LAUGHTER].

CINDY/LINDA: That's great, Debbi. We actually have a question from a listener. She wants to know who is *"they,"* what did you mean by *"they"* when you said *"they invest in us?"*

DEBBI: Ah, okay. It is how I express myself spiritually. [LAUGHTER] I am not religious. I am, however, deeply spiritual. I strongly sense that there are loving forces out there. For me, personally, if I travel this life path alone it can be lonely and hard. I know that when I rely on something greater than myself and acknowledge it, that I am entirely more successful. What I mean specifically by "they" is the Universe — I use Universe euphemistically however I could call it God. I could call that energy Goddess. I can call it All That Is, Source, Guide, Counselors, Angels, Unseen Friends. Whoever it is that surrounds us. Buddha, Allah, I could even say, something greater than I that cares about me. For all of us, it's about the caring aspect. Feeling cared and loved, that what we do matters. That we're important. That we're noticed. I've seen that when I agree to step it up, things start happening. For instance about two months ago, I got a coach. I had resisted it because I operate at a pretty high level. But I realized I was ready to expand even bigger and if I wanted to do that — I had to have somebody who was an expert in certain areas I was not. I can't be an expert at everything. I wasn't put here to do that. So that's a good time to start delegating, start hiring, and start getting your team going. The moment I said *yes* and set up appointments I had new doors open for me that was fantastic. And monetary situations show up that I had been trying to bust through, that just came to me. So things started to shift and I felt like the Universe was cheering, *yay — she gets it. We've been trying to tell you, Silly.* [LAUGHTER]. *You can only do so much and now you've hired somebody and that's great.* Because I created the space for something greater to come into my life. And that's what it's about. When we let go and let in the forces of those that love us and care about us, then we can let in pieces that we may not be able to do through our own intellect, or our own action and warrior energy. We allow the winds of the loving Universe to come in and help.

CINDY/LINDA: What advice do you have for those who have a hard time letting go — who feel like if they don't control everything it will fall apart?

DEBBI: That's such a good question and I get it. I know what that's like — to control everything because that's what makes you feel safe and secure. When in fact, you never feel safe and secure. So you hold on even tighter. It's an intense place to operate from and it's not beneficial [LAUGHTER] to be sure. It's really about taking contrary action. Part of our healing process is that we have to do things differently and at some point it becomes more natural to do it by flowing with life. What worked well for me—is when something came up, a circumstance or person that caused internal anxiety, I wanted to control it but it was out of my control, and the more I tried to control whatever I perceived was going on the worse it went out of control. What I learned to say is, "*I let this go. I turn this over to God, Goddess. I can't do it. You can.*" And in the beginning I had to do it every five minutes when something unnerving came up. "*I let this go. I give it up to God, Goddess, All That Is. Please handle it, I can't.*" Sometimes I would take my palms facing up and literally throw it up. A gesture to myself to show I was releasing. I did that over and over again and then at some point, the control was released and then things, of course, always worked out. Of course they did. I learned to use that technique of surrendering and letting go, and it was a great and freeing gift.

CINDY/LINDA: So practice any skill you don't already

have and then it will be available more easily.

DEBBI: Yes. If you understand what the issue is you can also understand the opposite of it. So if fear rules you then courage would be the opposite. Courage doesn't mean without fear, courage means doing something in *spite* of fear. You can label yourself a courageous person and when something comes up, if fear starts to take over as your default you can acknowledge, *oh. Okay. Fear is where I usually go. Well, we're going to respond instead as someone who is courageous.* And just step forward. Act as if. And if doubt is your usual pattern then the opposite way to behave is though certainty. You can just act as if — and it's brilliant to access what is actually already inside you. Even though it may be awkward at first at some point it becomes natural. It may be days, months, it may be years, but trust the process to hone new skills and experiences.

CINDY/LINDA: We talk a lot about intuition on this show. What role does intuition play in your work and how do you use it?

DEBBI: Intuition is an integral part in how i conduct myself in my personal and business lives. According to Freud, intuition is communication from the unconscious. A typical definition of intuition from a dictionary echoes Freud's explanation, explaining that it's a quick and ready insight or perception that bypasses cognitive reasoning. I also believe that intuition is a function of the unconscious – and most easily I'd call intuition a "knowing." I highly recommend using your intuition. How you start to connect with your intuition is through being sensitive to any internal nudging's that inform that you do this, or don't do that. Be with this person, don't be with that person. We've all had those feelings. Oh, I really shouldn't get in this relationship and then a year down the road you're in the very relationship you warned yourself about and wonder, what were you thinking? [LAUGHTER] I told you. Why did you have to lose a whole year with this person? [LAUGHTER] You're looking at your life and wondering, if only I had listened to that original intuitive feeling I had. I've had intuitive urges about a particular horse winning, or a boxer that would win a fight in Las Vegas – I'm not even into either of those sports – but if I had placed a bet when my intuition spoke, I would have made money that day, because my intuition was spot on. When intuition prods you, follow up on it and you'll have incredible results. Intuition is a Latin word for "into you." That means that all the answers already reside within us. So anytime I need to know things I go inside and ask. I get quiet, I ask a question and I hear an answer. When I decided to publish my first book—a colleague who teaches authors to be best sellers said, *"Deb you're thinking about publishing your book, it's already late November. To do this in November with Thanksgiving almost here, then Christmas, then New Year's. It's the worst time. As a first-timer it's near impossible to become a best-seller after Thanksgiving. Your timing is off unless you publish immediately, right now, or wait until next year."* There was so much Ii didn't know going into publishing my first book, I was so green. I didn't know what I was doing. I just knew I desired to publish a book. I didn't think anything through. But once she explained the statistics I realized, we really are right around the corner from Thanksgiving. I have a choice to make and I feel anxious about what she's saying, and I don't have answers. When we got off the phone—with much gratitude for all she had enlightened about the timing— I sat down outdoors and went inside myself to ask, okay ya'll. [LAUGHTER] Here's the deal. We have a week and a half before Thanksgiving, what do you think? And I literally heard the calmest, most beautiful energy tell me, put out the book now, we have your back. That's literally the knowingness I received. I'd never done a best-seller launch and I didn't have a team but I decided to do it. Okay. You've got my back? That's all I need to hear. And the rest is history. I did it. I learned on my own how to launch a book. I researched it, I took the steps. Things happened that were coo koo, ka ka, and things that were on the brink of disaster and almost went terribly wrong. Create Space suddenly had an issue and couldn't print books and their printer shut down for a couple of days. There were big things like that, that might have gotten in the way and every time a potential catastrophe popped up I didn't get upset, I let it go—because of intuition. I already knew: you've got my back—alright. I'm not going to get worried about that. I would just keep moving forward with faith, moving forward with faith. And bada-boom. The book was released on a Friday and I got a call from the same woman. She's an expert at best-sellers and she knew it was fairly nuts what I had set out to do. She called me a few hours later and said, *"I hope you're sitting down because your book is selling above Sir Richard Branson's, over Lisa Nichols, over Jack Canfield's Chicken Soup for the Soul."* And I was thinking, "holy-moly." I got two more calls from her that day, *"Debbi, are you sitting down? You're now a best-seller in self-help."* Oh my god. Three different bestselling categories that shot up. So that's the power of intuition. If we will get quiet and ask the question, then what's most essential is — trust what we hear. I could have said, *"Ya'll are crazy. That doesn't make sense."* I could have gone into logic and figured out it couldn't work, but I didn't. I just moved forward with faith knowing that intuition is truth and is the quickest way to get where we're going.

CINDY/LINDA: So Debbi, what have you noticed about the patterns and habits of highly successful people, since you're one yourself?

DEBBI: Successful people find opportunities where others do not see one. They find a lesson while others only see a difficulty. They are solution oriented. They consciously create their own success, while others hope success will find them. They are afraid like everyone else, but they are not controlled or limited by fear. They are not necessarily more talented than others; however they find a way to maximize their potential. They get more out of themselves. While most are laying on the couch, planning, over-thinking, sitting on their hands or going around in circles, they are out there getting the job done.

And, if I may, I want to acknowledge you guys here real quick and just say, you have the most amazing energy — both of you, Linda and Cindy. You really do. It's a pleasure to be on this show. You have a calm presence — very light, wonderful, energy, and I'm just appreciating you so much.

CINDY/LINDA: Thank you. The feeling is mutual.

DEBBI: I hope everyone will support you two in what you are doing, because part of being successful is to reach out and support people you believe in, enjoy witnessing their journey and seeing them make it. Know that if they can be successful, it means you can too.

CINDY/LINDA: I love that. I want to talk more about that. I love that you're saying a way to be successful is to step out and support other people's success. Could you just talk a little more about that?

DEBBI: Yes support other people, absolutely. Rather than be jealous of other people, or notice what others have and think it means we can't, what does it say about us when we live in separation like that? Because if you're doing that, that means you don't think you're capable. Instead when you show up for somebody else—perhaps you post social media on their behalf when you notice something they've achieved, or call them and say, *"Woo-Hoo! I'm so proud of you. I knew you could do it, that's wonderful news!"* Or if you hear about a dream someone is working to manifest and say, *"Hey, Cindy and Linda. I know you're working toward this. You know what? I'm going to send your link and mission out through my newsletter to let my people know what you're working to create."* Or, *"I'm going to introduce someone influential to you."* There's many ways we can show up for each other. By doing that you're being clear with your reality, if they can do this, I can do this too. By honoring their success it means you also honor yours. It means you are setting up reciprocity. It doesn't mean that person will show up exactly the same way for you, but it means stay-tuned because more will be revealed. And I betcha anything—like I said, the Universe is a 401K. It'll give you a hundred-fold back. It's always a great surprise. Don't sit there waiting, expecting it. Don't come from that. But do know that things will come to you. It may be unexpected money in your account, or you start a project and you start stepping into something and someone says, *"I know how to do that, I'll show you."* Or *"I have someone who is an expert in that. Let me set you up with someone great and trustworthy."* Let me do this; let me assist you with that. *"Oh, you're going to make that dream happen? I want to help you. I'm going to tell my friends."* Things will happen because that's how life happens. I've heard karma is expressed as an echo. We put something out there and it bounces again, and again, and again, in an echo. Know that with a pure heart when you show up to support someone in any way that is reflected back.

CINDY/LINDA: Is part of the pattern of successful people that they aren't afraid to support other people?

DEBBI: Yes. Successful people do what they love. They are committed; they follow up and follow through. Successful people ask questions, they know that by listening and inquiring they are learning and receiving information that will make them productive. They innovate rather than imitate; they take calculated risks, and they don't spend time with toxic people. The next one is they turn their wounds into gifts. Some of the most amazing stories—names you would know—when you know their background it just—ah, it touches your heart. Someone who had a severe learning disability and was told you'll never amount to anything and they left school and became homeless. I'm thinking of someone in particular and I don't have to mention names. When they decided to walk through their wound and heal it and deal with it, they came out the other side. That was the gift they came here to give. They're huge; they have a big name and are now known as one of the world's greatest educators. I love that. You think about so many stories of people who had such issues. Wayne

Dyer grew up in foster homes and had an alcoholic father. He had so much going against him. But when Wayne dealt with it, mindfully worked on forgiveness for his father, dealt with the issues he had from his upbringing, he came out the other side—my goodness look at where he operates from today. And the last thing is that very successful people move forward with trust. They don't know for sure. They don't see it yet. But with faith, like jumping out of that nest like a baby bird, they really somehow choose to believe that they can fly.

CINDY/LINDA: That is lovely. We have another email question for you Debbi. This person says he's a little confused about the relationship between goals and deadlines. He sets deadlines but when he doesn't make it, he goes into a downward spiral. Should he set deadlines, or leave it open-ended?

DEBBI: Wow. I don't know if you feel the energy of the words that were used, what a great question. Deadline has the word dead in it. [LAUGHTER] And a goal—is alive, expansive and open? I like your question and I want to feed it back to you. How are those deadlines working for you? Because I hear you saying that you create them and they're not being fulfilled and it is frustrating. It sounds like it's a setup for you not to succeed. I want to offer you another way of approaching goals since you brought up the idea of being open-ended. Maybe there's somewhere in between that can work for you. I know there are people out there who like to ask, *"Where do you see yourself in five years"?* [LAUGHTER] I dislike those questions. Personally I leave things most things open-ended. Now realistically, there are some goals that need to have some kind of date attached to them. For instance I'm about to speak in another country as a keynote speaker. I must have deadline dates attached to that, such as when my speech will be prepared, right? Otherwise we create anxiety when we procrastinating. We create anxiety because we're not in action and the way to quell that anxiety is to start doing something. An example from my life is that recently I took the day off. A mental health day—which meant I went to the gym, I meditated, I took a hot bath, and once I felt nurtured I then worked. I sat down and said *alright girlfriend, you need to figure out what this speech is.* It was less of a deadline and more of an awareness to feel good inside and to show up for me because no one else is going to handle this. I'm the one alone on stage with the spotlight [LAUGHTER] and hundreds of people looking at me. And the last thing I'm going to do is be a fool who's asked to speak and not show up prepared and profession. The other action I took is—I have a girlfriend who does presentations all over the world. She's been a speaker for decades. I shared with her that I felt anxious. And she said, *"Oh, Deb, this is what you need to do."* She gave me three pointers that were extremely helpful. Sometimes we invest in other people who know better than we do. As soon as she gave me pointers it broke the spell of concern. So yesterday I put together what I'm going to hand out, I wrote out the essence of my speech in bullet points. Once I get bullet points I know where I'm going. The rest of it will be to rehearse it. So again, it's not a deadline but I took action to get a handle on it because there definitely is a date attached to this. And if I start now with a week and a half ahead of me, I will be fine.

CINDY/LINDA: He just emailed and said, *"Thank you, thank you."* Now we have a question for you from a caller, Tim from Chicago. Tim, what is your question for Debbi?

CALLER: I've been exploring crowd-source funding. Kickstarter is one. You put up a goal and if you meet your goal, people pay a contribution. If you don't meet it, they don't pay anything. Also indiegogo.com. There is a chart here that says you raise eighty percent more money with a team than you do by yourself. You get a hundred percent of whatever you get by doing it yourself, but you get almost two hundred and fifty percent of your goal if you work with four or more people. People helping people. Do you have anything to say about that?

DEBBI: Well, I don't know much about crowd-sourcing funding sites, although I do have colleagues who use Kickstarter and I always contribute to help. I sense this is an intuitive question more than anything because statistics are wonderful but they're not fact or truth. If you have an amazing project that is ready to go out into the world, you need to intuitively ask inside is this a team effort or a "me" effort? If it's team, what does that look like? What kind of team and who does it consist of in your world, or do you know them yet? If it's a "me" effort what does that look like? Trust what you hear and feel because that is what's going to lead you to success in your efforts.

CALLER: That's good advice.

Wonderful, and I wish you the best with your goal.

CINDY/LINDA: Can you talk to us about the laws of the Universe that govern dream and goal manifesting?

DEBBI: There are several. There's one that's not a law but if I may add this: Failure isn't to be feared because if we don't fear failure we'll jump more often, we'll try things more easily, we'll trust life and ourselves a lot more. And if we go out there on a limb—because that's where all the fruit is—and we fail, big deal. Because it's an awesome opportunity to learn. Now none of us ever embarks towards a dream and says, *woo-hoo—I'm going out and fail today.* [LAUGHTER] But if we consider it, that's a possibility. I may succeed, I may fail. When I give myself permission to go big and strong to my goal, boy does it take the pressure off. And also, it lets us start a lot sooner to do what we need to do instead of trying to figure out all everything in advance. You can now choose a whole new tact and realize: This is why that didn't work and this is what I need to do differently, and then you will. Learn from failure – it's highly educational.

To answer your question, there are many laws. Laws that govern us and laws we talk about in quantum physics. And laws we talk about as there is the law of vibration. And the law of reciprocity, and reversibility. There is the law of attraction. The law of cause and effect. Law of resonance. The law of growth, law of abundance, and law of polarity. Each of them has a different energy to them that we can utilize to create more abundance if we understand how it works. Cindy and Linda did any of those speak to you as I said them that you want to know more about?

CINDY/LINDA: Did you say reversibility? I want to hear more about that. This may be a good way to wrap down the show.

DEBBI: Wonderful. It's funny you picked up on that one because guess which one is my favorite? [LAUGHTER] It's a beautiful idea to end this on. Reversibility means just that—it's the law of doing things in reverse. Like a rubber band—I'm here, my goal is there. You stretch the rubber band out to there and let it go "*boop*," and it jumps back. How we utilize the law of reversibility is when we write our list, our action steps, we do it in reverse. We start as though the goal is already achieved and write the action step that preceded that and the one that created that, and the one that led that, and the one that came before that, all the way back to where we are right now with just a dream and an idea but not the completion of it yet and now we know exactly how to proceed forward. That is the law of reversibility; energetically it happens just like that rubber band and snaps what we want back to us.

CINDY/LINDA: Wow. Debbi this has been wonderful. Thank you so much, we are going to have you back.

END

Transcript

Debbi Dachinger:
Interview with KAREN LUNIW

KAREN LUNIW: Hello everybody, Welcome. You are listening to the very first Shift Shine Grow with the Experts series. We have a great expert with us today, her name is Debbi Dachinger. Hello, Debbi are you there?

DEBBI DACHINGER: I am Karen, thanks for having me.

KAREN: For everybody that is listening in, the interview title for Debbi's call is *Showing You How Far You Can Go*. The magic bullets to hit your goal every time. Debbi has received many amazing awards and worthy accolades to mention. Welcome Debbi. It's so great to have you here today.

DEBBI: Yes, I'm ready to shift and shine and grow and provide some excellence for your listeners.

KAREN: Debbi, what are the benefits of goal setting?

DEBBI: The benefits are that you're going to feel alive. If you're not feeling so alive right now, or you're feeling halfway alive and dead, [LAUGHTER] by starting the goal journey in earnest, will help you feel alive, which means it shifts what you can bring into your life. Karen, you teach law of attraction and in law of attraction we know we magnetize from within either positive or negative. So you know these aren't just vapid words I'm speaking, I'm going to ask everyone to choose a dream that you have already successfully created. Something in your past that was a bit challenging for you and that you manifested in your life: a job, relationship, hobby, experience? Whatever it was that you *said I'm going to do this*, and you did it. Now in reflection, do you notice when you look back—did you feel an increase in your energy and your passion when you created that dream come true? Were you the driver in the car of your life with the ability to generate your destiny? In other words you weren't the passenger, you were the driver who created that dream? Did you feel when you were going after your goal it gave you a purpose and it kept you excited throughout each day? And when you were in the midst of going after that, did you begin to magnetize and attract other opportunities, some that were actually surprises. You weren't even thinking you were going to pull it in but the Universe just said *here you go.* Did you feel like you fully enjoyed your life because you designed it? Now that you've reflected on a past success, do you understand the benefits of goal setting and goal accomplishment? That space is what I'm going to be talking about today. Why it's amazing to create your dreams come true. To go after a goal that feels bigger and more challenging than you and in the midst of all that, even though you're not entirely sure it's going to happen, you're willing to take the steps to make it happen. Just to realize how truly limitless you are, and the potentiality that's out there that is informing you at every moment, you are steering your life, you feel excited, you have purpose, you attract unexpected opportunities, and your energy and happiness increases. So those are the benefits. Remember with any dream: I am possible.

KAREN: I love that, I'm possible. I think that's a great statement.

DEBBI: And think about it, Karen; think about the word, impossible. When you break impossible down, it spells I'm possible. It's looking at dreams through a different lens. Nothing is impossible. I am possible.

KAREN: I love that because so often we stop ourselves. I think that's just a great thing to bring up. I am possible. With regard to dreams and goals, why do you think we're here?

DEBBI: I think more than any other era, reflect on the fact, has time sped up? Oh, indeed. Because we're all experiencing and feeling it and we're sensing the quickening forces of manifestation, right? We're manifesting left and right. Some things we don't like, some things we do. This is the time of putting our preferences out there and what that means in regards to dreams and goals is that we're here because each of us has a unique contribution to humanity. I believe we all agreed to be here right now because the planet needs us. The world needs us and we are powerful beings down with unique gifts and talents and proclivities, and it's going to help our planet and beyond. It's been said that the purpose of life is to discover your gift, and the meaning of life is to give it away. We're given this lifetime to step it up, to express who we are, to choose our life. And hey, if it doesn't feel good in the moment, just re-choose. We can alter how we want our experience to be.

KAREN: Can you reiterate the difference between purpose and meaning? I've never heard that before and I love that. It's a great way to put that.

DEBBI: Yeah, sure. The purpose of life is to discover your gift. And frankly, a lot of times when we go on the journey of going after our goals we actually start to find our purpose and other things. So it's said the purpose of life is to discover your gift, and the meaning of life is to give it away. I'll share one illustration from my life. So the purpose of life is to discover your gift—when I was born, I knew the moment I came out of that womb I wanted to be an actress and a singer. It's all I did; it's what I went to college for. I went around the world performing in several mediums. I loved being on stage, period. [LAUGHTER] I liked being in film. I didn't anticipate the other passions that would come up for me. Passion is that thing inside of you urging, "*Oh, I want to do that. I want to experience that.*" And it's a good thing to allow yourself the freedom to move forward and have that experience. In allowing passion to direct me, I found things revealed that I didn't know were going to be my calling. My getting into radio was a huge surprise. So our backtracks, you understand, the purpose of life—is discovering your gift. I was a motivational speaker and I suddenly got a call to audition for play a lead cartoon character, then I see a job listing for radio, for a station. Now I have no interest in radio—really. I have no interest in radio and I think, maybe I'll get my voice out there—and here is where the Universe comes in with divine manifest destiny, and the sentence about the meaning life is to give it away. I am given a one hour talk show. And it poured out of me: Dare to Dream. This is my metaphysics combined with my desire to be in front of people and entertain, to connect with people and to help the planet—to assist in some way because I feel there are so many amazing people doing amazing work, and it's time listeners know about it. So now, I'm telling you this is six plus years later. My show goes from zero listeners to two million and in the interim I write a book. Everybody wants to know: *why did you write this book?* This best-seller book. Well, I wanted to give it away. I felt I could only reach so many by radio so let me share more through this book. Again, opportunity. [LAUGHTER] And it has opened up another world to me that I did expect. I'm interviewed a minimum of one time a week, sometimes interviewed up to four times on various telesummits and radio/television shows because now I'm known as a goal expert and I've also done keynote speaking. So saying yes to each opportunity completely switched around my world again and again. This morning I received a beautiful email from somebody who wrote *Debbi you're changing my life.* That is meaningful and it was sweet, he said *"When I write my book, I'm going to write an acknowledgement to you because I've learned so much from you."* So you can see from being a motivational speaker and saying yes to this voiceover job which made me say yes to this radio show, which made me say yes to my listeners, which made me say yes to write a book, which made me say yes to speaking, yes to being in a mastermind group, yes to being interviewed. And

Karen, I'm not even done. It's continuing to expand and grow because I keep saying yes and trusting the Universe to move forward. And that's what that means: It's been said that the purpose of life is to discover your gift, and the meaning of life is to give it away.

KAREN: That's fabulous. By continuing to say yes that next step opens up to us. When you say *"give it away,"* to clarify you're not giving it away for free?

DEBBI: Great question because I am all about boundaries. And you learn what's for free and what's for charge quickly if you're in business. Listen, a lot of us spiritual types, that's what we'll do. And I've been guilty of that too — we, give-give-give, people ask-ask-ask. And pretty soon you don't have much in your bank account but boy are you helping people. [LAUGHTER] In life there has to be a balance. You know, we are here to live a good life. There are some areas of my life where I do service and I do service for free. And I know intuitively when that's the right thing to do. There are a lot of other times when I don't. It's true reciprocity, and I am a firm believer in doing business with love. I call it loverage. [LAUGHTER] Leveraging others in business with love. So trust me, they get a gift from me of my information which is helpful and I know affects change and it's always delivered with love. So you're right, when I say I give it away it is a balance and yes, I do get paid for what I do.

KAREN: Again, I wanted to make that clear because there are people out there doing great work but they keep giving it away and end up not getting what they need. It's so important to give and receive. So tell me why it's important to live by design?

DEBBI: In the very beginning when we did that exercise I talked about being in the passenger seat or the driver's seat. If you were in a car and it was moving quickly, which seat would you want to be in? In the passenger's seat. That's terrifying. A lot of people live their life like that. They're living their life from the passenger seat. They don't really decide, they don't steer or shift gears or step on the gas or brake—they let other people make decisions for them. They don't really step it up or do the brave thing, the courageous thing. That makes for a difficult life. And those who are willing to have their feelings, of whatever their patterns are—fear, doubt—anything like that, come up but still move forward anyway are the ones who live an empowered life. The bottom line is our dreams are worth dreaming. They're worth working towards and they're worth enjoying. We can live by design, and we can drive our lives based on our decisions. I'm all about making decisions and choices. We have to take charge of our lives and we do so by living with deliberate intention. It makes for a very exciting life.

KAREN: So where do you think people fail at achieving their goals?

DEBBI: You know I was thinking about this, this morning. Let me offer this illustration. For anyone who has watched the Olympics on television or in person, we've seen the athletes—for instance amazing world-class runners who are spectacular at jumping over hurdles, right? So when these world-class runners are racing on the track and they have hurdles—what do they do? They are trained to jump over them, right? They run and leap over each hurdle so they can get to the finish line. I use this illustration since it is much like pursuing a dream. [LAUGHTER] It's what we all go through because when people have a dream, they're at the starting line and then as they're moving on the track toward their dream, hurdles may come up. Now what most people do is they run and they run, and they get up to the hurdle and they say, "*Oh my goodness. This hurdle is huge. I am full of doubt. I'm not certain this is going to happen. I'm convinced I don't have what it takes.*" And they walk off the field, defeated by their own thoughts. And yet other people run up and perhaps see repeated failure as their hurdle and they say, *I don't know how to get over that, I can't get over it, I don't have the legs to jump over it so I'm going to go back to the starting line.* So they go back to the starting line and do this over and over again with the same pattern and stop at the hurdle, or they just walk off the field. [LAUGHTER] I literally was thinking about this this morning. That's how powerful these dream busters are, this is the kind of empowerment we give them. Look for the people who figure out how to get over those hurdles, they are the winners. They change during the journey. They change at the finish line because now their life includes their dream come true. What happens as well is they take on that hurdle, that issue in their life which is probably everywhere in their life. To go over and past their personal hurdle they agree to do something about it, find a way to heal it, to deal with it, and in doing so, they positively shift everything because now certainty and faith is in their arsenal. Then they move forward to the next dream with new and stronger resources at their disposal.

KAREN: Fabulous. What are the magic bullets to hit your goal every time?

DEBBI: Decide. Write. Take action and let go. Heal and deal. And last, achieve and celebrate. To decide, that's pretty simple, right? You have a desire and you say, *"I'm going to do this. I don't know how I'm going to get there yet but this is what I desire to achieve."* And the second magic bullet is to write. I like the track and field analogy so I'll use that again—how are you going to get from where you are at the starting line to the finish line? Well, you need to write the steps that it's going to take. For example: I have to make this call, I have to write this paper, I have to take a class and learn something new—whatever it is you have to do to make that happen write those action steps.

Now you want to keep that paper with you because the third bullet to hit your goal every time is to take action. So each day you look at your sheet, you take an action. And that's how you start to get there. You also need to let go. I'm fierce. I could take action twenty-four seven. I'm the one who is always learning to surrender, to let go and release, let go and release. It's a beautiful gift in my life. The action is the fierceness and the letting go is the softness. When you move into letting go, you've done everything you can, now you just release it. The next bullet is to heal and deal. I talked about that in the previous question about the dream busters. That means when you come up to your personal hurdle you don't run away. You stay and figure it out. Now either you can do that on your own—or if it's overwhelming, work with a therapist, do energy healing, sign up for an Avatar course, or take an Access Consciousness class or learn a releasing technique. There are ways that will help you move forward—it's not around— it's through it. Then the last one is to achieve and celebrate. My coach has been after me because I expand my business and these great things happen and she'll say, *"Okay. What did you do to celebrate"*? For instance last Friday some really great things occurred for me and my goal was accomplished. So I went out and I got a ninety minute facial; I also met with a woman who does hand readings which was so much fun. That was a day of celebration for me. I can always look back on that. Let me tell you those little rewards are important, appreciate what you have achieved, acknowledge your efforts and where you've been; what you've done — that's a really nice place to be. Those are the five magic bullets. Above all just remember don't be pushed by your problems always be led by your dreams.

KAREN: I love that. Most people know how to take action but don't know how to let go. How do we do that?

DEBBI: We can do it several ways. No time like the present, right? [LAUGHTER] Shall we experience letting go right now? Everybody take a big inhale and a full [EXHALE] exhale and just let go. Allow a big release. As you release let go of all pressure and any ways that you are riding yourself or being unkind to you. That's the first thing. Release that and breathe. Being successful. What if you are up and coming or are nearly there and not quite yet? And is that okay? Can you breathe and let go and let it be enough and okay? Everybody experiences something—Steve Jobs who got fired from Apple, Bill Gates who created Internet Explorer and combined it with Windows 95 and when someone said to him, *"Bill, why don't you add a search engine"?* He said, *"I don't think that's such a good idea."* [LAUGHTER] But Google thought it was a good idea and look at Google now. Thomas Edison created the light bulb after ten thousand failures. So failure is not final. Failure is just valuable feedback. Here is another clue to letting go. You don't have to figure it all out. If you have a dream or a goal just by proceeding forward, it's enough. As you move forward in earnest, new information arises and you can make adjustments or add to your reserve. Let down the walls and the need to figure it all out. The next tip is let go of discomfort with changing directions because attachment is a hindrance and you can expand out instead and trust what comes along. You don't need the answers, just the desire and the willingness. Detach and allow a different direction to present itself when needed. I have had this happen when I'm moving toward a dream, and it seems like something amazing is going to happen but instead

I keep hitting a wall and then I realize my tact isn't working. So I have to go with the flow basically, and follow that energy instead. The next one for all you worriers [LAUGHTER] let go of worrying your dream into being. On the contrary it is being in a state of relaxation, it's playing that brings in the great opportunities, so lighten up. Lightening up is a welcoming quality that invites your dream in. And please give up thinking you need to be anyone else in order to succeed at your dream. Being yourself, your authentic self, is all that's needed. What contribution did you come here to be? Just ask your soul: *show me the divine design of my life?* And when you hear answers, act on it. Finally, what's helpful in letting go is to ask more questions. *What do you really love? What do you want to say yes to? If you were the most generous person on the planet what would you gift yourself with? How can you give yourself this, starting right now?* Because ultimately you have divine inheritance. You're called by the Universe, by Source, into an epic heroic performance just by taking on your dream. Your role is irreplaceable, unique and important. Never give up on a dream just because you don't feel you have the time you think you'll need to accomplish it, because honestly time is going to pass anyway. Do take action and always let it go. And letting go is the greatest gift.

KAREN: So, can you lead us through an exercise on letting go?

DEBBI: Yes, okay. If you would please close your eyes and just take a deep breath in and a deep exhale out [EXHALE]. And again, breathe in and on the exhale out release any worry, any fear, any have-to's, any anxiety. Just let it go, just let it go. And if there's anything that's going on in your life right now that is causing you fear, or concern that doesn't feel good, just locate where that is in your body. And locating where that is in your body-- imagine a window in front of the discomfort and can you release that feeling right now through the window? Because all it is, is energy. And when energy comes up it's asking to be released. Not to be pushed back down but to be released. So right now, can you release that feeling through the window and you can answer *yes*, if the answer is yes. And can you release it a little more? Yes. And can you release it just a little more? Now this relaxed state is the real nature of you. Choose to let go of the things you can't control, and take control of the things you can. You can't control all the events of your life but you can control your state of mind during them. [EXHALE] And now in these last, delicious breaths remember that when you let go, all you're letting go of is clinging to desire. You're never letting go of acting or taking action, you're just letting go of attachments and expectations. With your breath bring yourself back to the present with your feet on the ground. Ground yourself. Be here. Open your eyes. And if you like — bring the earth energy up through the soles of your feet and into your body and be here now. Safe, whole, complete. How was that for you, Karen?

KAREN: Nice. Boy. Very relaxing. That's amazing. Fabulous. Thank you so much for doing that.

DEBBI: You're welcome. From this space you can go out and create the rest of your day and know that any moment you can tap into this. It's really that simple to remind ourselves to let go and use our breath.

KAREN: Why is taking action so critical to being successful with the goals?

DEBBI: It's critical. It's like having a car and

going out and kicking the tire and saying why aren't I driving to the next town when I need to get there? Well you have to get in the car, you have to turn the key, you have to put your foot on the gas, you have to change and shift gears. You have to take action to get there. It's the same with dreams. Everybody knows this, by the way. [LAUGHTER] You probably have heard "take action," but I'm hoping today the light bulb will go off and you'll realize, *"Oh. It's not a secret — and I should have been doing it. I can start following this sage advice now."* [LAUGHTER] So whatever is stopping you, know you can shift into action because that's the way out. If you're experiencing discontent, you can channel your dissatisfaction into immediate action. If you're wondering — *"Oh, I don't know. Should I go after that dream or shouldn't I? Should I take action or shouldn't I"?* Just take action! [LAUGHTER] If you're thinking about taking a class, do it. I cannot tell you how many times in my life I've thought about things and not done them, to the point where I finally go, *"Augh. I surrender. Let me just do it. Why am I holding myself back? It's so silly."* You know people who create their lives from the filter of resistance know that resistance is like starting out to do something while at the same time pushing against yourself. So you basically stay stuck. If what I'm saying isn't resonating, let me refer you to a team of experts: Dr. Phil has said, *"Life rewards* action." Tony Robbins says we should *"take massive action."* Action is – it's like wildfire and it catches. Take concentrated action. Take small steps each day because eventually it does cause your dream to ignite. All the things you've been doing—the power of thought—can be amplified through the power of action. We have to invest in our future through the action we take today, and we absolutely have the power inside of us to align with our destiny and action is the way through.

KAREN: So, I'm going to shift a little bit. Can you share about the idea of gratitude around dreams?

DEBBI: Yes, there is gratitude around dreams. We all know that an attitude of gratitude, to express thankfulness—is so important. We can shift our attention to all the things we have accomplished and all the ways we've really showed up for ourselves and for others. Recognize that you have accomplished a lot of things and celebrate that. The other piece of that is, if we are grateful, if we spend our life—appreciating, then more will show up. You can turn your whole day around by employing sincere gratitude. My best friend and I talk on the phone every Wednesday. One Wednesday about a month ago we were having a poopy day—both of us—and she was thinking about how we might start to feel better and she suggested, *"Why don't we spend the day just being grateful"?* I said, *"Oh. Brilliant."* So we agreed to spend the day in gratitude and that's what I did the whole day. Every time I spoke with anybody, corresponded by email, passed someone in the hall, paid for something at a checkout counter—I expressed sincere gratitude. And in fact, if I can be honest—there were times I thought *"I have never thanked this person like this."* Like the man who runs my radio station. I thought I've never really taken the time to say, *"Wow. Thank you for all you do. I work at a rocking place. Thank you for showing up anytime something's broken. Thank you for helping me have the best show imaginable."* With some people—I could feel them soften in the moment. Coming from gratitude totally changed my day and my mood. I got a client that day and received some unexpected money which was a huge bonus. Didn't even expect that. I'm telling you that story because if you use gratitude with your dreams it has the same effect. Because again, you're amplifying, right? Using the power of thought through the power of action to create great things. It helps in your dream and will also start to attract new opportunities to you.

KAREN: Wow. That's great. So that process would be going through your day really grateful, acknowledging what to be grateful for, which is everything. [LAUGHTER]

DEBBI: Yeah. Be grateful, exactly, it'll shift you around.

KAREN: I would like to get as much of your wisdom as possible. I think that was a great process—going through your day being very thankful. What other tips do you have for moving into our dreams?

DEBBI: You really want to desire the goal. Just notice when that feeling comes up don't push it down. I had a client once who said, I really want to have a dog but I'm terrified to have a dog because every time I express it somebody—*I want a dog*, somebody says, *oh you're going to lose your life. Oh, it's like having a child.* The comments were crushing that passion she had, and giving her tremendous question about *do I really want to go forward with that? Maybe that isn't so good for my life.* I would encourage anyone who has a dream, no matter the feedback on the outside; you really owe it to yourself to investigate the desire, the dream. So here is the action she took: she aligned herself with friends who have dogs to experience them further. As soon as she opened her mind to the idea—no kidding, her stepdaughter got a dog—her stepdaughter is a young adult. She's in her twenties. The stepdaughter travels. So what happens is the stepdaughter drops off the dog for three days, or ten days while she's away. Is that awesome? So she's having the experience. She now knows what it's like to walk the dog, pee and poo, get it fed, the love, the attention, the playing, for anywhere from a few days to a few weeks consistently. As she goes along she's creating this particular dream slowly which is okay because that's an important responsibility to another life. She's starting to see if this is something she indeed wants to do. Of course there are also ways to foster animals too. I'm just saying you desire the goal, you decide. You have to make that decision. I would also set goals that are grand enough to challenge yourself. It could be really easy. For instance I have a male client who wanted to try ballroom dancing. That's an easy goal for him. He's going to find a class in his area and he will sign up to take dance classes. He might be scared the first time to attend but generally it's not hugely challenging. But when you do something like join a dating site, or change jobs, or change where you live, or a million dreams we can fit in the blanks, many of them can feel hugely challenging. It usually feels like you're not quite sure you're going to get there. That's okay. I suggest visualizing yourself experiencing the goal. Something I do every night when I go to sleep when I put my head on the pillow is I see my life with my goal already in it so I'm living my future life now. It's the most beautiful way to slip into beta-theta waves as you're falling asleep. It's been powerful for me. And you do have to take action. There is a reason why in the movies that have that little clapper that says "action." [LAUGHTER] You've got to do that in the movie of your own life too. Don't lose sight. Keep moving forward. There can actually be profound ease when you do it. I guess the other thing is I would highly recommend meditation and gratitude on a daily basis. I meditate daily. It's life changing to be in that stillness and quiet and reconnection.

KAREN: Fabulous, that's fabulous. Debbi, any final thoughts before we wrap up today?

DEBBI: I guess what I want to say to anybody who's listening, to anybody who's inspired is, what do you usually do? Is this the time you usually click off and think, *oh, what she said sounded good*, and then move on with your day? Because this is an opportunity. It's a call to action, right? To do something different. Is it time to do something different? Because that's when you shift and change your story. It's not where you came from, it's not your circumstances; I believe you took human form to stand and live in the imprint of the divine template that your soul created for this life for you. Let your light shine through your goals and your dreams. You didn't just come here to dare to dream, you definitely came to dare to make your dreams a reality and I support you in that.

END

~ Quotable ~

"It is not because things are difficult that we do not dare, it is because we do not dare that they are difficult."
- **Seneca**

"Every great dream begins with a dreamer. Always remember, you have within you the strength, the patience, and the passion to reach for the stars to change the world."
- **Harriet Tubman**

"There are people who put their dreams in a little box and say, Yes, I've got dreams, of course I've got dreams. Then they put the box away and bring it out once in a while to look in it, and yep, they're still there. These are great dreams, but they never even get out of the box. It takes an uncommon amount of guts to put your dreams on the line, to hold them up and say, How good or how bad am I? That's where courage comes in."
- **Erma Bombeck**

"Throw your dreams into space like a kite, and you do not know what it will bring back, a new life, a new friend, a new love, a new country."
- Anaïs Nin

"Be careful what you water your dreams with. Water them with worry and fear and you will produce weeds that choke the life from your dream. Water them with optimism and solutions and you will cultivate success. Always be on the lookout for ways to turn a problem into an opportunity for success. Always be on the lookout for ways to nurture your dream."
- Lao Tzu

Transcript

Debbi Dachinger:
Interview with CECILIA LI

CECILIA LI: Thank you for being here with us. Before we start off our journey today, if there are any distractions please move them aside because our special guest, Debbi Dachinger is going to share some helpful tools to achieve your dreams. Welcome Debbi. How are you?

DEBBI DACHINGER: Oh, Cecilia. I like what you said—put everything aside to be present for the journey we're about to take. Thank you for setting that up. Any listener who has taken time out of their day today can absolutely make that choice, by being present now. Let's take a journey so that we offer fantastic content for people for the next hour to help shift and change. That's what I'm all about. And thank you for having me.

CECILIA: I am very excited for this call because this is one of our favorite topics. It's all about achieving your dreams and goals. Debbi, you are such an inspiration in helping people, teaching people how to make their dreams a reality throughout your life. Were you always on the path to living your dreams or was there ever a time that you were not so successful, happy and fulfilled?

DEBBI: I have always been happy, fulfilled and successful. [LAUGHTER] I'm kidding, I really am. Wouldn't that be fantastic if you asked somebody that question and they said—*yeah, always*—and meant it!

CECILIA: Right. We all wish we were successful, happy, had all we want, never struggle, never suffer-*augh*.

DEBBI: I basically transformed what was aberrant inside of me to become the very thing I am here to teach. That's my story. I didn't know how to be successful. Did I have elements? Oh, yes. Of course. I was born with a lot of talent. I was born with the ability to sing. I was very musical, I was always very expressive. I loved being in front of people, I had a passion for that. I was definitely born to live out loud. I might have easily shifted into something successfully but I also had things in my upbringing that caused me to create limiting beliefs about myself, about my worth, about my deservability. Today I can look back and say, *wow I was really talented*, but back then, I wasn't that sure. I knew I wanted to be on stage and entertain. But I severely doubted myself and looked at other people, comparing and thought *they're so much better than I am*. I remember auditioning for plays and thinking, *oh my god that person is much more talented*. I was sure the part wasn't mine, and often when I was cast in the role I'd auditioned for --- I was shocked that they picked me. That's the level I was operating at.

CECILIA: Sure. You thought you weren't good enough. You didn't measure up to the standards. It's almost beyond your belief.

DEBBI: I had poor beliefs operating in my life, and those poor beliefs manifested on the outside through inconsistency. So I would get things and do things and not get things and not do things. The bottom line is I had moments in my life when I opted for and chose big changes; where I made new decisions. One of them was I had been in a relationship and living with somebody. I finally got myself out—because I really didn't want to be in the relationship—but I didn't want to leave him because I didn't want to hurt him. That's crazy, right? Because if you're not happy in a situation, you're going to end up leaving anyway. And for a long while I was stalling. When I left I was living on my own in my own place, and I realized while I was grieving the relationship that I had held myself back. No one asked me to. This man never told me, *put your dreams on hold—don't do anything—it's all about me.* He never said that. I chose it, something inside of me decided not to do the things I love and was curious about. So while I was alone I sat down and made a list and I was shocked at what poured out of me. I wanted to go on a whitewater rafting adventure. I wanted to travel to Costa Rica. I wanted to travel to Italy. There was a course for self-development that I always wanted to do, and for many years I did not allow myself to take the workshop because of the cost. I looked at a list of ten things that my heart was screaming for. My soul was saying *yes, yes, yes* and I had put the gates down. And I thought, *what has this cost you in interest, to not allow yourself?* And in that moment I vowed everything would be different and from that moment on I was going to do one thing at a time and cross each dream off my list. I want to tell you it was the best year of my life and completely changed the trajectory of how I did things, how I operated, and how I felt about myself and my life. It became the most amazing adventure.

CECILIA: Wow. What an amazing transformation. I think a lot of people can relate to that because they've put themselves as secondary instead of operating from a belief that they should always make themselves happy first. So many of us make decisions based on what other people think or will say about you. It wasn't even an authentic choice.

DEBBI: Absolutely. You know, I'm known as a goal achievement expert and I'm often asked to speak. My keynote signature speech is the five simple steps to achieving your goals every time. There really are five basic steps. And one of them is you have to heal and deal your obstacles because they're patterns in your life. It's interesting because one of the dream busters is "others." One of the things that people do, much like I did with this relationship, is look outside of themselves and think, *I can't — what will my family think of me? I can't because these people are depending on me. Or I can't — <u>fill in the blank</u>*. And what's really behind this is a way that we incapacitate ourselves; dim our light in the world and refrain from giving ourselves what we deserve. So we blame it on *others*. Chances are "*they*" haven't always asked us to put our lives on hold for them. [LAUGHTER]

CECILIA: Right. My mom would never say you have to do this or you have to be like that. Never. She really just wanted me to be happy. But I created a belief, thinking that if I did certain things she would be happy. So many times we don't even realize that we're replaying that pattern over and over again. And even if we're aware of it we don't necessarily know if there is a way to get out of it. So, Debbi, do you have any practices or exercises that you can share with us to help us release the negative energy and stop replaying the patterns?

DEBBI: Yes. There are a couple of things we can do and the first is we need to get honest. Whatever your thing is—and I euphemistically ask you all, what's your thing? Here's you, here's your dream: *I want to world travel, I want a new career. I want a relationship. I want a healthy body.* Whatever it is. You fill in what magic makes your soul sing. Now—what's between you and your dream? Admit to yourself—whatever you've been allowing to paralyze that area of your life. It could be I'm afraid. I am so fear-based that fear will stop me from everything. Or I'm afraid of failing. I'm afraid of being successful because if I'm successful I'll have to be that great and I don't know if I can step into my greatness. I'm afraid of not playing small anymore. Or I'm afraid of being visible. I'm afraid that if I put myself out there something terrible is going to happen or someone is going to see me and I'll be humiliated. Fill that obstacle to your goal in and notice, it's like an octopus, right? Threads coming out from different aspects of your life that this impediment affects and if you look at the whole picture and feel into it realize, this is controlling my life. Every time something comes up—a promotion at work, me stepping up into a larger version of myself. Me putting myself out there saying yes to an opportunity, shifting directions—whatever it is—you keep stopping yourself. We create it all, know it's you. Our beliefs are that powerful. So—that's the first thing. Be honest with yourself first and foremost. Now look at, how is it working for you? Is that belief doing great things? [LAUGHTER] Chances are you're thinking *no, this really doesn't work. This is actually not working for me at all and I prefer to experience something else.* Okay, what is that something else? That's a beautiful one. What would it mean to move through the world in conviction? Holy-moly. How about living through the world in trust. Just feel the difference in that energy. So now feel where you are. Now feel where that dream is across the space there. Now fill that space between you and that dream with Trust, with Confidence with Commitment, and with Conviction. Now when an opportunity comes, a promotion comes to you, a chance to shift, change or take action and do something different, the first thing is to say *yes,*

[LAUGHTER], and the next thing is prepare. Take action. Prepare so when opportunity comes you'll be ready and you'll do well. Comfort comes by saying *yes*, by preparing, and doing what you love and what excites you. We don't have to know everything but we do have to do things differently.

Here is an interesting exercise: Go to the thesaurus—the physical book or the Thesaurus on your computer—now type in the word which usually causes the demise of your dream. Type in, for instance, failure, doubt, codependence, fear, whatever it is. Next look at the antonym of that word. It's so expansive to see what the opposite is of where you've existed from. You can incorporate and practice the opposite, and know this is who you are from today forward.

CECILIA: That's so beautiful. Thank you so much for sharing with us.

DEBBI: It's my pleasure. And let me tell you, you don't know what you don't know. If you didn't grow up in an environment where this was taught, where there was a school or a home that showed how to make dreams come true—and how many of us did? This is why I teach what I do. When this interview is over it's just the beginning. It's just the beginning if you decide that. I hope for you all to succeed and I know you can.

CECILIA: Thank you so much for having one hundred percent confidence in us, and your commitment and your passion. This is great energy you've brought us. You've worked with many, many successful people. What do they have in common? What are their patterns that make them become so successful?

DEBBI: They do have patterns that over time became clear to me and I realized something is emerging here. *Pay attention, Debbi, if you desire to be successful.* [LAUGHTER]. The first thing I found they all had wounds that they turned into their gifts. As an example, Dr. John DeMartini—he's just amazing. His story briefly is that he had ADD and was dyslexic, he had a learning disability but they were unkind at the school he went to. His teacher said awful things to him, like *you'll never make it, you can't even be taught*—and he dropped out of school. He became homeless; lived on a beach and was headed downhill. And one day, on the beach a man came along—his name was Paul Braggs from the Amino-Braggs we know of in health food stores—and Paul found and helped John. As I said, John was told he was unteachable, he would never make it, he shouldn't be in school—and John is now one of the world's renowned educators! You see what I mean about turning a wound into a gift? I know other stories of phenomenal, inspirational people who took--what seemed like the worst piece of themselves, they dealt with it head on and that "worst piece" became their greatest gift to themselves and others. Successful people do what they love, right? They're not out there working at jobs they hate, they're not out there hanging out with people who don't serve them or are pulling them down and are vampires. They're not out there making subpar money. They aren't out there denying themselves their worth, deservability or a good life. They're doing the exact opposite of all that. They're fully living life.

Now of note, successful people experience periodic failure. I want you to hear that, so do not be afraid of failure. Successful people fail too.

What makes them different is that they're resilient. Successful people fail, they feel their feelings, and they figure out what happened and learn the lesson: *What did I bring to that party? How did I contribute to what just happened? Okay, what can I learn here?* They learn and they get up and they move forward. It's like Thomas Edison. Someone was asking about his success. He said, *"I had ten thousand failures before I had success."* Talk about resilience. Nothing was going to stop that man from inventing.

I would say the last thing to mention is that successful people invest in themselves. They take time to look for who is out there to be their coach or their mentor. What workshops, what telesummits, what or who is a couple of steps above where they're operating now? They don't stagnate. They're continually growing and expanding. They're always growing. Those are some of the principles you can look for in your life and if you see that some of them aren't operating as high, you'll know where you can start spending a little more time to improve that area.

CECILIA: They constantly learn and grow and that's how they become successful and not just a one time achievement.

DEBBI: Exactly. And you know what? I just took a coach myself recently and here is the bottom line. We can only know as much as we know. For me, I came here to live out loud. I came here to express myself. When it comes to something like creativity, I'm probably off the charts. If you tested me I would probably be out of the universe. But if you tried to talk to me about science, geography—oh, embarrassing. Math— embarrassing. There are just certain things. I could make it happen if I wanted to put my abilities there, or I could hire someone. [LAUGHTER]. So here I am, my whole business has expanded to a completely new level. I'm savvy at marketing but I was trying to maintain too much and at some level it starts to go out of control and I realized I need a coach. I know this. I teach this. I see successful people do it—it's my turn now. So, yes. I'm working with a coach and let me tell you, I said a decision changes all the energy and I'm telling you the moment we set up our appointments— the Universe went *woo-hoo, she's stepping into a bigger version of herself. Yes, she's going there.* I received new opportunities that blew my mind. And I knew it happened because I had said *yes* to myself. I said *yes* to showing up. I'm here to play a bigger game. That's what showed up mirrored right back to me. It's worth it. It's amazing what you can work out financially. These things, you know, it seems like, *I can't do that, I can't buy these products; I can't work with that person.* It does seem like that because that's the easy way out and that's incapacitating. When you look at all the coffees you buy and all the expensive movies you go to and all the clothes that hang in your closet, and I could go on. The credit card debt. Let me tell you when you start streamlining, when you start investing in yourself, there begins a shift in your world and your finances because the Universe receives the message that we mean business and we mean good business.

CECILIA: Yes. Take advantage of everything and learn and grow. Don't be afraid of failure because unfortunately, it's going to happen. But at the end of the day—learn from it and before you know it you're there, right?

DEBBI: Can I take everyone through a quick exercise right now?

CECILIA: Oh, that would be awesome.

DEBBI: Let's shift the energy because we want to give you a bang for your buck. Oh, that's right. This is free. [LAUGHTER] You get a bang anyway. [LAUGHTER] Okay, my lovelies. Just take a deep breath and close your eyes. Put your feet on the ground. Breath, relax. Just [EXHALE] relax and let it all go. Anything that feels like stress, release. Anything that feels like you gotta do or be or have, let it go. Anything you've been worried or concerned about, allow it to literally glide out of you. Let any negativity leaving your body to now transmute into a beautiful and magical energy into the world. Feel love pouring into your head, going all through your body and out through your feet into the beautiful Mother Earth who supports and loves us. Feel that love pouring in through your head and into your body, out through your feet and cascading again up into your head. Allow the Universe to bless you with lavish plenty. Within you is an inner-guide and teacher who's always speaking to you--who loves you. It's your soul; it's your highest self, saying, *Pay attention. This is best for you.*

Acknowledge that intuition, that gut, the inner-GPS—God Protection System—*I will listen from now on. I will listen as you guide me in my highest truth showing what's best for me. I only desire what's best for me. And I nurture this connection with my Highest Self and intuition.* Again breathe [EXHALE]. And know within you beats the message of your heart and the universal heart. Beloved, you have a unique destiny. You are an irreplaceable being and you are a beloved part of the All That Is. And truth, is this the time? If you're on this planet and it's time, you can positively take new risks and live more courageously. The good news is you decided to be here now — it's okay to embrace your greatness and be inspired forward and encourage yourself with positive messages. Know it is possible. That dream, it's possible. *I deserve goodness. I deserve happiness. I'm going to live as though my wings are grand enough to carry me anywhere I desire to go.* Any energy that does not support you is gone from you now. It's gone. It is gone. Let it flow through your feet, into the Mother Earth and transmute it into something magical and wonderful. Now listen inside for one word-- the one word your soul, your highest self, desires to gift to you. There's something you need now more than anything else. Is it peace? Is it ease? Success? Self-love? Self-care? Fun? All that's left is your word—your one impeccable word. Keep that. That's your treasure. And tuck the word into your heart to assist you as you carry forward into your grandest dreams. Understand: you always have more than enough. Thank the Universe for your great abundance. Today we expand our awareness of the abundance that's around us at all times. Enjoy a tsunami of prosperity growing and overflowing every day. Be filled with faith. Move forward in spite of not knowing everything now, but knowing that you are loved and cared for beyond measure. And right now, all is well. Everything you need is here [EXHALE] right now. And with that word tucked inside of you come back different with that word as your gift. Come back; open your eyes, breath. If you feel lightheaded at all, allow eroots to come out through your feet, that go down into the Mother Earth-deep, deep down--that bring up her beautiful energy into your body. Open up, choosing to be present, with your magical word in place for you. Lovely. How was that?

CECILIA: Wow. I feel so lighthearted and the freedom to do whatever I want to do. Debbi, so you really are such an inspiration. Question: you have achieved this level of success in your life and we assume you are a multi-tasker.

DEBBI: [LAUGHTER] You assume correctly.

CECILIA: So, do you have a to-do list or do you have something else that you use to help you do so many amazing things within a limited amount of time.

DEBBI: Yes, that's a great question. The first thing I use is lists. I write my to-do's down and put them in a semblance of order of importance of which task gets done first through last. The second thing is how I handle emails. The third principle I utilize are the words *yes* and *no*.

So, first of all: lists. Occasionally I get astounded by the amount of emails and requests that come to me -- it is a lot of information, a lot for anyone to handle. I'm pretty much on top of everything, so if I'm going to operate at this level I use a method to make it work for me. I can let emails and to-do's drag me around or I can be in charge of them. I choose to be in control of it. I put together a technique — I create a list that works on my behalf. I do this each day and it's easy. I write everything down on a list. Get it out of my head. Then I number it, one through whatever in order of importance. When I'm ready to start work I literally only work on number one. Yes, a little bit of multi-tasking does take place but basically, I keep my eye on task #1 until it's complete. Then I move into number two, next I move onto number three. I make myself a deal that all I do for today is the top three tasks. Everything else on that list is either a bonus or I let it go. Wow. Is that permission and freedom or what? Let me tell you, the best thing happens when you take contrary action because there is no pressure. So I finish task number one. *Woo-hoo.* I finish number two. *That feels great.* I finish task number three. *Yes. It's off my plate.* Then I can look at task number four if there's time left in the day and decide if I want to keep going. Or I can elect, *it's time to stop and time for me to play.* It's up to me. What I found, is this removes overwhelm or exhaustion. I write the day's list out like that, prioritize the tasks, and only take on the top three responsibilities; anything remaining on the list is a bonus to-do or means I am done for the day. This method organizes me, allows my to-dos to work and I get so much completed very easily.

Okay, the next thing. We are all weighed down with emails, social and professional media? We all have to get a grip. It is so addicting. Right? Guess who controls how much your email comes up? Your email doesn't control itself. It's set at a default, right? So perhaps every three minutes it tells you, *you've got mail, you've got mail, you've got mail.* Maybe you've set it up on your home computer, your work computer, your cell phone — I mean, Mama Mia. [LAUGHTER] You control it. You can make a new choice about when it is convenient for *you* to check in. I know people who make it work — by going into their email only two times a day — once in the morning and once in the afternoon to check in, handle responses and get back out. They give themselves an allotment of time. I know a guy who runs an unbelievably savvy social media machine and he has so much stuff coming at him and he told me, "*Yep, I go in for thirty minutes in the morning and thirty minutes in the afternoon and handle whatever I have to and I'm out.*" You must make it work for you.

And the last suggestion in handling a multitude of tasks is to employ the words *yes* and *no*. We talked about 'others' earlier, and it's very easy to make decisions based on what we *think* others want us to do, but what do *we* desire to do? You need to entrust yourself to say *yes* when you desire to do something and *no* when you can sense you do not want to. If you've written down your goals and dreams then you know that's what you keep your eye on. So if something else comes up and someone asks, *hey join my gardening group*, look at your list – is gardening on it? What if your list reads *I'm creating a trip to this amazing country*? If you're looking at gardening and your dream trip and they're not in alignment, you have the right to say *no*. In fact, anything that doesn't feel right or good for any reason, you have the right to say *no*, and you have the right to say *yes*. Once you start employing those words in your life, the yeses will be driving you forward to the things and people you love and that honor you. The no's will represent—*not right now*. It's your voice. You are fully empowered to say *yes* or *no* and you'll free up lots of time.

So use those boundaries: create the lists and order them in importance, set up specific times to check email and social media each day, and also take care of yourself by affirming what you prefer to do or bowing out.

CECILIA: That is absolutely amazing. I never thought successful people spend specific time checking their emails. If you aren't present with what you're actually doing, you'll feel like your energy is scattered and that way you're not as efficient as you can be. Right?

DEBBI: Oh, yeah. It's a great sabotage, isn't it? Your dream is over here waiting to have life breathed into it and if all you're glued to your email it's actually prohibiting you from moving ahead. Do you need your email for what you're doing? Absolutely. It is one form of communication. Can you do without it sometimes? Of course. And you decide when to engage by creating a timeline that works. Nothing's set in stone. You control it. So let's say you choose to handle email twice a day. You may sit back and say, *oh my goodness, pour me a glass of wine this is awesome. I just created so much time.* Or you may notice, *I missed something important in email today – checking it two times a day didn't work. Instead I'll add a third time, 3 checks a day and then I'll let it go.* You can design this however it works for you. That's the bottom line.

CECILIA: Thank you so much, Debbi. In your book *Dare to Dream, This Life Counts* you mentioned that you made a list of things you always wanted to do but didn't do. You decided to make those things happen, took action and actually made the dreams come true. One of them was a wonderful trip to Italy. Can you tell us how you finally went to this place you always dreamed about?

DEBBI: Wow. It was magical. That's the thing that is prevalent when we make dreams come true. It's a memory we'll have forever and it's a life changing experience when we fulfill it. I had always dreamed about Italy, and it was something I put off. First it was about money. Then it was about I don't want to travel alone as a woman. It was about so many things that I let take priority. I wasn't divorced yet but I had recently left my husband and in one of those defining moments I just knew—*I don't care anymore if I have to go alone. I don't care what it's going to take; life is too short. I don't want to be at the end of my life and think about, oh—all the regrets I have. If I'm breathing then I'm here to have fun and to live.* So I designed my trip myself. I didn't go with a group. I literally decided where I was going to go and for how long, and I would take trains between cities. Well at the time the book *"Eat, Pray, Love"* had come out and everybody said to me, *oh my god. You have got to read that book because the author also went through a divorce and traveled to Italy.* So there I was on my trip and it was—there are just no words for what it was. I'm going back there in my mind as I'm speaking. The trip started out with quite a bump because when I landed in Venice I was so exhausted from all the flying. I was just so tired and it took an additional hour in Venice Airport to get our luggage, and while waiting for my luggage I was robbed. My wallet was stolen, my cell phone was stolen, my American Express card was stolen, all my cash—the whole shebang. The only thing I had was my passport. It was quite a first day's start on my dream vacation, where I ending up in the El Capitan (Head of Policeman's) office in Venice Airport crying. The Police Captain was very kind to me and understood my distress and I had the presence of mind to ask to use his telephone, and used it to dial my (stolen) cell phone and changed my outgoing message to say, *if you're calling me I've been robbed, please call me at my hotel.* My girlfriend and my ex-husband heard the message and by that evening they were taking care of everything, they were amazing. They got money sent to me and all my credit cards cancelled and got everything handled. Now it took a while for the money to arrive so I didn't have funds to eat, so I lost weight. [LAUGHTER] I lived on the protein bars in my suitcase the first three days. But I didn't let it stop me — my first night there I sat in my room in Venice and I thought, *guess what honey. Here you are with nothing but damn it, you made it. You're in freaking Italy.* I picked myself up out of my hotel room, as exhausted as I was that first night and walked all around Venice by myself and it was just — I could cry telling this story. What it meant for me to be there was everything. From that moment on — the financial stuff worked out, it was fine. And from that moment on the adventure began. I was fully present in Italy. One of the things I did that was phenomenal is take the train to go between cities every four days. I would take a train to the next place. And I decided to do a speaking journal. So I would speak into this recording device and free flow whatever I was thinking or feeling and these stream-of-consciousness recordings ended up becoming radio shows. It was a six-part series of my travels in Italy which was very popular with listeners. During one of the recordings—I had been reading a chapter in *"Eat, Pray, Love"* and it really struck a chord in me. I was never going to say why my marriage did not work and why I left, but I was never going to do that again. I had started to date quite a few men back home and really I didn't have interest in them. They were fun, it was nice, but truthfully I knew I wasn't interested in a significant relationship with any of them and so I committed out loud – thank God I had my own train cabin with a closed door!—[LAUGHTER] that I would end those relationships when I returned home. I got honest with myself, so I'd be honest with those men. Next I was emotional and it was like my soul was demanding out loud, I said into the recorder *I am going to have an amazing relationship next time, I deserve to be loved. I deserve to be cherished. I desire mutual respect. I want trust. I want to look at that other person and just be mad, crazy in love with them. I want wild sex. I want someone who understands my intelligence, who gets who I am. Someone who's passionate about music and expression. Someone who's well-read, loves to travel and blah, blah, blah.* I let it fly. It just poured out of me. Well the entire Italy trip was beyond amazing. I spent some time completely alone. There was another time when I walked Cinque Terre. Cinque Terre was the photo that impassioned me in the first place that I had to go to Italy. I got to Cinque Terre and I walked all of it. It touched my soul. These five towns on these cliffs overlooking this water. I met people. I made friends and had an amazing Italian boyfriend who was this beautiful pianist-artist guy. I really had a fantastic trip. What I want you to share as a caveat is, one month after returning from that trip I met the man that I described out loud in those recordings. When he and I started dating he would listen to my radio shows and he stopped one day while my Italy show was on and said — *oh, my god. You're describing me. Everything you said while on that train in Italy is describing me.* I looked at him and I could only think the power of that moment. The power of saying: *Bring it. I'm showing up. This is who I am. This is what I desire. This is all of what I'll allow and I will enjoy the right relationship with so much relish because I deserve this and more, and even more.* And the Universe brought it. And I'm still with that man today. And that's just from making a vacation dream come true. [LAUGHTER] Who knew? [LAUGHTER]

CECILIA: This is one of the most beautiful stories I have ever heard. Thank you so much for sharing with us so openly. I really understand that anything is possible. Do we have any opportunity to go deeper into your work?

DEBBI: Yes, and I invite you. I invite you all to turn it around. If I can, we all can. While I encourage you to take your dream on the road — and I'll tell you how — if you come to a fork in the road, you have a choice to make. *Do I keep doing things the way I've always done them and getting the same results? How happy am I right now? Or shall I make a different choice?* Personally, I don't like pain, I just don't. [LAUGHTER] Pain is the great encouragement for me to change, so even though taking on a dream or a new path can be new and unknown, I do opt to take the trail I haven't tried before and do something that is positive—even though I've no guarantee for success or anything else. It's just our own worst thinking that advises us to avoid the unknown. And guess what? You'll get so far, and if you find there's an obstacle and it's not you—it's from out there—then you turn left and keep going, and keep on the path. Trust me it works, it works, it works. If you're here, if you're alive, if you're breathing, it's time for you to make your dreams come true; you will set a beautiful ripple effect on the planet. You'll inspire. People will be watching you. There is a reason why you feel those callings inside. It's not a mistake. You were given them for a reason. And if you were given the dream, you were also given the power to make it come true. Give all of us your inner gift. Because we are all waiting for you.

CECILIA: Wow. That's incredible. Thank you so much, Debbi. Really. It would be wonderful to have you back. Thank

you, everyone, for listening.
END

Transcript

Debbi Dachinger: Interview with DR. PHIL DEMBO

DR. PHIL DEMBO:	Hi everybody and welcome to Life Coach Radio--I'm Dr. Phil Dembo, your host—for conversation about the strategies we need to face the life that we have. We are bringing you the best people who have the best message, the bigger scope, so that you learn everything out there, including from our guest tonight, Debbi Dachinger. Debbi thanks for joining us on Life Coach Radio.
DEBBI DACHINGER:	I am happy to be here. Thank you, Dr. Dembo and if I may say, you gave away a secret right there at the beginning to making your dreams a reality which is, you have to have a bigger vision. Once you have that

bigger vision then you do whatever it takes to step into it. So I congratulate you for sharing that on your show.

DR. DEMBO: Well, I appreciate that, thank you. And so, that's a great lead in. You had a vision to write this book, it's called *Dare to Dream: This Life Counts*. Tell us about that. Tell us a little bit about you, and your transformation to what is becoming this large message that you're bringing to the world.

DEBBI: I'm living a fantastic life and it amazes me every day. How I got here was a great surprise -- as John Lennon once said, *Life is What Happens To You While You're Busy Making Other Plans*. [LAUGHTER] Ever since I was a very little peanut I only wanted to do one thing: I was an actress and singer — period. I never thought I'd end up an author. I never thought I'd end up a media personality. My book was born out of the fact that I was reaching people through broadcasting, and I kept feeling, the more I was speaking and the more I was being interviewed on radio and television shows, that every time I brought up the idea of goal achievement — I experienced a tremendous hunger out there and a frustration amongst people. They had big dreams but didn't know how to make them come true. They ended up becoming frustrated and giving up. Accomplishing dreams is not something we're taught in school. It's not something we often see modeled by our parents. So people just don't have the skills. It's not a wrongness about who people are, it's just a lack of information. I realized I had an opportunity to put together a book that would teach how to make a dream come true. The book contains everything from examples of people who have come from unbelievable circumstances and made dreams a reality, to the exact steps to take, with writing exercises and a lot of inspirational information. So if you're having a bad day, if something comes up, you can pick up the book, the chapters are short and everything keeps buoying you up and making sure you know it's not only possible, it's doable. And I'm with you every step of the way. So that was the birth of my book.

DR. DEMBO: That's awesome. Debbi in my journey in working with people, I find that so many people don't know how to feel their own feelings, let alone dream their own dreams. We know that they have them, and we know that they're in there. But it seems that more and more the world is too afraid to step into their dream. To step out of the script that has been set forth for them. What do you tell people about the fear that goes on in order to get the courage to do something about it?

DEBBI: People have different patterns about what stops them, and indeed fear is a really big one. From a detached perspective, I've noticed several things about fear and one thing I see is that it's a huge deterrent when it convinces us that something horrific is going to happen. And it convinces us so strongly that we end up abandoning the very dream we have out of fear. The other thing that happens is a lot of doubts come up. We're not certain it's not going to occur for us. And the interesting thing is that people are so busy playing out their dream *before* they even take action steps. They're so busy figuring it out, going into logic. Let me tell ya' I've done things that on paper were impossible. I've done two marathons and before I began the process I had no training. If I had believed all the doubts in my mind I would have completely given up. But what I felt in my belly, that sort of fire that you feel, that calling? That was there, that was enough for me, in spite of doubt, to still show up and take the steps and see how it plays out. The other piece about fear is that often it's mistaken. What's really underneath it, is this incredible excitement—something that calls to us. But we're so used to—by default—moving directly into fear that we lose touch with that, *"Oh that would be amazing to experience. I am excited by the prospect of what that is."* And the last piece is for many of us fear denotes a new possibility in our life which is just unfamiliar. We have a calling to know, be, do, perceive, experience something, and that is excitement. And then what comes up is—*I don't know that. That's unfamiliar. What if.* And we're so busy jumping out of excitement and into the default of fear that we've lost touch with what called us in the first place. I urge anybody to understand that fear is energy like anything else. It is only energy. And energy can be changed and transmuted. So with all of that in mind now, when fear comes up for you next time you can acknowledge to yourself, *okay. I feel afraid and how valid is that really? If I stay here how will I ever know what it's like to take steps toward my dream and possibly experience it?* It's just a matter of acknowledging and moving forward anyway. Choose to move forward anyway.

DR. DEMBO: What you're saying is really important because for me, when people talk about dreams they talk about a destination and outcome. And dreams aren't outcomes. Dreams are the journey, the experience. The quality of a moment that leads to an outcome. Because you could say I dream of being a professional actor. But you may not become a professional actor in the way that you experience yourself. It doesn't mean that you can't experience your dream because it's what being a professional actor would bring to you. The experience of being on stage or in front of a camera. The experience of having people applaud you. There is community theatre. There are other ways of moving in the right direction and sometimes the content overrides the intent. The intention to show up to that moment. And what I love about the work that you do is really helping people understand that when you set goals and you accomplish those goals toward your dream, you're actually living your dream.

DEBBI: One hundred percent. We don't know what's going to happen in the journey. We take action to get where we need to go, and we let go and enjoy the ride. And it must be a marriage—an energy flow back and forth—of taking action steps and letting go. In the letting go, that's where the journey unfolds. The beauty of the journey is where we are transformed. Everything we were so convinced couldn't possibly happen, all our self-imposed limitations, self-imposed sabotages, we come right up against them. We move past them and we look back. We almost feel like crying out of joy and knowing, *I am not that. I am so much more capable and limitless than I gave myself credit for. What else can I possibly do?* The other thing that happens on the journey that's exciting is when we let go, we sometimes end up places we didn't expect and opportunities come up we would never have known about had we been controlling everything. And so, the beauty of the journey is that things will be presented to us and they really are great gifts. We ramp up our confidence; our ability to be who we innately are becomes manifest in that journey.

DR. DEMBO: So Debbi, people are out there thinking to themselves, what if my dreams are unrealistic? Is that fear, or is that maybe a truth? Maybe what they're dreaming for is just an impossibility. What's your opinion on that?

DEBBI: Well, I am laughing. That means that people are thinking to themselves that their dream is impractical, improbable, and unlikely. Exactly. It is truth. Or is it? Take the Wright Brothers as an example. The Wright Brothers used to spend a great deal of time observing birds in flight. And they had a dream of making a flying machine for humans which was thought totally crazy by others. Over several years, they designed a series of gliders and flew numerous test glides. In spite of all kinds of problems, the Wrights determined that they could fulfill their dream. Finally in 1904, they made the first airplane flight. If the Wright Brothers had more realistic and ordinary goals at that time, they would hardly have achieved such success. Following ambitious dreams can not only make personal progress but can also prompt the development of a whole society. If Jules Verne had never written about space, air, or underwater travel, people could not soon have achieved air travel, invented practical submarines and devised practical means of space travel; if Martin Luther King had not dreamed of ending the racial segregation and discrimination, African-Americans would not have against discrimination; and civil rights in the United States and around the world would not have improved; if Bill Gates had not quit a famous university and started his own enterprise, we would not be working on computers. At first, all these ideas and goals were considered crazy and not realistic by most people, but it is the ambitious and unrealistic dreams that opened up a new era in different areas in our society.

I can tell you — if you're a fifty year old person and you're obese and you would like to be a ballet dancer, is it unrealistic? For a career, probably. However I would never dissuade you because if you have a passion for the ballet, you could work for a ballet company. Maybe you could team up with a ballet teacher and train. Maybe you can start dance classes and just see what is possible for you because I firmly believe that if you were given the dream – go make it happen! And the other piece is, if you have a dream and you're not sure it's realistic, I can give you so many examples from my own life where I was not clear about certain things but I knew I had a calling. I thought *well if I sit here and try to figure it all out, that will do nothing for me except waste a lot of time and energy. But if I actually take action steps and move forward, as though this is the right thing for me, I'll discover if it is or not.* I did that with public speaking. I wanted to be a motivational speaker, I wasn't clear if I loved it. I wrote a workshop and I was delivering it all over Los Angeles. It was awesome on one hand. It was great. But I realized quickly on: *I've been driven to do this and I'm so grateful I did. However, what I've discovered is this isn't it for me. It's something else.* And what's fantastic is, speaking professionally ultimately gave me many essential components that have created who I am today. I needed to be comfortable speaking in front of others. I needed to know how to write a workshop. I needed the pieces of what I discovered and the wisdom so that I'm able to disseminate what I do today. Pieces of motivational speaking are incorporated into what I do now. So – I say go out there. What else is life for? It doesn't have to be perfect. Let it be messy and wonderful but just go do it.

DR. DEMBO: So do we get ashamed? Do we get humbled to the embarrassment? A lot of people are so trapped with that Debbi. What is that moment when we know that we can dare to dream? That a dream can actually become our new reality.

DEBBI: You know for people who are existing in that--shame, embarrassment, trapped --that's a very, very small space to live in. Understand it's what's outside of that space that's compressing them in. So rather than trying to push yourself to a level that will create that level of stress, I would urge people start small. Trust your journey, start small. So let's say the best you can do is sit on the sofa and listen to Dr. Dembo's show. However, you've thought about how cool it would be to take a ballroom dancing class. Or what would it be like to walk on the beach every Saturday? What would that take to attend a ballroom class? Figure it out. Do you need to call several places in town and find out how much, when classes are, where it's located? What kind of equipment or clothes you would need, and then find the dance studio you resonate with. I say, follow the energy that you feel is right. Don't try to be logical, just follow that good-feeling energy. And the other thing I would suggest—and this is something I've done—sometimes I talk to myself like I'm a kid because I need to. When I really step outside of what feels like my comfort zone rather than push myself or bully myself, instead I'm kind and patient. I literally tell myself, *You know sweetie just go once. Go once, have the experience. If you hate it I promise you don't have to go back again. And if you love it…..* —and just take a wild guess what happens one hundred percent of the time? [LAUGHTER] Of course I love it and end up going back! As I step outside of my comfort zone; I'm always fascinated at how well everything turns out. And afterwards I look back and I wonder: *What was I thinking to try and stop myself? This was the most amazing experience.* Of course I'm going to keep breaking the barriers of my comfort zone. And you have the option that if something doesn't work for you, you don't have to experience it again. So start small, do the small things first. What I have found is when you start small and it works out and there is a feeling of success—like walking every Saturday on the beach — then a couple of months down the road you can dream just a little bit bigger and if you do that slowly and surely you'll start to expand out.

DR. DEMBO: The beautiful thing about everything you're saying to our listeners, which is so important and very much aligned with everything we talk about on our show, are the action steps. So many people today have more than one life within their life. They get divorced, they start over. There is some kind of transition. Changing careers either by choice or necessity. And these are the moments when these kinds of things come up. I remember when I got divorced years ago before I met Linda, saying to myself — and I do this for a living and I've worked with thousands of people over the course of thirty years — I remember saying to myself, *"Okay, Phil. It's time to practice what you preach. It's time to try something you've never done before just to see what it feels like."* I joined a tennis class and I gotta tell you it changed everything for me. Because what it does is give you the courage, a new view of yourself that you can actually try something different and see who you might be in a whole new context, a whole new identity. So let's talk action steps. Because you do a lot of that. What do you recommend? You say start small, then what?

DEBBI: Yes, it is all about action. Taking steps towards your dream. People talk about the Law of Attraction — so remember the last six letters of Attraction are Action. There's a reason for that. [LAUGHTER] You want to attract, you have to act. Maybe your dream is to travel; maybe it's to take a class. Maybe it's to start dating. Whatever it is, just write it on paper. Then write down underneath that what steps it will take. In general, from where you are right now — to the dream manifest, what needs to happen to get you there? You write it down. You must keep that sheet because each day you'll pull out the sheet and refer to it, for *what action step will I take today?* And every day you do something. No one is ever going make your dream come true for you. No one is going to take the action steps. The only one who can bring your dream into a living entity is you. When you start taking action it feels joyous. Celebrate it because this is your opportunity to do something different. In the past you've probably run away or given up the ghost. What if this time you just kept moving forward in spite of it and knew, *I'm going to be alright. It's okay to feel any feelings and do it anyway.* It's okay to start small, it's okay to take small steps, it's okay to accomplish your goal.

DR. DEMBO: That's wonderful. Debbi, you're wonderful. You're a dream come true for us. Thank you so much for joining us on the show.

END

Figure Out What You Want And Learn How To Ask For It

I love hearing from you folks. Please keep writing, I desire to inspire you forward. While we're on this planet let's bless ourselves and the world with who we are authentically. Why we're here and what we're meant to be doing. Be your amazing self now into the world, the planet sure needs us.

This is an excerpt from Steve Jobs' commencement address at Stanford University in 2005, which he called, <u>Love and Loss</u>. *"Sometimes life hits you in the head with a brick. Don't lose faith. I'm convinced that the only thing that kept me going was that I loved what I did. You've got to find what you love. And that is as true for your work as it is for your lovers. Your work is going to fill a large part of your life, and the only way to be truly satisfied is to do what you believe is great work. And the only way to do great work is to love what you do. If you haven't found it yet, keep looking. Don't settle. As with all matters of the heart, you'll know when you find it.*

And, like any great relationship, it just gets better and better as the years roll on. So keep looking until you find it. Don't settle." Steve Jobs lived from 1955 to 2011.

The one guarantee we all have in life, is that we are going to die. Each of us is going to leave this body, this incarnation and it is up to you to decide what kind of legacy to leave behind. We don't have an expiration date stamped on the bottom of our foot, so we need to decide what we want to be, what we want to accomplish and experience while we're here. What blueprint for your life do you prefer to leave behind, and in what condition do you desire to leave this planet when you go?

I was watching a movie this weekend and the protagonist decided she would go to go see a therapist. She doesn't actually carry through with the appointment. She leaves the appointment because she's too afraid to open up, and just as she's about to exit the office she steps back in and addresses the therapist by asking, *"Hey. You've been doing this a long time. You've seen thousands and thousands of patients. What's the one thing – the one secret that you can impart to me that you've learned"?* The therapist thinks and replies, *"That's a really good question."* And he considers this for a moment and replies, *"Figure out what you want, and learn how to ask for it."* So find out what you love, then inquire and make a request – of you, of others, of life. Figure out what you want and learn how to ask for it.

Next, I urge you to manage the minutiae in your life. In other words, just stop spending so much time on Facebook and Twitter, and instead keep your eye on the ball. Life goes by so fast. Right? *Tic-tic-tic.* The minutiae attempts to pull us away like a pretty shiny object. We can mindfully—instead—place our responsiveness, and our focus, back where we intend to end up. What do you want to achieve? Move your attention there instead. I laughed when I heard that the word "social-networking" is actually "social-*notworking*." When it comes to social networking it's said we're amusing ourselves to poverty. Time is up to you. What you do with it is based on decision. Choose to allocate your time since getting ahead is often about mastering time. You can mindfully choose where you're going to put your attention.

In his book, Through the Looking Glass, Lewis Carroll wrote, *"Sometimes I believed as many as six impossible things before breakfast."*

Remember, all you Dare-to-Dreamers—life isn't about finding yourself. Life is about creating yourself. The secret to managing life and success? Figure out what you want and learn how to ask for it.

Transcript

Debbi Dachinger: Interview with MARIBEL JIMENEZ

MARIBEL JIMENEZ:	Hello and welcome, everyone. This is Maribel Jimenez, your host, for the Dream Launch series where I have brought an amazing lineup of eighteen high level experts who are really out there living their dream. I brought them to you specifically to hear their expertise, to share about their journey, and any secrets to launching a successful online business that is full of flow and abundance. As you may have noticed, we have a theme for each day that encompasses parts of the journey that I have found in creating success online. Here we are in day one, and what we are focused on today is the dream. I'm super-excited to introduce Debbi Dachinger to you today, who is doing amazing work around Daring to Dream, as her book is called. Debbi's abundant career is in

using her voice to live out loud, teach and inspire others, to dare to dream, and make their dreams a reality. I'm so excited to have her with us kicking off this event, welcome to the call, Debbi.

DEBBI DACHINGER: Thank you Maribel. It is a pleasure to be with you and everybody who is listening. I'm excited to be part of this.

MARIBEL: Thank you Debbi. I want to start us off by asking if you could share a little about your own journey in creating your dream business online.

DEBBI: First of all, those of us who are doing business online, how blessed are we? Everything is online and available on the web. For those of us who are doing online work, it's great. I have a varied background, whether it was the period of time when I was a jewelry designer selling in high-end stores and online, singing in bands and selling our CDs online, when I was an actress, as a voiceover artist, and today, doing online radio and television and speaking and writing books –all of these creative careers used the Internet for customers, sales and to connect. What I love about being online right now is it has been successful for me. I find that because I'm doing work that people like - and this is a key - I'm providing a service that people need, so the work I do is well received and well followed. You can be amazing but if what you offer is not solving somebody's problem through information and the assistance people require, maybe that's why your business is having a tough time. It's helpful to figure out how to translate your message into something compelling that people need. I teach how they can create their dreams to come alive. I'm providing a service that people desire and I love teaching. Another key is that the more I am being myself and sharing the ways and methods I have learned, the more energy and volition my business gains. It keeps expanding; then the next piece unfolds and reveals the next piece. It's my job to step into the next piece. Holding oneself back never works. So when opportunities present themselves it is my job to figure out how to move ahead. I would say my journey in creating my dream business has been a pleasant surprise, to be living my dream in this way, is an amalgam of everything I have ever been and done, and I'm loving where I'm at.

MARIBEL: Yeah. I feel it. Are there any other areas or specific breaking points, or "a-ha's" that really started to shift your business dramatically?

DEBBI: There have been markers along the way that presented themselves to me and made significant differences. One a-ha was recognizing what I was meant to do. In the beginning when I started doing this little radio show, frankly I thought I was just trying to get my voice out there in a bigger way to get more voiceover work. That's the only reason I did it. Plus, I had just separated from my husband and everything was fairly emotional. All I knew was to keep moving forward. As time went on and I started to see the level of people coming on my show, the level of what I was capable of, something clicked. I realized I have a real gift here. As I was saying before about how dreams keep revealing themselves? I didn't know I would write a book. However, I did. It's always about recognizing, *I'm deeply interested in doing this, let me bring that into my life.* Opportunities are important. You don't have to have all the answers, which means if an opportunity presents itself and you think, *wow I think I would like to do that* *but I have no skill there,* or *I don't know how that will work out--* put all that aside and have faith in the fact that your desire can carry you through and you will learn what's needed along the way. Your true north is different than my true north. Another breaking point I have found is when I step into opportunities; I'm fascinated at what is possible. I'd like to share a story, if I may, of something I experienced this weekend that speaks to that. I've had a dream about doing a television show. For a long time I was writing to stations and networks to introduce myself and my show and say: "*Hello, I'm here.*" When Oprah was on TV and I knew she was going to start her OWN station, I sent out a: "*Hello.*" I felt like I got some interest but mostly I was only hearing an echo and crickets. [LAUGHTER] I have always had this *je ne se quois* about myself which is; *don't you see who I am and what I can do?!* I believe in myself, what I'm here to do, and what is possible. I'm a big proponent of taking action and letting go. So I let the TV show go and put my focus on other creative endeavors because I wasn't hearing back, and wouldn't you know when I released my dream, it's then that I heard from someone with a history in film and television who had been following my show. He said, *I think I can make both our dreams come true because I have been looking for a project such as yours. I want to put something on television that is going to make a difference at the level we're ready for, and I think you're the person.* I thought, "*life is good.*" So the director and I are working toward that goal. An event occurred this weekend that was of assist toward our goal. An event called GATE--Global Alliance for Transformational Entertainment—was created by John Raatz, a producer, who got together with his friends Jim Carrey, the actor and activist, and also Eckhart Tolle, the spiritual author. They created GATE, which brings Hollywood and spirituality together. These are my people! I was invited to interview celeb attendees at the affair. We were also invited to work the red carpet. My director came with a cameraman. This was the moment, I was working toward. The celebrities are lining up. The publicist is coming up and saying, "*it's time.*" But something's wrong; the camera is not operating. I have a big-time cameraman there, and he is spinning into anxiety because the equipment's not working and time is starting to tick by. In that situation when something is going wrong and someone is growing increasingly anxious, if I were to also get anxious I would compound the situation, thereby paralyzing the energy. Nothing is going to get better if I spin out of control too. Knowing that, I was patient until I realized the equipment and the cameraman's emotions were not getting better. If something didn't change I'd miss the opportunity, celebrities are already being interviewed by others; a publicist is coming to me and asking, *"what's going on? They are waiting to be interviewed by you?"* I had to step in; I could not accept what was going on because I had come too far for a failure at this juncture. The cameraman was telling the director all the things that were going wrong with the equipment, but this was the moment – we'd use it or lose it-- so I told him, "L*et the anxiety go. There is no place for it now. Right now you have one thing and one thing only to do: You have to make this work. We are going to start filming now. Whatever your Plan B is you must shift into it now."* Literally a minute later I had the microphone in my hand, the camera and lights functional and on, and we are filming, it's working, Plan B is in full force – we are filming and I am with Reverend Michael Bernard Beckwith, James Van Praagh, don Miguel Ruiz, Barbara Marx Hubbard, one transformational leader after another. And that's what's possible when you step into your power and own a moment, we all shifted and it all worked. Beautiful. Now, another thing that happened that day is, when I was changing into my red carpet dress, I lost the questions I'd written out to ask during the interviews. Losing the written questions turned out to be the best thing. It forced me to be fully present and connected with each guest and ask questions out of genuine curiosity. We ended up getting the most spectacular interviews. A lovely moment occurred once the red carpet was done, when the cameraman came to me and said, *"I really appreciate your professionalism. Thank you for getting me out of that mess by what you said."* I was grateful for him and for the experience. The evening was a great success. The specific break through was that we were able to create a Sizzle Reel to pitch to television networks from that evening's event. The making of this reel is impactful and in shopping it around and taking meetings and hopefully creating a television show based on my talk show and book – this will dramatically shift my business! So when I say that opportunities come up, how we show up, who we show up as--should always be as ourselves – our best selves. There is genius inside each of us. Instead of trying to act like or do business like anyone else, the genius of who you are is that you can be yourself take advantage of breaks that come your way by being prepared and find your niche in business. That's how you shine. Only you can do your thing in a way that nobody else can. You will get recognized for that.

MARIBEL: Wow. That was an amazing story. I would love to move into what you prepared to share with everyone, the big dream, and getting out of your comfort zone. I'd love for you to share more with us about that.

DEBBI: There are so many things that entrepreneurs can do. This is our time, isn't it? The old business model has changed as we once knew it. And we can conduct our business with love. We can get out of a comfort zone by connecting with the dream and those we do business with. I have amazing experiences and connections; tremendous results coming from that place. It's not an act - *if I act loving, I'll get such and such*. It really isn't. I believe in relationships. Influential people have at times stepped forward on my behalf and offered *I will do this for you* or *I would like to show up in this way for you*. I have received so much generosity and kindness and I'm the elephant who never forgets. [LAUGHTER] When people assist me like that I remember kindness, so when they express: *I need such and such* - I'm the first one in line to help. I will do what it takes to assist. Another thing of importance is when you have the big dream -- never wait for permission to do what you love. You don't need anyone else to grant your status. It's not about being the world's greatest expert. It's about being expert enough to accomplish your goals. A comfort zone is created when we believe: *I can't go into the next thing because I need all the answers first*. That thinking will never serve you. Instead learn to leap more, jump more and trust in yourself, and you'll be pleasantly surprised at how well things turn out. An example from my life is the story I just shared. A year ago if you had said I would be working a prestigious event with a camera and crew, filming at that level, operating with so much ease – well, what a difference a year makes! [LAUGHTER] It was the culmination of a lot of prep work coming together in my life. The day before the event, my boyfriend asked me, *Are you nervous?* I said *I'm not nervous, I'm excited.* The day came and because of everything I had done previously, both inner and outer, I felt calm and very present. I didn't need permission to be myself or do what I love doing to accomplish the goal I set up for myself. So it's ok to not have all the answers. I promise when you step forward anyway, you absorb much. I think it's about giving yourself permission to learn on the journey. What we don't yet know, we will pick up. That leads me to another point. Asking for help. Asking for help is everything from: Hiring a team. Handing off things you don't like to do, you don't want to do, or bring you down, slow you up, and you don't even care to learn about. Hire someone who is phenomenal at those tasks and loves doing them, anything that will free you up. I think time is money and it's important as we make more money to contract out our work and acquire a fantastic team. In addition, we can ask for help in little and big ways. For instance, I have a professional relationship with a wealthy individual and I had never gone to him for help. I had a project I was working on with a question I couldn't find an answer to when I realized, I'll bet he'd know. I asked him for assistance on this question and was touched by the caring information he provided in return. His response will influence and change what I am going to do. So it's ok and strongly suggested to ask for help.

Another thing for entrepreneurs in getting out of their comfort zone is -- don't be afraid to change direction. There are times when it's important to stop and re-assess. Consider that the way you're doing aspects of your business are not achieving the results you prefer, and maybe you need to look at what you're doing from a different angle and consider a change. Allow yourself and your business to be modified. Most people don't like change. No matter what, change is a natural occurrence in your life and you can actually initiate the transformation so that when something is not working you can make new decisions. Do you need a coach? Do you require a set of skills you don't have? Do you need to attend workshops to free you up? Do you need a mastermind group? Do you need a different tactic? Do you need a team? Are you trying to do everything on your own? Whatever it turns out to be, allow yourself the grace to ask yourself those questions from a permissive space, and be sincerely interested in the information that comes back. It's ok to change directions. I've certainly had to do it many, many times.

I also want to talk about fear. What happens if we're heading towards this amazing dream or entrepreneurship and we experience fear? Fear is paralyzing, as we all know, because it compounds itself. Fear is like the greatest lawyer in the world in the court of our lives. It starts making all sorts of claims and talks to the jury in our brain and starts convincing us we can't possibly do *that* because look at all these facts, and of course these factoids are correct in fear's estimation, even though they may have zero backup or statistics to go with them, but fear is so compelling we believe what it tells us. We can know we are living through the filter of fear if we recognize that we would rather stay where we are, even if it's unhappy and we're deteriorating, even if we really dream of being 'over there,' because at least we know *this* place. Instead can you allow yourself to move forward understanding this is not fear, this is just unfamiliar? So you can walk through fear and do it anyway. You were given the exact composition of who you are for good reason. So step into the dream. Just go there. Fly.

With fear comes the negative mind, which creates conditions for us to feel unworthy to move forward, because it basically lies to us. The truth is each of us is so magnificent that we are blinding. Remember the little bushel we are pretending to hide our light under? From Matthew 5:14-16: *"You are the light of the world. A city set on a hill cannot be hidden. Nor do people light a lamp and put it under a basket, but on a stand, and it gives light to all in the house. In the same way, let your light shine before others, so that they may see your good works and give glory to your father who is in heaven."*

Understand that you have the power to move through fear, to recognize it, to go out there and do your thing and prove to yourself, not only is it ok to get out of your comfort zone and manifest your big dream, but you are a rock star. You got this.

MARIBEL: What are you feeling right now that you want to do next, Debbi?

DEBBI: May I take you through some questions to shift the energy and possibilities? So here we go.

What talents, abilities and capabilities do you have that you are not acknowledging? What have you decided is not possible and refused to ask for that is truly possible that if you ask for it, will allow the universe to give you the dream life you desire to have? If you had any idea of how big a gift and contribution to the world you truly are, how much money would you allow yourself to receive? What are the infinite ways the universe can gift you? What would it take for your dream to show up? How can you be the energy that would allow the universe to give to you beyond your wildest dreams? What invention are you using to create the not-enough-money you are choosing? What invention are you using to create the neediness as motivation, are you choosing?

So you have this amazing dream, and

then what happens? Do you experience doubt? Do you abandon and sabotage your knowingness? Do you back off because you're afraid to fail? Do you know that no matter what happens you're okay? You have way more resilience than you give yourself credit for. Is it possible that deep inside, you sense you were born for greatness? Not ego-driven stardom but real greatness. That truly you have talents and gifts and things you naturally excel at. Is it possible that you were born to be a trailblazer and light at a time on this planet when leaders and chiefs are needed? Do you play small? Do you hope you are almost invisible? Which, by the way, means you don't have to be the person who changes the world?

What silliness are you using to create the defense of the valuelessness of you as the justification for being the unreal, fantastic, and phenomenal being you could truly choose to be? What foolishness are you using to create the defense of you not being the valuable product you are as the justification for being the unreal, fantastic, and phenomenal being you could be choosing but never choose to be? What if you knew that you are capable and that you will succeed at anything you decide to do? What if it really is that easy and joyous to move forward and generate your deepest desire? What if you are worthy and deserving and there is nothing you need to do except breathe and be yourself?

Thank you for allowing me to share that.

MARIBEL: Thank you for allowing me to participate in that. That was amazing. Beautiful. Thank you. I feel grounded and peaceful.

Debbi, what one piece of advice can you give our listeners that will support their journey in creating their dream?

DEBBI: I think your greatest magnificence is in who you are. I think most of us are so busy looking outside of ourselves for the answers. You were given the proclivities, the desires, the talents, and the exact makeup that you were for a reason. I know many of us grew up feeling incredibly different, like we don't fit in. We grew up wondering *who am I, and how does this all work?* I want to impart that what you perceive as you being dissimilar is actually what makes you unique and beautiful. We adore your authenticity, and strangeness and fabulousness. So whatever it is that makes you the freak that you are [LAUGHTER] whatever it is that comprises the genuine, stunning you — be that — be you---and that's how you'll be your greatest success.

MARIBEL: Beautiful. Thank you for that. That was a wonderful piece of advice. I want to thank you Debbi, for everything you shared. Thank you for joining us today on this first day of the series.

DEBBI: This was a positive experience. Just remember to turn your cant's into cans and your dreams into plans.

END

Transcript

Debbi Dachinger: Interview with Debra Poneman

DEBRA PONEMAN:	Hello, Everyone. This is your host, Debra Poneman with New Transformation Strategies. Now more than ever we need knowledge and tools to get us through these times. For this series I've brought together amazing people so we can learn from them and really thrive not just survive. And I know that if there is anyone that is beyond amazing, it's my beautiful, loving and open-hearted friend, Debbi Dachinger. Deb, Welcome.
DEBBI DACHINGER:	Hey Debra, it's so great to be with you today. A beautiful opening, thank you.
DEBRA:	Well thank you, thank you. I am just so happy that you're going to teach people how to Dare to Dream. And

we're going to have fun for the next hour. That I know for sure. So, here we go. Deb is here today to help you realize what you're able to create in your life. We'll cover a lot of topics, including how to gain clarity on your dreams; how to deal with doubts and fears and other dream busters. She is going to share easy-to-learn goal achievement systems; and--did I even tell everybody that you're a best-selling author? I said you're a best-selling author, and I didn't say the name of the book, which is Dare to Dream—

DEBBI: Yes. *Dare to Dream, This Life Counts.*

DEBRA: This Life Counts. And I know the book because I got to read it in pre-publication, and I was so blown away that I asked if I could give you an endorsement because it's an absolute gem. You are a gem, and now I want you to tell everybody about your journey, because a lot of people would love to be multi-award winning radio hosts. They would love to be best-selling authors. They would love to hear where you started and how you got to be where you are today.

DEBBI: Well, I believe that anybody can be anything. If you feel a passion or desire for your dreams--then dare to make those dreams into a reality--I believe dreams were given us by our soul and we can choose to experience it. That means our career, our job. That means our service. That means the hobbies we enjoy. Also owning something, our health, our education, family, something to experience, learning a language and health are other dream possibilities. We design our life spontaneously from day to day. If you will hone in for a moment on one dream you have already created, whether you have climbed Mount Everest, or maybe you got up in front of people and read your poetry, or there was a trip you dreamed of and went on. Or, maybe you desired to find real love and you manifested that. Or, a dance class. Anything at all. If you remember that feeling, what it was like to desire it, take the steps to acquire it, and then experience it, you know the joy of a dream and a goal come true. And just imagine if your life could look like that all the time.

I had to combat a lot to get where I am today – where I now understand how to make my dreams real and do whatever it takes and then enjoy my goals achieved. [LAUGHTER] I came from a very interesting place and often the thing that hurts us becomes our life challenge to realize that it's not okay to live like that or feel like this. For me, I developed the goal achievement tools so I could access what felt important to me, and ensure any childhood predicaments would not be the victor in holding me down. I ultimately desired to live my dreams out loud.

DEBRA: Well, you know you already have given everybody so much. Because, I just learned something from you and you might not have even noticed it. But usually when people teach others to live their passion, it's narrow. It's like it has to be your life's work. Discover your life's work. Discover what you were put here to do. And then people get very disappointed because they feel that their life's work is to write the great American novel but they're working as a legal secretary. But what you just said is, it could be your service, it could be your hobby. It doesn't necessarily have to be your career. You could be passionate about anything—and you can you can go and be the legal secretary but find and live your passion somewhere else. That's huge,

Deb. You know that?

DEBBI: We are told all the time in this life that we are here to learn, but life is not necessarily about lessons. Life is also about being happy. And when we hear those words--joy, happy, love--and then you look at your life. Is it being reflected? Do you experience that most of the time? And if not, where is there a lack of that? And how can you put the joy, the love, the happy back in? My experience is that it is intimately connected to the urgings to have certain experiences. If I give up my dreams I will ultimately be unhappy and on the wrong path. Some people give up dreams for their children. They say, *I can't, I have no time, it's all about my kids.* But the truth is when you see parents who are attentive and show up for their children and also pursue what brings them joy, you'll find a much happier family. And you'll find children who learn, by virtue of watching their parents fulfill their dreams, what it means to care about yourself at that level and how to accomplish a goal.

DEBRA: Two things. One is, you know my story that I did have this amazing career and my seminars were being taught all over the world, and I did give it up to be a mother at home. I always say to people, *"That doesn't mean that you're supposed to do that."* It's just that I followed my heart and I knew that I was put on Earth to be at home with my kids for those eighteen to twenty years. But don't think that that's what you're supposed to do. There are no supposed-to's. Like you said, just don't give up your passions or your dreams for anyone. And I have to ask you one other question because it is just bothering me. Are you going to tell us what it was that that you had to overcome? You don't have to, but are you willing to, or if not, that's okay.

DEBBI: Yes. I was conceived in Israel and I was born in New York. My mother had left my father and moved back to New York while pregnant with me. My father was a holocaust survivor and his story is incredible, what he went through, what he endured. So much of his identify had been crushed as a child because his experience surviving the war was severe, and as a consequence he chose not to show up, so I was a fatherless girl. I had a mother who was difficult to be around with a lot going on emotionally. And an older brother who was unhappy as a child in his circumstances, so I did not have an ally in my household growing up and there was much dysfunction. Those were the dynamics. I got tons of messages, whether they were intentional or not. What I felt was that I am not special. I am invisible. No one wants to hear me, and I felt dreadfully alone and abandoned. Dad was not in our life before I was born without saying goodbye or why he was leaving. And Mom would leave each morning to go to work and I'd be crying at the window everyday *"Please don't leave me, please don't leave me."* She would not turn around and kept walking to her car to go to work, which was traumatizing. Although there was chaos, my brother and I were also blessed because we had amazing grandparents who adored us, loved us, and showed up - they were incredible. We were close to them. From my home life I manufactured lots of beliefs that I decided were true about life, and about me, and most of the beliefs were not very nice thoughts about myself, so naturally that's what I established in my life. Back then, believe it or not, I was socially awkward and shy. Meanwhile, I had innate talents. What was fascinating was that the Universe, my soul and its blueprint gave me the ability to sing and act and be onstage with little fear, and it was actually a great joy. It was the happiest place I could be. As I got older and I went out into the world as an actress and singer, it was hit and miss. And everything that ensued in my life, whether it was about money, about love, about friendships, about travel, jobs, it always came from that core place of *I am abandoned. I am not enough, I am unlovable, I come from no family that wants me.* And that was what I had to overcome – the idea that I was broken. I talk about the gift and the wound concept because my sense is that we each have an opportunity, if we take it, to do a spirit-walk. It's a pilgrimage of the soul. And, if we choose to take on that inner darkness or wound, we can see if there's truth in what we originally decided about ourselves. *Am I really all those things? Am I really unlovable? Am I really not wanted?* I decided a long time ago to walk through anything in my way and do the inner healing work, whether through workshops, belief work, twelve step programs and energy work

- anything to go deep and change. And lord, I did it. I showed up for myself time and time again, and I cried and I raged and I expressed and I went inwards and I found horrible beliefs I had created about myself, probably when I was very young. I unearthed them, and when unveiled I saw all of the threads that had influenced my life. The doubt and the fear and the terror they created. And I dis-created them. It was such relief. And in that beautiful empty, sweet blank space, I instead put in a positive belief I preferred. I put in the belief that was going to serve me in my life. I did many years of work. The upshot was through that spirit walk; I came out on the other side, willing to be happy, to feel good being me and to fulfill my dreams. I tell this story because there are people who look at me today like, *boy that Debbi is successful. Whatever she does turns to gold. She works in radio and it becomes this. She writes a book and it becomes that. She gets up and speaks in front of people and that happens. She creates a product, etcetera.* And I want them to know it wasn't always like this. It was work and I made changes. Again it was the injury I was originally living through as a filter, which was transformed into a pearl; I am sure my soul set it up like this. Isn't it funny that some of the things I thought – *no one wants to listen to me*, and now look what do I do for a living? [LAUGHTER] It's a career based on being listened to, and also to intimately listen to others. And the issue of being loved, wanted and valued, and today there are people like you, Debra, and others in my close tribe who are such gorgeous people traveling this planet helping, assisting and shining a light along the way – you are my kinfolk. I have also had much healing within my family of origin in that I have a decent relationship with my mother today, and I consider my brother to be a close friend and someone I think highly of. We've been able to come together in a whole new and better way. Also, the amazing friends I have today, how fortunate I am to be connected with a soul family that I resonate with. I find that all those original wounds were the reason for me to walk through the emotional fire, to choose to reconcile and rebuild, to come out the other side, to live the life I always dreamed of, and then to offer what I learned to anyone with the same desire to achieve their dreams.

DEBRA: One of the things that is so inspiring

about that is a lot of people think there is a quick fix. And sometimes it seems that those are offered. I for one don't believe in quick fixes. Although there are technologies that can speed up our progress on the pass immensely, what you're saying is, do the spirit-walk where it takes you. And even if it takes you years, don't quit. Keep walking and you will come out on the other side. For somebody it might be a few months, for somebody it might be a few years, for somebody it might be a decade. But you will find your tribe, you will find the techniques that will help you through and your greatest challenge will ultimately be your greatest blessing.

DEBBI: Indeed. Absolutely. Different things work for everybody. You always have to take somebody from where they are, where they came from, to where they are willing to be today. Zig Ziglar said: *"You don't have to be great to start, but you have to start to be great."*

I received the most incredible email today. There is a gentleman who lives in Minnesota; he's a young dad whom I helped. He was trying all the success principles to change and he heard me speak, *"I give you permission to fail. You go for it, put it out there. If it doesn't work out, fantastic."* Because in our society, we have these ideas that it's only about success. But if failure comes up, we don't want to talk about it, and a lot of people get depressed and letdown. So disappointed that they turn their backs on their dreams. I say, instead, go for it. *I give you the freedom to fail*, I told him and the whole audience at the event. *In fact I want you to embrace it.* The best people in history, the greatest inventors, and athletes have all failed. One thing we can do is brush ourselves off and get back up. We have all failed. So what? One of the positive aspects of failure is, you learn from it. I have. Every time something has looked like I started out on this path, it didn't work; ooh, failure. *Wah-wah-wah* and then, I get back up and ask, *what is to be learned from that? What did I do? What did I bring to that party?* Or, *who did I invite to that party?* [LAUGHTER] So the bottom line is the freedom to fail. This fellow wrote me the most beautiful email and said, *Thank you for sharing the idea of embracing failure because it gives me the power to do anything I want. If I'm not afraid of failure, I can do anything. If I fail at something, I can learn from it, go out and do it again.* And then he said, *I am going* to use this to cure my terror of public speaking. With my brain and ambition, I could be anything in the world but the one thing that has always held me back is public speaking. I hate meetings, I can't give speeches, I freak out talking to more than a few people at a time. I blush, I stammer, I can't do it for fear of looking like a fool. You just taught me I can give myself permission to fail, and just do it. For the first time in my life, I am going to do it. I am going to talk in a meeting, I am going to give a presentation, and I am going to get a better job that includes public speaking. OMG, right? Total life change. That email made my day.

DEBRA: I know you teach what holds people back from attaining their goal, and that's failure. What else holds people back from attaining their dreams and goals, and what can they do about it? [LAUGHTER]

DEBBI: The umbrella is "overwhelm." The feeling comes up, and people go into overwhelm, and there is total back-off from the dream or goal. Forget about trying to accomplish any dream perfectly. Relax on the rigidity. [LAUGHTER] There's no such thing as all or nothing. Pay attention to what lights you up, not to what you're "supposed" to do. Start right now. What would you do, how would you share your inner light if you were willing to just fling it out there in the world? [LAUGHTER] Stand in your courage and give yourself permission to dare. If what comes up is "overwhelm," ask yourself *"am I coming from love or am I coming from fear?"* Fear and overwhelm is what destroys the dream. What if instead you decided that your dream is an inspired adventure, this moment has no limits and everything can happen right now, no matter what? Start *being* successful instead of *becoming* successful.

DEBRA: This is absolutely powerful. What do you say to those of us who have a little bit of those dream busters going on? [LAUGHTER]

DEBBI: It's like a dream buster's stew, isn't it? [LAUGHTER] Here's the deal. You actually do not have to have all your ducks in a row. You don't have to have it all figured out, all your beliefs settled and aligned and correct. You don't have to be fully healed and re-birthed and everything else. You can just know the goal and dream and take action steps, and it is enough. I am a firm believer that our soul chose a blueprint before we came into this life of generally what it was going to be like and why. It's up to us to execute it. God/Goddess would never give us the dream without the power to make it come true. If you hear nothing else today, just know that. With that desire and taking the right steps, it will work by the way. Some dreams are super easy and manifest quickly. Some take longer, some take years. But do you have what it takes? To show up for your dreams and take a step? Yes. Take a lot of steps? Every day do something else toward your dream? The feeling you get inside when you show up for yourself and your life in that way will completely change you. All those little problems start to self-correct. Fear? Fear is like a horror movie. We watch a horror movie and we suspend the moment to pretend it's not a movie, to pretend that person we're watching in the horror movie isn't so stupid to go downstairs when the big monster is there. We do the same things to ourselves with fear. We terrorize ourselves with fear of the unknown and then pretend it's real. But it's an illusion. It's just an energy we use to sabotage ourselves. We make-believe fear is real. Okay, cool. Take steps anyway, and see who is right. Because I know for sure when I've shown up, those catastrophes I was certain were going to happen? They never happen. That's when fear starts to diminish; its voice loses validity.

DEBRA: Very powerful.

DEBBI: You picture a horse at a race track, and they're behind the gates ready to run. As soon as they lift those gates, off the horses charge down the track. These horses are built to race. It's like that with our dreams and goals. They are just sitting at that gate building momentum. What happens to that dream energy when it is not allowed to run free? It self-implodes. Or you can shift your attention, lift the opening and create the life of your dreams.

DEBRA: I love that you said we wouldn't be given the dream if we didn't have the power to make it come true.

DEBBI: Exactly. If we were given the dream, we were given the power to make it come true. If you desire your wildest dreams to come true, you have to remain wildly true to yourself. And remember that you're a big, giant answer to someone else's prayer.

DEBRA: When your book came out, I did a mailing to my list, and even I got thank you letters from people. I did too. [LAUGHTER]

DEBBI: Thank you so much for that, Debra. I hear from coaches who write and say, *Your book is now required reading for my clients. Anytime they start working with me, they have to read Dare to Dream: This Life Counts.* I am humbled by that.

Moving forward, there are some life rules such as: 1) If you do not GO after what you want, you'll never have it. 2) If you do not ASK, the answer will always be no, and 3) If you do not STEP forward, you'll always be in the same place.

DEBRA: Yes, powerful! We talked about how lack of worthiness plays a role in whether people can attain success. I think you said you're going to take the listeners through an exercise, I think around worthiness? I think I'm ready for an exercise. [LAUGHTER]

DEBBI: Yes, let's do an exercise on worthiness. As I talk, close your eyes and breathe.

Just take in the air and then release through your breath everything you're carrying and don't need to. Take a deep breath of air and breathe out to release anxiety and stress, time, limits and worry. Take in another beautiful breath. Release the air, effortless. Hold onto nothing. You have everything you need right now. Regardless of where you are or what is going on in your life presently, continue with your breath in and your breath out. Breathe and go back in your life ten years. Ten years ago. We're sending you back one decade to yourself then. Taking all of who you are now and what you know today, back. Ten years ago. When you get there, remember your age then, where you lived, what you were doing, spend a few moments observing yourself then. What were you like? What were you doing? Where were you physically? Spiritually? Where were you emotionally? Make note of where you lived, the relationship you were in, and how you made money. Now observing your past self, think about how much you have changed, how much you have learned. Think about how much you have grown and how far you have come. How have you evolved in the past ten years? Have you survived changes and perceived crises? Any challenges or obstacles? Did you make it through? Back then those situations felt insurmountable, didn't they? Look at who and where you are now. From who you are now, what wisdom can you impart to the now you? Can you see a through-line that any pain or difficulty you experienced actually shaped and made you who you are today? What do you notice looking at yourself then compared to who you are today? Is it possible that going back instills a feeling of magic and miracle over the amount of awareness you contain today? In the midst of that, do you feel some faith in yourself and in life?

Now in your visualization, I want you to fast-forward ten years from where you are today, go forward ten years. Given your current intention to create, evolve, I want you to imagine at ten years past your age now ~ where you see yourself, physically, spiritually, mentally, and emotionally. Be there now. If today you are going through any challenges in your today, can you shift your perception to the idea that your current challenges offer you the opportunity to grow into who you want to be? That what you perceive as a challenge will assist you to overcome and grow into who you are meant to be in ten years? Allow your future self, who is already everything you desire to be today, to observe you now. Allow that loving future self to give you some advice and tips, and just breathe and listen. Perspective is everything. You are worthy. You are valuable.

Come back to today, the present, with the information from the past and from your future self. Take those gems that you just received and be complete. Wiggle your fingers and toes. Breathe. Come back, and if anyone feels a little light-headed, imagine roots growing out from the bottoms of your feet and going into the earth and grab big giant rocks and soil. Be present here now, perfectly okay. Fine. All is well.

DEBRA: Wow. Very, very profound. Can I share something?

DEBBI: Yes, I would love that.

DEBRA: What was so interesting for me was when you told us to go back ten years ago. I realized that ten years ago, almost to the day last weekend, my daughter and mother and I had a triple bat mitzvah. My mother was in her eighties, and my daughter was thirteen, I won't say how old I was. [LAUGHTER] It was almost exactly ten years ago. I realized that through the knowledge that I gain from the people on this telesummit, and from amazing teachers like you who I have had the privilege of being in contact with over the past years, I looked at myself and I saw that my huge challenge has always been speaking up for myself. No feeling that I was worthy enough to speak up for myself. Ten years ago, I saw some things that happened during that wonderful time that I didn't speak up for myself or ask for what I wanted, and I realized how far I have come using the techniques I have learned from all my wonderful guests. I also realized how much further I have to go with my talent in the insight that I have, is we continually do our spirit-walk. It's not that we cross that one off the list. It's that we make progress and then we can see even greater progress that we could make on the issues that we came in here into this lifetime willingly, the challenges that we willingly came to deal with. Is that right?

DEBBI: Debra, that is so profound. Thank you for sharing your insights. Absolutely. You have been given profound gifts. Speaking up for yourself is an area that plagues you, and the fact that with detachment you could see the through-line from ten years ago where this issue was, to where you are today, and that it's not gone but it's profoundly changed, is commendable. The spirit walk gets easier and it does continue.

DEBRA: I love that word. You see the "through-line." We have our challenges and we see our through-line and see how far we have come, and how much more we have to do to continue on that path. Wow.

DEBBI: Did you know that courage means in spite of fear? Can we show up for big things in our life in spite of fear? I like to use a metaphor - when you think about baby birds, they're born somewhere up in a tree in a nest. They have mommy and daddy bird to feed them worms. All is well. But one day they've grown just enough that it is time for them to leave the nest. Mom and Dad with their little beaks are pushing their baby toward the edge for their first solo flight, and the baby bird gets to the edge and goes, *"Oh my God. Don't push me because if you do, I'm gonna fall."* But Mom and Dad know better because it is in the DNA. It is what birds are meant to do, and they push. Little bird is not cool with looking over the edge because they are scared. They feel the instinct to fly, and from fear they go back into the nest. Back and forth, until they just jump and go for it. The little bird leaps and the wings open. They may be awkward at first, but they sort of fly. The baby bird lands and they realize, *oh my, that wasn't so hard, I have what it takes, I can fly; that was pretty cool.* Then they do it again. You watch the baby bird a couple of months later, and that little bird is like, *oh, I fly all the time. Wasn't it silly that I was afraid?* And that's how we can treat fear. *Oh how interesting.* It can be our through-line. We can get to the edge of our nest, or comfort zone, and know, *it's time to jump*, and when you leap it will be okay. Always.

DEBRA: I know you said a loving net will catch you, and there are angels and guides and unseen friends there also to catch you, so you land softly.

DEBBI: Can I tell you a beautiful story about

belief in a loving net and faith? One of my favorite writers, John Irving, who writes about amazing, quirky characters, wrote a book called *A Prayer for Owen Meany*. In the story, two young boys grow up together, Owen Meany and John. Owen deeply believes in God. John, not so much. John never understands how Owen could have such an unwavering, strong belief in a God that can't be seen; John finds it very strange, but still Owen and John are the best of friends. One day they are playing basketball. They are at a church with a basketball court and several religious statues are around. As they are playing basketball, Owen Meany asks John if he can see the statue of Mother Mary, which is just off to the right of the basketball court? John says *Yes, I see it, she is right there.* They resume playing. An hour later, Owen asks John if he can see the statue of Mother Mary? John turns and looks at the statue. *Yes, she is still there.* They turn around and they keep playing. This goes on for hours, every so often Owen asks the same question if the statue is still there? And John looks to see the statue and confirms the statue is still there. Now the sun is gone down, it's dark, they are still playing basketball, and

Owen asks again, *can you see the statue?* And by now John is getting exacerbated by the same question and yells, *"No I can't see the statue."* Owen asks, *"But is the statue there?"* John yells *"Yes, it's there."* *"But,"* Owen asks *"how can you tell? It's too dark. You can't see the statue?!"* John said, *"Yes, that's true I can't see it, but I know the statue is there."* Owen asked *"How do you know?"* John yelled, *"I do! I just do. I believe with every ounce of me that the statue is there. I just know!"* And Owen says *"Exactly John, that's how it is with me and God. I can't see God, but I absolutely know that God is there."* That's a scene from my all-time favorite book.

That is what it's like when we create a dream. We can't see it yet, but we fire up our faith anyway. It's not here yet. But will it come? Absolutely. Chances are it will be even better than your wild imaginings. Part of what we have to do and understand is that, it's often the journey. It's what happens between us and our desire. It is part of our soul's walk. We have to go through that before we get there. It's often humbling and magical and surprising and it is the journey we have to take. It is about faith, knowing even though we don't see yet.

Believing with absolute certainty. Not being able to see because it's still too dark, but just knowing with every fiber of our being.

DEBRA: Well, Darling. This is definitely one of the highlights of my series. Before we sign off is there anything else you want to share? Any final words?

DEBBI: I want to impart to everybody to keep your eye on the ball. Always keep your goals in sight. If you falter, if you're having a tough time, it started to manifest but then it feels like an obstacle came in your path. Or you didn't start, or you're almost there and you're getting tired and you don't see the light. Here is a little something you can remember. There was a woman — she's actually the first woman who ever swam from Catalina Island to the California coast. She was also the first woman to swim the English Channel in both directions. Her name was Florence Chadwick; at thirty-four years old she attempted to complete the swim. It was a big deal. All the boats were around her, they're taking her picture, they're charting her swim, her trainer is in a boat, her mom is in a boat, everyone's encouraging her, "Go Florence, go." And she's swimming and swimming and then—she had been swimming for almost sixteen hours. She felt tired, the sea was icy, the fog was dense. She could barely even see the support boats around her. And people were watching on TV, they want her to accomplish this, right? Don't we all want to see people succeed? Her mom and trainer saying, *Florence keep going. Seriously, it's not much further.* But all Florence could see was a giant wall of fog. She said; *please just pull me in to the boat — I am going to quit.* And you know what? They pulled her into the boat and she discovered she only had a half mile more to swim. A half mile to her goal and she chose to be pulled out. So they pull her out, she's thawing [LAUGHTER] on the beach hours later. She's being interviewed by a reporter and Florence said, *I'm really not going to excuse myself because if I had seen the land I would have made it.* It wasn't fatigue; it wasn't even the cold water that ended up defeating her, it was the fog. It was that she was unable to see the end of her goal. Remember what I said in the beginning about failure? We learn from our failure. So Florence learned and said, *oh. I see what happens with me. So if I don't see something I don't believe it's there and then I quit on myself. I'm going to do my next swim differently.* Two months later, Florence was a strong woman. She went right back out in the ocean to swim again. And as irony would have it, again there was some dense fog. [LAUGHTER]. Florence is swimming and there is fog but this time her faith is intact. Her goal is in her mind—so clear. She knows that somewhere behind that fog is land. And because she knew that, she had faith; she fired it up and kept going no matter what. She made it, she completed the swim. Florence Chadwick became the first woman to swim the Catalina Channel. And she eclipsed the men's record by two hours. Go Florence. Remember you may not be able to see it yet, but it is there. We all have the same capability to have faith and to choose to keep going. If you can conceive it, you can truly achieve it. Don't stop before the miracle.

DEBRA: I am inspired. Deb, thank you so much.

END

Quotable

"Be silent and listen to the powerful wisdom from within. Trust and follow that knowing."

"Find the unique answer to why you're here. You will resonate with it deeply. Act on your purpose."

"Mediate on your goals, write them down and start taking action every day. Each step will take you towards what you dream of."

"Feel your fear, and go after your dream anyway."

"We are capable of achieving the most tremendous goals if we believe we can achieve them."

"The saddest words in life are: "I could have been..." Taking action boils your goals down to self-discipline."

"What is the one thing in your business that if you just get it will change your business? Now focus on that and only that."

"When nothing goes right, go left!"

"Your biggest challenge isn't someone else. It's the ache in your gut and the burning in your soul, and the voice inside you that is chanting 'CAN'T'. Don't you listen, just push through until you hear your inner voice murmur 'can', and you will discover that the person you were is no match for the person you really are."

"When feeling overwhelmed by a faraway goal, repeat the following: I have it within me right now, to get me to where I want to be tomorrow."

"All glory comes from daring to begin your dreams."

"Dreams don't work unless you do."

"There are 1,440 minutes in a day. Use 20 of them to take action towards your dream."

- Debbi Dachinger

Transcript

Debbi Dachinger: Interview with Farhana Dhalla

FARHANA DHALLA: Welcome everyone to Instant Transformation. I'm Farhanna Dallah and I am excited to be the host of this event. We're exploring this question — *is instant transformation possible?* I am really excited to bring to you, Debbi Dachinger. Welcome.

DEBBI DACHINGER: Hello, Farhanna. Good to be here with you.

FARHANA: The name of our series is Instant Transformation. What's your take on that? Do you think instant transformation is possible?

DEBBI: I know it's possible. I think it's predicated on what goes on inside of a person - how hungry is somebody? I like that you use the word transformation. Transformation to me is alchemy, right? You're taking one state and you're transforming it to something better. You're taking it from a lesser state and making it into gold. Throughout our lives we all have transforming opportunities. *What am I going to do in this moment, what am I going to decide? Am I going to go for the Big Kahuna here, or am I going to slink back into the stasis of who I have been?* Those who take the road to their dreams are the ones who transform. So is it possible? You bet. We can alter and makeover our life and our being. It's all about decisions and choices.

FARHANA: What is the moment for you where you had that shift? Where you knew that you had created alchemy. What was the moment before you've created the alchemy that created the alchemy?

DEBBI: I have had a lot of them, and those moments literally change one's trajectory. I remember when I was young and was unable to accept a compliment. It actually felt uneasy for me to be complimented. I was coming into my looks; I was just starting college and it was awkward whenever somebody said, *"You're pretty."* I had traveled back home to New York and I was very close to my grandfather. I was visiting my grandparents and while outside their house we were talking to their neighbors. I remember their neighbor, a man who owned race horses—I'd known him since I was a little girl. After our conversation, my grandfather and I went back in his house and grandpa mentioned that his neighbor told him I was pretty and I confessed, *"I hate when someone compliments me. I don't know what to do with it and it's really uncomfortable."* My grandfather was very wise and with lovely insight said, *"You know what, sweetheart. I understand. What you can do when someone gives you a compliment, is just say thank you. Say thank you until you mean it ~ it may take years. But keep saying thank you until it becomes a part of you, and when you are complimented feel appreciation for the gift the person has given you through their words."* It was a huge turning point. From that moment on, when people said nice things to me my response was a heartfelt--*"thank you."* The alchemy came decades later when some good friends told me, *"You know what I like about you, Debbi? The way you accept and receive a compliment. When we give you kudos or praise it feels so good because we can tell that you really let it in."* Wow—mission accomplished. My friends did not even know the back story to where I had once operated from, the wisdom given me by my grandfather, and the ensuing transformation. I completely, with ease and thankfulness, believe and receive compliments today.

Another time alchemy was created, was a time when I took dance class five days a week and I had dance teachers who, for whatever reason, couldn't stand me. [LAUGHTER] I would attend dance class every morning—I majored in Performing Arts at U.S.C.; I would show up every day at the dance studio—and every day the woman of this dance teaching team would say demeaning things to me. And I took it; for six months, five days a week she would speak to me in a way that you'd never want said or done to a student; I would boil inside. And so it went, I'd go to dance class and the dance teacher would put me down. It was a performing arts requisite to take dance class five days a week, and each of those days I was being undervalued. One day, I cannot tell you why it was different, but I had had enough, I had surpassed my breaking point and said, to myself, *no more. I will never take this again.* I asked both teachers if I could speak with them after class. We walked outside the classroom, the dance teachers: husband, wife and me. I was shaking. My heart was banging—*thump, thump, thump*—because I had not spoken up for myself before. I told them what it had been like to be treated in that way and said, *"You will never speak to me like that again and you will deal with me appropriately from now on. It stops here."* Now, because my energy truly matched my words it was clear to all three of us I was speaking the truth. And that's what happened. Not only did she not treat me poorly again, but frankly, she stopped speaking to me altogether. The silent treatment sucked [LAUGHTER] however even that was manna from heaven compared to the bullying. A month later I was performing in a musical and had a leading role. Unbeknownst to me, the dance teachers, husband and wife, were in the audience. The next day of dance class when I walked in as usual, instead of receiving the silent treatment, they both came up to greet me and expressed how much they loved the show and how moved they were by my performance. They were gushing and saying I was a star. Apparently they were surprised by my talent, and realized this girl (me) they had been picking on had talent with a lot to offer. Our entire relationship changed and thereafter they became mentors to me. I look back on that moment with such gratitude; that dance teacher taught me how to have a voice. I could have continued to choose to be a doormat, however the alchemy, the transformation in that moment was when I said, *not me, not ever again;* I learned a big lesson from that experience which goes out with me into the world; self-care and boundaries are an integral part of where I operate from today.

FARHANA: Wow. One thing that strikes me is that it was your decision to have a different relationship with her. It doesn't mean that you won't have these things come up; it just means your decision was stronger than your fear.

DEBBI: That's what it takes to live our lives. From my estimation, everything is predicated by decisions first. Frankly this man and woman were extremely talented and had much to offer me as teachers and choreographers. And in that flash, when I spoke up, shaking and full of fury for the judgment I'd received, I was kind of amazed with myself. [LAUGHTER] I was so happy that I stuck up for me and expressed myself and that I meant what I said and said what I meant. After that momentous day, all the pain surrounding that event was truly gone. My favorite part is that I never set out to prove them wrong, to convince them of the depth or level of ability I had. It was a God-incident (co-incident led by God) that caused them to be in the audience in a show I was performing in and finally, really see me – singing and acting – and get it, who the heck I was. I was moved by their response after the show and it was clear from then on they were fully on my team. It all had a very happy ending. And honestly if they had not played their part so well, I would not have had the opportunity to learn that lesson and be changed for good. So I am grateful.

FARHANA: Fantastic story and outcome! Thanks for sharing that. About a month ago I heard you speak and one of the things you mentioned was when you decided to become a marathon runner. At the time you were a smoker and you had never even run before. It was bold. [LAUGHTER] The boldness of the vision, even though the current state didn't match the vision, your commitment to the vision was so steadfast. Part of the process for us to merge with the instant transformation we already see in our mind's eye is to actually have a plan.

DEBBI: Exactly. By the way, I'm not a smoker anymore. I've been off of them over fourteen years. Thank you lord. And it was a very bold choice, you're right. My marathon experience contains all the elements of making dreams come true. I completed my first marathon—because it was my dream. It didn't seem attainable, and that's a component of dreams. The dream feels bigger than us and challenging. The idea of doing a marathon was huge. I thought *twenty-six point two miles? Come on.* [LAUGHTER] I wasn't sure how to get there, but I wanted it. The passion was in me and I felt a crazy longing to do it. I did everything right. I did the research. I found out how to train for a marathon. I aligned myself with institutions already set up for people like me where I could train, and I showed up for the training sessions twice a week and also kept up with the mileage training on my own the other 5 days of the week. Eight months later came the big day, I was well trained, I had all the right equipment and shoes and I completed the L.A. Marathon. When I crossed the finish line it was ginormous and informing to me of what's possible. What I'm really capable of. So the next year—this is where it gets juicy. I had a friend come to me and say, *"Do the marathon with me this year."* I really didn't want to because I felt like I had succeeded the previous year. But I adored her and knew it would allow me to have fun friendship time with her. We started working out together and four months into the training she said, *"I can't complete this, I have to bow out."* Here we go: the precipice. *Oh my god, what am I going to do? Am I going to tank this whole idea and four months of training, or do I create a new dream and a goal?* I decided, *I'm going for a big, juicy, almost unobtainable goal.* I decided, *I'm going to cut thirty minutes off of my time at the finish line.* Anyone who has done twenty-six point-two miles knows that to take thirty minutes off your finish time is a big number to go after. But it was exciting. I trained well. I aligned myself with a new teammate who was an unbelievable race-walker. She was so fast. And two weeks before the actual race, every day for five minutes in the evening I would visualize myself crossing the finish line, seeing the time as I crossed and feeling the phenomenal feelings having thirty minutes shaved off the time. Every night, two weeks, that's what I did, visualize and feel it. Come the day of the race—the actual marathon—the day has begun quite early, as usual and the day's going well, I feel good and strong. The miles are ticking by, Mile ten, fifteen, and --I do what my body always does for some reason, I'm very slow in the beginning, in the start of the marathon, and it takes quite a few miles for my speed to kick in. Then at Mile eighteen my body comes alive – at a time when everybody else's body is falling apart. *Tic, tic, tic.* I'm starting to go so fast the gal I've been training with can't keep up and tells me, *"Go, go."* At Mile twenty-five I realize I don't know if I'm going to meet the goal time I set for myself but I do know I'm going to finish faster than last year, I can tell. I don't think anyone's going to see me at the finish line because I didn't tell anyone about my goal - bummer! So no one knows I'm attempting a new finish time. I'm coming around the final street corner almost at the end of the marathon, when I hear a voice in the crowd shouting my name, and I look over and there is my mother who has somehow intuited that I'm going to be early. And there she is, witnessing the moment; having someone there to see it meant everything. And I'm running towards the finish line ---just as I did in all my visualizations --and I look up at the clock and I see my final time. I cross through the finish line and I start to cry. The volunteers come up to remove the chip from my shoe and ask, *are you okay?* —because I'm crying and I said, "I'm happy, I'm happy, I'm full of joy." Because when I crossed through the finish line and looked up at the clock — the time showed that I had cut one hour off my finish time. Not thirty minutes as I imagined every night for two weeks, but one full hour taken off my end time. Talk about alchemy.

FARHANA: Oh, my goodness. Wow.

DEBBI: And that is the power that we all contain. In quantum physics we can shift anything. You bet. And I was willing. I was willing to do whatever it took to experience that. So what else is possible? How big can we each transform....

FARHANA: Wow. There are so many lessons delivered in that example. Okay, so I love the correlation of your visions and goals. Tell us more about that and the impact that has.

DEBBI: We have to use all our senses when we want to move forward; we have riches at our disposal. For each, some senses are more powerful than others. Whether it's listening, feeling, or touch or visualization. We can use all of these to access the power inside of us. Also time has sped up. We're being called to play very big right now which is why dreams and goals are so important. I know that a lot of your listeners enjoy receiving energy work because we all want those quick changes. My work is spiritually based, plus the earthly tools so it's a combo platter of the spiritual energy and the pragmatics. Both are what is needed to effectively move forward.

FARHANA: You keep using the word alignment. Tell us about that because I really want to understand that language distinction and what that means practically.

DEBBI: Alignment is how we position ourselves, how we arrange ourselves in regards to our values and our dreams. If you've ever heard somebody say *I want to lose weight* but they remain the same weight, it's because they have not aligned their outward action with their inward intention. It's words; it's a wish. They're not going to get very far. But when you have a plan, you have a knowing of how you're going to get yourself from here to there. You make the decision to do what it takes on the inside and the outside and then it happens. The same thing if somebody wants to quit a habit. The same thing if somebody says I'm going to travel or I want to take dance classes. There's an "I want," dot, dot, dot, that doesn't go far. Or instead someone can create an I Am which has an *"I am totally going to do this. Bring it,"* distinction to it.

FARHANA: You're so right. There is totally two different power streams behind them. I Am is a very powerful statement to create an alignment.

DEBBI: "I Am" is the name of God. "I Am," is what Moses brought down from the mountain when he said *I just met Yahweh and I can tell you what the name of God means, it means I Am.* I Am is the point of all creation. I also want to share that for some people there are elements of confusion in moving toward their dream because they think, *"Oh, I just have to affirm this and it's going to happen,"* and again that's wishful thinking. Rather, make a decision, create a strategy, put it into a strong I Am and a decision and from there you can execute the steps—take action to get there and I can promise you, if you do that it works. It works every time.

FARHANA: Wow. I just thought of something that I haven't thought about in this term before. This whole thing about the goals I had actually achieved. It's important to be clear on our goals so we can actually know when we get our upshot of energy.

DEBBI: Exactly, Farhanna. The truly exciting thing is that it's really never ending. It's exponential. For anyone out there who has been invested in suffering or struggling, if you're thinking, *oh my gosh that's me. That feels like my life.* That's all it is. All it is is a story that you tell yourself and have bought into. You can take the same passion you've had to live a story of struggle and suffering and shift gears. Just like you're driving a car, just shift those gears and align with a new intention. [LAUGHTER] Here's what to do to align with your dream and goal: 1) Trust that you will always be looked after. Act as if there is an infinite energy that is there to protect and guide you. 2) Tell the Truth. Is anything worth sacrificing your vital spirit and joyous experiences for? 3) Accept Responsibility for your life and the events in it. 4) Come from the Heart and rid yourself of Fear. Fear constricts the wellness of life. If you truly come from the heart, you cannot have any fears. 5) Have Sweet Dreams...When you go to bed at night picture the life and circumstances you desire to create. Drift off to sleep with these positive pictures being the last idea and imagery in your head as you fall asleep, this technique works wonders.

FARHANA: When we feel fearful perhaps we're actually excited.

DEBBI: Agreed, a hundred percent. There's really nothing stopping you.

FARHANA: One of the questions for so many is *why am I here?* What are your thoughts on that?

DEBBI: I think we're here because each of us is a delicious, unique contribution to humanity, to our planet, and beyond. It's been said that the purpose of life is to discover your gift, and the meaning of life is to give it away.

FARHANA: I love that. I'm so going to Facebook quote you today. [LAUGHTER]

DEBBI: The truth is we are divine. We're a piece of the design and we're blessed with this lifetime --it's time now to step up and express who we are. How can we choose to live this life? Remember, at any moment you can re-choose anything, you can decide to alter how you experience your life. You can choose joy and delight and prosperity and adventure. You can change your decisions at will. You can change your direction; you can decide what you want to think, feel and do. You're here to treat yourself well and with love. You are here to be of service, through your gifts, and you're needed. Drink in your bigness, your love, and the exhilaration of your own nature. Your dreams and goals, they're not frivolous. What was instilled in your soul is a call to you to live your dreams out loud using your voice, your gift, your humanity. And that's why you're here. You committed before you ever came into this body to be present in this life, living your full potential, using your entire beingness. That's what's called for, is to express your unique contribution.

FARHANA: Often we discount the impulses that come into our head of *I want to try this,* or *I want to experience that.* But those are actually the conversations we're having of course that help guide us to why we're here, and the gifts we have to give.

DEBBI: That's why it's important to embrace your inclinations. Why you are built the way you are, and I'm the way I am. Rather than denying the guidance we receive, we can instead welcome all of it. [LAUGHTER]. Including all of who we are and all of what is.

FARHANA: It's a come as you are party. Life is come as you are. [LAUGHTER]

DEBBI: Exactly. [LAUGHTER] To embrace who you are because your involvement in life has impact.

FARHANA: Wow. Do you have any thoughts as to why we fail at our goals?

DEBBI: People fail to achieve their goals because of several reasons. They don't have the correct resources. That could be an education, funds, knowledge, research or training. Next is procrastination. When you say *"I will do that tomorrow"* generally you won't complete it tomorrow. By the time tomorrow gets here, it is today. You have to act in today in order to accomplish anything tomorrow. The third reason for failure to achieve goals is from lack of or improper planning. It is a good possibility that you have not paid enough attention to the details. When setting goals, keep in mind these three truths: life happens, constraints exist, and details matter. Life happens around you, to you, and through you. Life will interrupt your plans, it will challenge your abilities, and it will cause you to question your ideas. Therefore, you need to build flexibility into your goals so you can pivot when these challenges occur. That is paying attention to the details. A large percent of success comes from how we handle failure and from making adjustments. Along with factoring in life happening to your goals, you need to work within your constraints. You only have 168 hours in a week. Possibly you are working with a limited amount of income. You also have obligations, necessities, commitments, and personal desires that require a large percentage of your resources. These constraints can cause you to underestimate what it takes to achieve your goals. Planning requires you to consider the details, which allows you to create some flexibility into the process, providing an easier pathway towards achievement. Failure to execute is the fourth reason. We are really good at setting goals and we are well-meaning but failure to execute is less about the goal and more about actually developing a plan of execution. Setting goals is easy. It is more challenging to devise a strategy for how you are going to accomplish that goal. And the strategy is also essential.

So when all of this happens, sometimes it's one, sometimes it's several of these at once, it waylays us. It pushes us off the path, we give it up. Overall, it's so important to remember not to be pushed by your problems but instead to be led by your dreams.

FARHANA: That's profound. Now, what are some magic bullets that we can use to hit our goals?

DEBBI: The magic bullets to hit our goals are, first, to Find Your Dreams. Write down your dreams on a sheet of paper. A sheet of paper helps us to make absolutely clear what we really want, and makes our dream more real and practical. The dreams written on a sheet of paper will remind you about your daily targets. The second Magic Bullet is to Break Your Dream Into Smaller Goals. All great achievements consist of many small achievements. Our mind operates easier with many little goals, than one great dream. You'll feel the sense of liberation, once you break your big dream into smaller goals. The third Magic Bullet is to Develop An Action Plan. Ask yourself questions on how best to proceed. Allow the action plan to come; wait for an answer. Fourth, Define What Person You Can Be To Achieve This Goal. Imagine you have already reached your dreams. Do you see the new you? Probably you are quite different, more confident, smile more often, and will treat yourself and other people better? Experience the new you in detail, what your new traits are, the clothing you wear, the relations in the family, your attitude to life and how it will be. Fifth, Visualize Yourself Already At Your Goal. Practice it daily. Make your subconscious work for you, and support you, by visualizing. The sixth and final Magic Bullet is to Define The Goal That Comes After The Current One. What happens when you reach your goal? Is it a final destination point? Generally not. Some people stop after they reach one goal. They just forget to set up another goal. This is a small part of the overall road to success. The dream is not the destination point; it is a part of the course of our life. Enjoy your success once you have reached the achievement of your dream and when ready, dream again and set up the next new goal.

FARHANA: Wow. Beautiful. I'm excited because you're going to take us through one of your processes, and one of the things that struck me is when you were talking about letting go. It sometimes seems counter-intuitive to have your action steps and your goals and to also release. It's an ongoing dance. I would love it if you would be open to taking us through a process so that we can have an experience of how opening that can be in our own world.

DEBBI: Thank you for inviting me to do so. Let's experience letting go and release. With deep breath in and out and if you're in a position to put your feet on the floor to keep yourself grounded, please do so. Now close your eyes. Close your eyes and put your attention on your heart. As you deeply breathe, release all tension, just breath it out. Any anxieties—breathe it out. Any stress or *"I need to do,"* just breathe it out. I'll talk to you as you deeply breathe, about letting go. You don't need to figure anything out. You can let go of discomfort anytime and change your direction. Let go of any worrying, because in the past maybe you've tried worrying your dream into being which hasn't worked so well. Let go of thinking you need to be anyone other than who you are in order to succeed. Let go of your story that you're stuck, let go of your story that you give up. With your attention on your heart just repeat to yourself, *I am not my body. I am not my mind. I am my soul. I am my soul.* This is the nature of you, since the beginning. Reflect on the possibility that that little voice prompting within you is your guidance. That the little voice that tries to attend to and direct you, that we sometimes ignore, is actually our greatest ally and truth. Choose right now to let go of anything you can't control. You can't control all the events of your life. You can't control other people, places and things. You can control your state of mind. Your state of mind or spirit is what determines your happiness, not the events of your life. You're the master of your happiness because you're the master of your state of mind. Take control of that. Keep breathing deeply, in and out. Let yourself sink even deeper, even deeper, and even deeper and we will do a series of I Am statements together. Focus on the energy connected with these letting-go statements as you're breathing. The first part of each statement is the same, just repeat it on the in-breath, and the second part of each statement is different and you repeat it on the out-breath. I'll start the sentence and just repeat these words after me.

On your in-breath: **I am.**
Out-breath: **Completely safe.**
(In-breath) **I am**: *(Out-breath)* **Right here, present now.**
(In-breath) **I am**: *(Out-breath)* **Knowing that all is well.**
(In-breath) **I am**: *(Out-breath)* **Safe.**
(In-breath) **I am**: *(Out-breath)* **Loved.**
(In-breath) **I am**: *(Out-breath)* **Whole and complete.**
(In-breath) **I am**: *(Out-breath)* **As God created me.**

Remember as you keep breathing and vibrating the "I Am" statements that you are safe and all is well. You are loved beyond measure. You are already whole and complete. There is no place else you need to go, nothing you need to do; you are as God created you. It is safe to align with your dreams. You're called and invited by the Universe into an epic and heroic experience by taking on your dreams. Resources have already been set aside that will ensure that you have more than enough success. More than you've ever imagined. Just release any self-created obstacles. Know that in a moment's notice you can dream and communicate with Source energy in a heart-to-heart talk to embrace your soul's highest plan. Let go, let go of clinging to desire. We are here to take action and let go. Life is about the act – and the surrender. [EXHALING] And so, surrender. Surrender. It. All. Now. [BREATH]

Let the breath bring you back to be here now, bringing up energy through your feet, from the Mother Earth, imagine roots from the soles of your feet going down into the center of the Earth and be here now with full energy, bright with the beauty of this now-moment. How was that for you?

FARHANA: A feeling of peace entered my mind. I didn't know I was in constriction in areas until you took us through those I Am statements.

DEBBI: Your hidden treasure isn't hidden anymore. [LAUGHTER]

FARHANA: This is just so cool. I guess having two

million plus listeners tuning into your show each week, there is something to be said for that [LAUGHTER] that you know what you're doing. And no wonder you're such a sought after coach for those in the media as well. I'm definitely excited. What is the impact on gratitude, and the gratitude process, around our dreams?

DEBBI: We all know that when we express gratitude it energetically opens the door for more good to come into our lives. Dr. John DeMartini is famous for saying *"What we think about and thank about, we bring about."* Thankfulness brings in good, so if we have a list of goals we want to create in our life it's important to stop and celebrate what we have already accomplished. We can use the principle of expressing gratitude and thankfulness with the goals we have already achieved and just reflect on the past year. Besides writing up new goals, and knowing how you're going to get there, also have a list of what you've already accomplished. A gratitude list of what you've completed and attained. That's exciting. Do you feel that? [LAUGHTER]

FARHANA: Totally. Shift into also writing a "Done

List." It inspires me to do my "To Do List." This is my new "a-ha."

DEBBI: To create the Goal Gratitude List, ask yourself, *What have I done in the past year to improve who I am as a person? Have I broken off any toxic relationships? Have I become more assertive? Have I given my time or energy to a charity, or money? Have I donated blood? Have I been a soft place or shoulder to cry on? Did I show up for somebody and listen to them? Did I teach a child to ride a bike, to swim, to play a sport, or to tie their shoe? Did I finally clean the garage? Did I finally get rid of clothes; organize my desk or my files? Did I plant the garden, fix the car, or paint a room? Did I take the trip I've always wanted to take, write the book I've always wanted to write, learn a new language, land my dream job, graduate from college, buy a home, get married, have a baby?* Do you see as I'm asking these how you begin shifting inside, and recognize what you've already accomplished? The anxiety goes away, a rush of competency and good comes in, and this becomes a good foundation for attaining new goals. This is the process we can do to understand, *Moving forward isn't that daunting, it's actually exciting. I can connect with my confidence, that I have the ability to do this.* So write a list of what you've already done and have gratitude

         for all the ways you've already shown
         up.

FARHANA: Are some of these examples available in
         your *Dare to Dream: This Life Counts*
         book?

  DEBBI: Yes. In my book there are many types
         of exercises to do and also some lovely
         meditations. The book was purposely
         laid out with the intent to not just
         disseminate information but to give
         each reader a visceral experience. So the
         reader can take a goal, work it through
         the book and know that at the end they
         will have succeeded in creating the
         dream.

FARHANA: We're just so grateful that you're here.
         For all you have shared and offered us
         today, I thank you.

  DEBBI: It's been a pleasure. I wish you all the
         unconditional knowing that you will
         achieve success.

                        END

Transcript

Debbi Dachinger: Interview with CINDY BRIOLOTTA and LINDA CASSELL

CINDY BRIOLOTTA LINDA CASSELL: Welcome to the Art of Joyful Living. What interests us most about Debbi Dachinger's work is, she has a very unique way of combining practical techniques with spiritual approaches to help people live their lives out loud, and to inspire them to dare to dream. And today, she's here to talk about if you were given the dream you were given the power to achieve it. How do you tap into it? Debbi knows. Debbi, thank you so much for being with us today. So can you tell us what's been going on with you since you were last on the show?

DEBBI DACHINGER: Since I was last on the show the work I do has expanded. First, my radio show is now syndicated on eight stations so I am nationwide and global, as well. Which is awesome, it gets the message out there even more. I've also started to move more into various media personality roles, which I've found exciting because one of the things I thrive on is working with masses of people. When I'm connecting, the magic, the synergy, there's just something amazing that occurs. I've also had the opportunity to do that at some extremely important events which enabled me to make influential connections. I met key people and am working with them, and that's been incredible. I have at least one book coming out this year. I just started my first book editing when Spirit called me and said, *"I love you but please don't think it's one book. I'd like you to publish two books this year."* When I heard that, I knew I needed to get on board; it will be an interesting year. And finally, I'm starting work on a television show. It was a dream and you know, everything with dreams, is timing. *My* timing is always *now, now, now*. But God's timing, life's vibration has a different rhythm than I do. The bottom line is when the timing was right someone approached me and already was familiar with what I did. How perfect is that? The television footage we shot is being edited and it's incredibly exciting. Juicy, juicy time.

CINDY/LINDA: I love it. That's what's possible when you live according to the principles that you're going to teach us today. People often fall into the trap of thinking that there is nothing to do when there are things to do. It's just all joyful doing, right?

DEBBI: Yes. I'm getting more and more into this interesting mindset that if it looks like a "*no*," it becomes a bigger "*yes*," inside for me. And if everybody else is turning left and having issues getting there, I sure as heck am going to turn right instead and create a new trail and a new opportunity. I am all about forging my own path and having utter belief that if I'm given the dream there is a reason. I just don't think it's random. The dream may not happen immediately but it will happen. I just keep at it and I keep saying *yes* to opportunity and following the next right thing.

CINDY/LINDA: What do you mean by if it looks like a "*no*," it becomes a bigger "*yes*"?

DEBBI: A *"no"* does not define me or my circumstance. I am the captain of my life's experience and if I decide to do something I will. Just because someone out there says *"no"* to me, doesn't mean I crumble or cave. I will find a way to do it. If I sense it is for me, it becomes a yes and I will find a way to make it happen. Along the way, I've had people who have underestimated me. At times it was a little difficult because, for instance, in one case I desired to break into a new avenue for my work at a much bigger level but the decision people initially held me back. When that happens and my abilities are underestimated, if you look closely there's a little bubble over my head that says, *"Don't you know who I am? Don't you know what I can do"?* [LAUGHTER] Although it can be frustrating for me to initially get a "no" response on something I want to do or be, I live from the space of the "yes"—*Let me in the door. I'll bring it.* Sometimes it's interesting what it takes to turn things around. In one case it took a person with clout to watch me working, to see me in action to completely bring them around. They observed me working and then they got it—there I was connecting with "name" people and the kind of conversation and friendship we exchanged. After that they understood who I was. Sometimes we just have to show people for them to get it. Everything turned around after that and this person is now a colleague and a supporter. That's a huge win because it could have been a situation where I gave up and said *It's just not working out. They just don't get me and I'm trying so hard and I'm doing everything right and this doesn't feel good.* I could have gone into that head space, or I could have held strong to the notion that I know who I am and what I am skillful at. I know that what I do makes me feel joyful. I'm not going to stop. I was given a dream and I'm going keep going forward and even if it's not this door, another one will open. There's that saying that goes, *"Whenever God closes one door he always opens another, even though it's sometimes hell waiting in the hallway."* [LAUGHTER] ….or until a window opens. Or what if it's that we're waiting for this one particular door to open for us but it's actually that *other* door across the hallway instead? Surprise, surprise. That has certainly happened to me.

CINDY/LINDA: Not to talk about you, Debbi, but that great self-confidence just oozes from you. [LAUGHTER]

DEBBI: I love that you brought that up! [LAUGHTER] Self-confidence exists in us all. I've experienced a lot of the same things that other people do but I have tools. I'm sure anyone who does anything for the first time — can be full of exhilaration — and approach new experiences with the idea that *this could be wonderful*. Or you react when don't know how something new will turn out with the response that *this is terrifying*. Whichever one creeps up, the truth is you will never know until you have the experience, and until then you cannot know the territory. Anyway, I hope my self-confidence is encouraging and feels inviting.

CINDY/LINDA: Yes your confidence is full of poise and assurance. You know, fear so often paralyzes people.

DEBBI: The great thing about continuing forward and having more expansive success is that it keeps showing you how silly fear is. *What am I thinking? Why am I afraid, why do I even go there? That's such a time waster.* Everything *works out. I'm capable. If I flub up, I just recover and keep going.* Nothing is really life or death. It's actually just more of an expression of joy.

CINDY/LINDA: Right and you talk about your fear of your own greatness and power. I would love it if you would talk a little bit about that because that's intriguing for people, you think?

DEBBI: I have this new point of view that is very interesting right now that I'm existing in and that I'll share, which is whatever your biggest dream is, you're playing too small. Every time I think about what I want to put out there in the world — let's take for example, the TV show. I think — that's too small, Debbi. Think more global and think more universal. How can you affect the whole Universe? This takes the onus off "the dream." All this energy we put around the dream and fulfilling the dream and what does it mean if I get there, and what will it mean if I don't? What if we're all playing too darn small? What if we all came here to be the captains and the influential, the ones that this planet and Universe needs? What if we're the beings who signed on and in our soul blueprint agreed, *I'm going to show up during this lifetime because I know the planet and humanity needs me?* I know we're all paying attention and have noticed—this is a crucial time; we have the opportunity to make choices to create a new way that works in our global society, cohesively as a Oneness, and to generate a healthy ecosystem. We can make a different, holistic choice or we're potentially going to self-destruct. What if we each signed on—and knew *this is our time for humanity and for the planet. We're choosing everything in a better healed and altered way,* and for our soul blueprint it's about living out the dreams. What if it was important for us to put our talents and gifts forth because in our small and tremendous ways we're going to change the planetary tides and amend the ripples currently going on? So I suggest, whatever you think is your big dream—go bigger. Because the truth is we're infinite beings and as an infinite being can you can make your dream come true? Of course. As an infinite being is there anything in your way but you? As an infinite being is it possible that you have a permanent green light from the Universe with angelic cheerleaders calling, *yes, yes, yes?* Wherever you are in pursuing your dreams, bigger and bolder is where you can now exist. We have a complete connection with everything, the All That Is, the Oneness; therefore we are all truly that big. If we are part of the One and the All—then we are the size of the Universe and beyond. We are already that.

CINDY/LINDA: We have an email question from a listener. She says when you were saying whatever your biggest dream is you're playing too small, *I want my work out there.* She says *it's an uncomfortable thought for her because it feels like boasting.* Her question is *how does she overcome that when talking about her work in such a big way?*

DEBBI: When we feel boastful it's because the ego has gotten involved with what we're doing. The ego likes to look in the mirror. The ego likes to say *me-me-me. Look at me.* The ego likes to take credit and be given credit. The ego is what separates us. So when we function from ego we're separating from the infinite and the All That Is. If the Universe told this listener to put her work 'out there,' then they also told her *we're going to give you this specific dream because you are the magnificent being we'd like to carry this* out at this time. That's a beautiful thing. So she can shift—it's just a shift. Nothing else has to be done except a shift to the comfort of: *I am here to do big things and release my gifts to create much needed good on the planet at this time.* Whether you're a painter, whether you clean houses, whether you work on cars, whether you have a radio show, whether you're a teacher, whatever it is—to do that the very, very best you can. I'm recommending a shift out of the vanity portion that desires to boast, into a shift of *I came here with abilities, and I'm going to illuminate that.* And the other piece of it is when we are aligned with putting our work out there for the joy it essentially is, then we are not boastful, or self-important, rather we also recognize everybody else. We see everyone else's light and gift. We're just equal and a part of the beautiful heaven on Earth puzzle. I hope that helps.

CINDY/LINDA: I know you're all about living by design and knowing that you can manifest your dreams because you wouldn't have them if you couldn't, right? I run into people who gave up their dream because they lost hope that it was ever possible. What advice do you have for people like that?

DEBBI: I would say do what makes your heart beat a little faster. When I was very young I knew I wanted to be an actress and a singer. I remember being in high school and other students would say, *I wish I was more like you. I'm going to college and I still don't know what I want to do.* I had no answers for them at that time. However some of them, who were not clear on their direction then, are crazy-successful now. We just don't need all the answers. Sometimes it's about following the energy. So for people who have forgotten—for whatever reason—they stopped dreaming. Maybe they didn't think it was probable. Maybe they didn't think they had the right to dream and chose a pragmatic and logical progression to their life. Maybe they felt dreams could never come true. Or they had the desire but didn't recognize their talent or the means—whatever it was, allow yourself to go back in that dreaming space because it really is quite exciting. To dream and act on it is the juice, the nectar of life. One of the ways you can start to dream again is to make a choice. You can put it out there, speak to your own soul or highest self and ask, *I'm ready to go back into the energy of knowingness of what makes me happy and excited. What makes my heart skip a beat? What do I like? What dream shall I fulfill?* Frankly, that's enough to know right now. You don't need conclusions. You can just allow the questions. And the questions will deliver informing energy. For example if someone were to ask what area they'd enjoy working in and the energy is, let's say animals. They can acknowledge *I love animals. I'm crazy about animals.* Well follow that energy and if an opportunity presents itself, follow that work with animals. Maybe that will take you down a path that will ultimately be something amazing for you. Or maybe you'll go down that path and something entirely different will present itself and you'll realize instead—*I really love science. It's not exactly animals; it's biology that I enjoy.* And because you were working with animals, you happened to meet someone who is renowned in science and is looking for an assistant; you start to investigate or work in that. What I can promise you is if you follow the energy presented and trust it—you'll have a great life. You'll never be bored. You'll be full of joy.

The second thing is energy will always lead you to the next right thing. My life, often, has been like skiing down a mountain of switchbacks. I'll be heading down one way and it seems like it's *that* but then something else presents. I'll go the next way and it feels good like that until something else presents. My life has been predicated on experiencing something full out and then transitioning to the next right thing which ultimately got me here today. So if you've given up on dreams, go back and trust where energy leads you instead. As long as you're happy and expressing yourself, you're in the right place doing the right thing. Re-engage that 'dreamer' muscle by making a new choice. Choose now to dream and recognize your dreams and start to follow what presents itself.

CINDY/LINDA: I love that. I love when you said do what makes your heart beat faster. This can also bring up fear with it. Is that also a sign of that's where you need to go?

DEBBI: Yes, exactly. [LAUGHTER] It is. We're not talking about the kind of fear that informs that something is going to harm you, that is one to pay attention to. Rather, it's when you feel, *ooh this is an opportunity and I'm afraid* then yes – do it! Take the opportunity because it's exactly where you need to go.

It's fun to look at people who have preceded us in history people who did great things and see where they started. How did they get there? What kind of choices did they make? History can inspire us. I'll tell you a story about a woman who was in her late seventies. She was struggling with severe arthritis. She was a farmer's widow from Eagle Bridge, New York and she loved to do needle work. But because of the onset of severe arthritis in her seventies, her fingers no longer worked for the small detail work of embroidering. Her arthritis became so painful she could no longer hold the needle. Instead of letting the arthritis be an obstacle to stop her, this elderly woman found that she could hold a small paintbrush. The paintbrush was easier in her hands than a needle. So she decided to try her hand at painting. She painted pretty farm and country scenes and felt they were good enough to enter into a contest at a local fair. Unfortunately her art was not recognized by the judges. Funny enough she instead won prizes for her preserves and her canned fruit! [LAUGHTER] This woman took her signature folk style paintings to a local drugstore to be displayed in their windows. One day an art collector noticed her paintings in the window and he loved them. He bought all of her paintings and was very excited about this new artist, so he showed the newly acquired paintings to his friends in art circles in New York City. They found her to be very talented and all wondered—who was the painter? And now for the big reveal! The artist was Grandma Moses. Her real name was Anna Mary Robertson Moses, but the press dubbed her "Grandma Moses," and from that moment on she gained an international reputation. You might remember that her widely collected works of art were featured on calendars and greeting cards, expositions in leading galleries including the Metropolitan Museum of Modern Art in New York City. It's reported that twenty-five percent of Grandma Moses' more than one thousand five hundred paintings were done *after* she had turned one hundred years old. So for those who have fear, whose heart beats fast at the idea of their dream but they give in to any mental or physical obstacle? In this real story from history, notice what Grandma Moses did with what she had, and in spite of her initial physical handicap she made choices that created who she became! So isn't it time you got started? I'm just sayin'.... [LAUGHTER]

CINDY/LINDA: That's so beautiful. So many people say they're too old, but as long as you're breathing, right, it's never too late?

DEBBI: I've noticed more and more people in their forties, fifties and sixties having these life changing epiphanies. Whether it's *I don't love this corporate job anymore,* or it's because they feel the call to a new way of dreaming and being; people have gained enough inner wisdom to admit *there is something completely different I desire to do with my life.* I know a couple of corporate people, Mark and Liz, who started traveling the world and saw many things that pulled at their heart strings until they realized, it's not enough to do the corporate work I'm doing. They preferred to contribute and make a difference. The couple left their corporate jobs and started a fair trades company. Now they travel all over the world and help out depressed areas and support women artisans. They buy and sell gorgeous goods that these skilled handicraft women create. Everything from home décor to jewelry to scarves and they bring the goods back to be sold with the proceeds going to helping these women in these countries. What an amazing impact their lives are now having. It reminds me of the previous listener's question when the woman asked about being boastful. I think the emphasis, the focus for all of us can be on what kind of contribution do I make? How I do I leave this planet different than I when came here? If I'm thinking about how great I am, how cool I am, or what I imagine anyone thinks of me, it's not going to cut it. We're living in a time when our involvement, influence, support and contribution to society and the Earth and its people is essential and meaningful. So for all of us—one hundred plus years old, or teens through forties, fifties, sixties, seventies and beyond, it really is about being in the moment and trusting what comes up as your new path. Things will speak to you and show you the way. What will you do when you hear the call?

CINDY/LINDA: You're listening to our wonderful guest, Debbi Dachinger. So Debbi, tell us about your own practices that keep you on your path for choosing your dreams.

DEBBI: I've been involved in self-development since I was a teenager and it's definitely changed forms over my life. Most recently, I'm involved in energy healing because I find it to be immediate. Sometimes it's about taking the threads of whatever has been in place for a long time and disentangling those threads so I can create what I select instead. Energy work has been profound for me. I know pain can be paralyzing for many people. To me, pain is a great motivator so I'll do what it takes to get to the other side. I'm not afraid to be who I am, and I'm okay to be wise and I am comfortable to be in wonder and interest, to not know; to ask questions. So I'm very hungry and willing to do whatever it takes. I also surround myself with people and opportunities to continue moving forward. When I find something that really excites me and I feel the potential positive change, I just immerse myself in it. Specifically I did the Avatar course for ten years and that was life-changing. More recently I work with a gifted Master Theta Healer, and I also attend Access Consciousness courses which are beyond amazing. And last, I meditate. I have a mantra and I meditate for twenty minutes a day. It's good for my personality because I'm such a doer, and it's important for my physical and spiritual being to have that peace. That complete disconnect and that reconnect with the All That Is. It's a pretty amazing state to go into.

I've had an interesting history of various healing modalities I've experienced. I recently attended something that had a surprising result. I know someone who is in recovery and attended their family therapy for addicts. I understand twelve-step programs, and actually the therapy session turned out to be great. Anyone could share so I spoke up to express myself in a room with a lot of people—and the therapist made a comment to me that was very helpful. She asked me if I was speaking about *my* feelings. And how much did I focus on how *others* feel, as opposed to where *my* feelings were? Busted. I do often do for others first. Then the family therapist made a comment about those of us who are connected to the addicts and how we are extreme givers, so much so that we might give to other people before we consider taking care of ourselves. This recovery group illustrated the issue through an image of a person who has arms that are so long that those arms are always reaching out and giving, giving, giving to other people. Except their arms are so long that they can't wrap around themselves. I laughed and said to the therapist, *Wouldn't it be beautiful to have one arm that is long like that, and one that is normal? This way you can give and contribute with the long arm and also hug and contribute to yourself as well.* It seems that is the ultimate balance. What I came out of the experience with is to notice how this plays out in my life: I can aspire to giving to myself first more in my life, to paying attention to my needs, not just the needs of others. More emphasis on filling my own inner cup.

CINDY/LINDA: Love it. I know you have a gratitude

process. What does gratitude have to do with dreams?

DEBBI: It's interesting because we can often forget what is here right now. Everything from did I say I needed to clean out the garage and I did? Did I give away clothes? Was I a soft shoulder for someone when they needed it? Did I do a service for somebody? Have I done a kindness to myself? Did I say I was going to take care of things on my to-do list and actually do them? Have I changed? Have I lost weight? Have I started a program that I've followed through on? All these things, they're not to be disregarded. Recognize them; it's important to have gratitude for all we have already done and for who we are and how far we've already come. My best friend and I ensure we have a weekly phone call together, and it's awesome. One day we were connecting on the phone and we were both in the poopiest mood. It was like *eh. This is awful.* And she said, *I know, why don't we spend the whole day expressing gratitude? We're coming from a really bad place, let just see what happens.* So we agreed to do it. I spent the entire day saying *thank you*. No matter what the interaction was I made sure to dip into my heart, connect with the person and then express what I was thankful for in that moment with them. Of course, this started to happen with people who had never heard gratitude from me or people I didn't have that level of connection with and it was amazing. I could feel everybody going *oh, oh, that's so nice*. It was all over the map; I ended up completely shifting myself and the gratitude changed everything. All the relationships, including the one with myself and my day. So never underestimate the power of gratitude. It's totally free. You can do it without even a piece of paper or a pen. You can do it with your mouth, and you can do it right now. What if each one of us just decided to spend the whole day in gratitude and whoever comes in your path you find something to thank them for that you sincerely mean.

CINDY/LINDA: I love that you said not just gratitude for what we have, but gratitude for who we are and what we've done. That's really amazing.

DEBBI: Yes, life goes by fast – how about we acknowledge what is big and juicy right now? Can you say I was the best parent to that child or animal? Or I'm really impressed with how I show up. Or I've been a good partner. Or I have a really good business practice. Or I was honest. Whatever it was there are many things we do every day and if we can take in the panoramic view of our life—this can be heaven on Earth right now. To notice all these wonderful choices you've made and all the ways you've shown up. Be grateful and operate from that place. Coming from a full-of-thanks place, thank-fullness, it will change everything. It lets you know that right now everything is okay.

CINDY/LINDA: I want to go back to something you said earlier in the show when you said *"Spirit called me."* For people who may not know what you mean by that, what does that look like to you?

DEBBI: Wow. What a good question. Let's see if I can answer this—the best I can. When I say *Spirit called me* it's about my connection to the loving power that moves in and through me and is my being and is everything that surrounds me. For some it may be God, for some it may be All That Is, Source, or knowingness. I remember being told when I was quite young, by a gifted psychic that I had a telephone to God and I could pick it up anytime and just say *howdy*, and ask questions and get information. I was so young at the time. It was very nice to hear but I had no idea what to do with that information. It took decades for me to discover what was being referred to. I'm an intuitive and I'm a clairsentient. We all receive information differently. For me, it feels like a download, using a computer term, and there is this absolute knowingness. I can ask questions and have a sense of where to go and it works well. There is a great deal of trust that comes in. Essentially direction can be received in pieces and we don't necessarily get the entire picture all at once. That's okay. Take the piece you have and run with it, more will be revealed, it always is. So when I say *Spirit called me*, it's because—I was starting to write another book. I was heading in one direction, when I decided to pay someone to transcribe my previous interviews and when the material came back to me I felt this is a way people can get this dream material in a whole different way than a straight write-a-book. I got excited and we kept transcribing and that's when I had that *boom*-knowingness, which came in and said, THIS is your next book. There was a moment when I just went O*y*. *This is a lot of work.* [LAUGHTER] Once I accepted the new direction and got excited about it, then the book cover totally came to me. I knew exactly what the cover and the rest of the book was going to look like.

When I say "*spirit called to me*" I mean that I'm being guided. I think so much of life, with the changes for us all, is for us to stop resisting. We are built to know. We are built to receive. We are built to allow. All we need do is allow that knowingness to come in. Receive—allow—know.

CINDY/LINDA: Yes, and I just want to repeat we are built to receive. I think that's so important, Debbi. And also things come to you in pieces so you don't have to have the whole picture before you start to act. You don't have to know the whole answer. So I think that's one of the themes today. Thank you Debbi.

DEBBI: Yes, it's a misnomer to think *if I don't*

know everything and every step and every action and every way of how this is going to turn out, then why even bother going forward if I don't have the full vision? We are taught to visualize and we are taught to affirm. We think we need to have all the pieces in place first before we'll go out and do anything. But we don't need all the pieces and in fact, a lot of the joy is in *not* having them and just trusting and moving forward anyway. When we let go at that level, the Universe creates a thousand times more brilliantly than we ever could. If we will stay out of the way and move forward in knowingness and are open to receiving, the Universe will deliver the greatest unimaginable, unfathomable—unfathomable means we don't even know the depth of what the Universe will gift to us-- surprises. Move forward in knowingness and allow the rest to fill in as it will in its own time.

CINDY/LINDA: What about people who perceive they have failed over and over again? How do they recapture the trust to move forward?

DEBBI: People who fail need to know they didn't create that club. They need to know that every single one who is listening, including me speaking, have been in that club. Including some of the greatest minds and athletes and inventors who have ever walked this planet. We've all failed. But the message is don't let failure define you. Let failure inform you. So when a failure occurs feel whatever feelings come up—the disappointment, the sadness, the anger, the frustration—whatever that is, allow some space to accept and feel that. And once that's through, which doesn't take much time—move into action and ask, *what was my involvement in creating that?* Because there is a lesson. Failure is a great teacher. Something happened that didn't work, that's all it means. It doesn't mean *we are* a failure, it just means in that situation *there was* a failure. Maybe we chose to align ourselves with something or someone that wasn't right for us, but we did it anyway. Maybe we tried to control something and force it to be something it wasn't. Or maybe we didn't have everything we needed and maybe we need to take a class to learn. Maybe we need a coach. Maybe we need to buy a book. Maybe there are things we can do so we have all the information. Or maybe we made a right turn and we needed to make a left. It really is about figuring it out. That's what resilience is. Resilience is asking, *what happened? What did I bring? What occurred?* Just globally looking at the situation. And once you've learned the lesson, get back up. Now you know better so do better. It's not about what happens to us, it's about what we do with it. Remember you define your life.

And if you have a history of failure, what kind of pattern are you repeating over and over again that you're not stopping long enough to understand its message to you? The divine message is never that you're wrong, bad, or not enough, or that you don't have what it takes. Never, never, never. Divine message is just another piece of the puzzle you're currently missing suggesting that you stop in order to recognize how to make that new adjustment and go forward successfully.

CINDY/LINDA: Wow. I think we've had a lot of divine messages from Debbi today, don't you Cindy. [LAUGHTER] A lot. Wow.

DEBBI: Cindy, what is your big, juicy, dream

CINDY/LINDA: birthday girl? I feel like I'm a beacon of love and light and want to shine it everywhere, to every corner. I'm all about helping people transform their lives for the better.

DEBBI: We're lucky to have you. Thank you for being here to do that.

CINDY/LINDA: Thank you. I'm so happy to be here now and be living in these amazing times.

DEBBI: Me too. Absolutely strange and wonderful and amazing times. This is the most amazing time -- what are you going to do with the gifts you've been given, because it truly is your genius. You can utilize it and harness it. If you have dreams there is no greater time to help them come true. We're not living with the density that we did at one time. This is a manifesting, magical time.

CINDY/LINDA: Just listening to you Debbi, this has been a gift. I have a rule that I don't work on my birthday, but this is not work. This is pure joy, it has been a gift. Please come back when your next book gets published. What would you like to leave our audience with?

DEBBI: Every time you say, *"I can't because,"* you're giving your power away to someone or something else. It means you're giving yourself away. Don't underestimate your dream. Don't under estimate the limitlessness, the tenacity and the potency that you truly be. Because power is a foundational, spiritual, quality. Pretending that you don't have power or that you're not responsible for your life, is the quickest way to frustration and misery. It's the ultimate self-sabotage. I return to what I said in the beginning. Wherever you are in your life right now just surrender it all, and receive it all. It's that easy. Go with the flow and what is, and trust — just trust that when you get excited and your heart skips a little faster that you're headed exactly where you are supposed to.

CINDY/LINDA: Debbi, again. Thank you so much.

END

SPIRIT

Literally "SPIRIT," an English word derived from Latin, means *Life-Breath*. We are comprised of energy and our radiant energy is a physical force which is conscious. Consciousness is the head of all creation. Spirit is the manifesting power which brings into our range of sensation all the appearance constituting our environment. Everything we know is an appearance of the One Spirit, the Life-Breath, the energy, consciousness becoming creation, becoming physical. Spirit is pure consciousness, that which integrates and disintegrates forms by means of words and thoughts.

Spirit is a definite natural energy which appears in the world as the various objects we perceive. Every single *"material"* thing is really the One Spirit expressing itself through a combination of vibrations.

The desire to create does not go away, it continually seeks expression.

Healthy desire is never about perfection. It *is* about

going deeper than your mood, deeper than your stories of what is allowed or possible, diving into the sensations and energy of desire itself, and letting that move you into inspired action.

Every day, remember who and what you really are. You are not separate from anything. Release any falsehoods that your life is determined by external conditions. Sub-consciousness is always amendable to suggestion. It is magnetic and compelling to orchestrate your mind first and then experience what you have set up and intended.

An extreme instance of this is what occurs in a hypnotic demonstration. The hypnotist tells the subject, *"You are a dog,"* and the subject tries his best to act like a dog. Reverse the suggestion and you reverse the consequences. Watch your mental processes and you will see that your present expression is the principle; subconsciousness always obeys.

Remind yourself that your personality is an instrument for the limitless life-power which works through you to create a particular demonstration of its ability to produce beautiful results. Practice and you will overcome. This begins the way to freedom.

Do not get discouraged. Every one of the wise, kind souls who has gone before you has also shared uncertainty and has lacked clarity. The early stage of anyone's dream work has been fraught with problems and perplexities. By precisely practicing and keeping committed and taking steps to move toward their dream, they have won through achievement. You can do the same.

The wealth expert, Robert Kiyosaki said, *"Everyone wants to go to heaven, but no one wants to die."* And everyone wants to have their dream come true, but what will you do to get there?

At this very moment you are fully equipped. You have the seed-forms for all you need in order to express perfectly the special tendencies of the life-power concentrated in your being. You don't have to get anything. You have to discover what you already possess.

We are the masters of our universe. It's time to step into the potent role you came here to play.

- Don't worry, everyone who participates in social media just pretends to have happier and funnier lives than you. They don't.
- Forgive yourself for not being perfect; there's no such thing; embrace your imperfection and your uniqueness.
- Thank the Universe in advance.
- Have a sense of humor, especially when it comes to you.
- Be grateful for what you have right now.
- End every complaint with the words: *"And I'm so blessed."*
- Tell someone you love them, right now.

Truly you are the magician in your own life,

Debbi

"You have brains in your head. You have feet in your shoes. You can steer yourself in any direction you choose."

❖ *Dr. Seuss*

Debbi Dachinger is an expert in goal achievement. She is a radio and TV personality; a three-time bestselling author, keynote speaker, and coach (for goal attainment and in coaching to be exquisite talent while being interviewed on radio). Debbi's *"Dare to Dream"* is a syndicated, multi-award winning radio program with 2+ million listeners offering inspiring information and methods on how to achieve goals and dreams. She's a top-notch radio personality, was an award-winning actress and singer, a successful motivational speaker, a professional voice over artist, and was a popular jewelry designer. *Awards*: Editor's Pick: Featured Intriguing Creator, Broadcasting Industry Lifetime Achievement Award, featured in multiple news sources, Inducted into the *Who's Who Hall of Fame* for entertainment, seen in the documentary film *"Girl's Rule,"* about self-esteem and confidence, author of the bestselling book: *"DARE TO DREAM: THIS LIFE COUNTS!"* (won the Motivation Book Award of the Year from the National Independent Excellence Awards and was awarded the *Missy Bystrom Sponsor NIEA* book award), she's an International speaker, and has an inspirational video channel at: **www.YouTube.com/debontheradio.** Debbi's abundant career is in using her voice to live out loud, to teach and inspire others to *Dare to Dream and make their dreams a reality.* **http://www.deborahdachinger.com**

Get your free audio gift ~
At: **www.deborahdachinger.com/freegift**
Description: *"THE SUREFIRE METHOD TO ALWAYS ACCOMPLISH YOUR GOALS"* ($49.00 Value) from Debbi Dachinger, a goal achievement expert teaching the practical and spiritual techniques to achieve dreams and goals. She's a radio and TV personality; a three-time bestselling author, keynote speaker, and coach *(for goal attainment and in how to be an exquisite interview on radio)*. Audio is an instant download.

Debbi Dachinger

Bestselling Book: http://www.amazon.com/dp/1467930814
http://www.deborahdachinger.com
http://www.YouTube.com/debontheradio
http://www.Twitter.com/debontheradio
https://www.Facebook.com/DaretoDreamRadiotv
http://www.Linkedin.com/in/debbidachinger

Radio Coaching: Debbi coaches individuals and groups on how to be exquisite while being interviewed. Perfect for beginners, for those who have already been interviewed, and for advanced guests who are consistently interviewed. From soup to nuts, A-Z, Debbi coaches the advanced and the beginner alike how to be superb on air and how to get on the radio. Many people want to be interviewed on the radio today. Do you want to do get on the air waves? Know how? Learn it all from start to finish – become the best radio interview guest; learn from an expert who shows you how to be amazing on the radio! Be at the top of your game and very professional on all fronts. Generate great marketing and advertising for you and your business through radio.

~ Designer: Sandro Flora

NOTES and IDEAS to Remember

CPSIA information can be obtained at www.ICGtesting.com
Printed in the USA
LVOW13s0000190913

353047LV00019B/375/P